# AGILE MARKETING

# AGILE MARKETING

## Implementing Scrum in a Marketing Environment

**Greg Kihlstrom**

**MERCURY LEARNING AND INFORMATION**
Boston, Massachusetts

MERCURY LEARNING AND INFORMATION
121 High Street, 3$^{rd}$ Floor
Boston, MA 02110
info@merclearning.com

G. Kihlstrom. *Agile Marketing: Implementing Scrum in a Marketing Environment.*
ISBN: 978-1-50152-357-1

The publisher recognizes and respects all marks used by companies, manufacturers, and developers as a means to distinguish their products. All brand names and product names mentioned in this book are trademarks or service marks of their respective companies. Any omission or misuse (of any kind) of service marks or trademarks, etc. is not an attempt to infringe on the property of others.

Library of Congress Control Number: 2024952351

242526321   This book is printed on acid-free paper in the United States of America.

Our titles are available for adoption, license, or bulk purchase by institutions, corporations, etc.

All of our titles are available in digital format at various digital vendors.

*For my father,*
*who first taught me the value of agility*
*while also teaching me so much more.*

# CONTENTS

# *INTRODUCTION*

Agile marketing is becoming increasingly important because marketing teams should have the process, discipline, collaboration, and communication methods that will help them as the brands they support increasingly take on more complex work and initiatives.

The work and collaboration required to create the personalized and orchestrated experiences that customers increasingly want means that better methods of working together are needed. Thus, Agile principles and approaches such as scrum have been increasingly beneficial, and those that have experienced approaches based on Agile have seen stark contrasts between teams that use those approaches versus those that stay with more traditional methods.

The goal of this book is to provide a foundational understanding of Agile and scrum practices while providing some practical guidance on approaching the implementation of Agile marketing within an organization.

## THE TREATMENT OF AGILE AND SCRUM

Those who fall into the "die-hard Agile proponents" camp may find more than a few things to criticize about this book, as the philosophical approach of this book is that a thorough understanding of Agile principles is necessary, but a dogmatic application of them is not always beneficial. The following paragraphs explore a few caveats.

First, it should be made clear that Agile is not a methodology; it is not synonymous with scrum, SAFe, or Kanban—all of these, while related by principles and desired end goals, are very much unique interpretations of Agile principles.

In this book, in particular, the die-hard Agile proponents may feel that the terms *Agile* and *scrum* are used a little too often in conjunction with the other. Since this book is written for those less experienced and familiar with the nuances of Agile principles versus scrum practices, this was done to simplify things and to best serve the topic of Agile marketing.

## WHO THIS BOOK IS FOR

This book is for marketing executives and professionals who want to understand how to implement Agile principles within their marketing to increase their effectiveness, including chief marketing executives (CMOs) and marketing leadership, marketing management, and other marketing team members. Of those professionals, this book will be most useful for marketers with little understanding of Agile or for those who may be tasked with exploring whether or not Agile practices would be a good fit for their organization.

Also, this should be thought of as a *guide* to Agile marketing, not an encyclopedia for it. Therefore, it is intended to be an introduction to the topic and to give readers a good understanding quickly and easily, with examples for guidance along the way. To get more in-depth knowledge of Agile marketing, more reading and training will be required, but it is highly recommended to also get *experience* as soon as possible.

## WHAT THIS BOOK IS NOT

Those who have years of experience with scrum and other Agile practices may find some elements of this book to be a helpful refresher, but it may be too elementary in places for seasoned practitioners. Thus, this is not an advance Agile or scrum guide, although there should be some beneficial elements for those that don't consider themselves advanced, as well as those who are tasked with managing teams comprised of people who are a mix of novices, intermediate, and advanced Agile marketers.

Also, while the concepts and definitions of scrum elements, team members, and even how to do scrum well may benefit teams of all types, this is not a guide for teams other than marketers.

Finally, there is a brief mention of the scaled Agile framework (or SAFe) in this book, but this is primarily a discussion of the scrum approach. Therefore, if one is looking for a deeper guide to SAFe, this is probably not a good reference.

## A RECURRING EXAMPLE

Readers will be looking at a hypothetical case study that will help frame some of the opportunities and challenges inherent in Agile marketing adoption. The company used as an example is called AgileCorp, a software company whose engineering team has been using scrum and applying Agile principles for years, but whose marketing team is just beginning to explore how an Agile approach can be beneficial to their work.

## WHAT IS COVERED

This Agile Brand Guide is divided into two main sections, with several parts in each:

- **Part 1: Introduction to Agile**
  This will give those new to Agile and scrum an overview of the practices and roles of scrum, as well as some basic guidance on how to use them.

- **Part 2: The Elements and Roles of Scrum in Agile**
  In this section, readers will look at the different activities and parts that members of an Agile marketing team will play, and the important connection between people and the successful implementation of scrum.

- **Part 3: Implementing Scrum in Your Organization**
  This section discusses how to transition from a more traditional marketing organization and operations to embracing Agile principles and scrum practices.

- **Part 4: The Marketing Scrum Team**
  Based on our broader understanding of the roles of scrum teams and the components of scrum, readers will apply what they have learned specifically to marketing and how to be successful in each role.

- **Part 5: Adopting Agile Practices As a Marketing Team**
  Beyond the fundamentals of adopting Agile marketing, this part will explore ensuring that leadership is bought in and that teams embrace Agile principles in a holistic way. Readers will also explore how to determine and measure business value.

- **Part 6: Working Collaboratively with Scrum**
  Whether a team is working alongside other teams that have adopted scrum, or are working with non-Agile teams, readers will explore how to be successful in different types of environments.

The author has tried to strike a balance between giving an overview and discussing practical examples of implementing Agile and scrum.

# ACKNOWLEDGMENTS

As with any book, countless people have a hand in the thoughts and ideas that are contained within. I will endeavour to thank many of them, but a full list would take up its own book, so please excuse this abbreviated list.

Thanks to Anthony Coppedge, Jascha Kaykas-Wolff, Steve Moubray, and the many other Agile Marketing experts that I've had the opportunity to learn from over the years, whether it is as an interview guest on my podcast, or in other conversations.

Thanks also to Lisa Guhanick, Brandon Coy, Lauren O'Neill, and the Association of National Advertisers (ANA) team who worked with me on my 4-part course and certification on Agile Marketing which enabled me to explore these topics in greater depth.

Also, thank you to Melissa Reeve and the team at the Agile Marketing Alliance for their feedback on my writings about this topic over the years. They are a great organization full of insights, education, and community, which I highly recommend anyone truly wanting to embrace Agile Marketing consider joining.

I am forever grateful to my wife Lindsey, who is always supportive of me, no matter how many books I write during the course of a year. She is forever an inspiration, and I'm thankful to have such a great partner in all things.

Finally, thanks to everyone reading this book and anyone who has listened to my podcast, read an article, and supported me in any way over the last several years. I hope that the thoughts and ideas shared by myself and others have been helpful in your work.

Let's move forward and create great things together!

# INTRODUCTION TO AGILE MARKETING

Whether readers are familiar with basic Agile or just getting started, gaining a better understanding of the rationale and principles behind the approach can help when it comes time to put Agile marketing in practice. Even if they haven't been part of a team that has used Agile approaches, they've likely run across the term—maybe from a software team that they've worked along-side—but as readers will see, there are some key terms and principles to learn, as well as some common misconceptions to break through.

It's time to get started on our journey of exploration to look at how Agile practices can apply to marketing teams and their work. The book begins by answering a simple question: What exactly is Agile, and how is it different from other marketing methods?

The book goes on to explore the twelve Agile principles and how they can transform the way one thinks about team collaboration and the work product one delivers.

Then, in the next section, readers will look at how Agile relates to marketing practices before the book goes into more depth about specific Agile practices, specifically scrum.

All along the way, the book will be following the marketing team at AgileCorp as they take steps toward adopting Agile marketing for their work.

1

# *WHAT IS AGILE?*

Those who have started reading this book most likely did so because they have a basic understanding of Agile, although many definitions and misunderstandings are floating around.

By definition *Agile* is an iterative approach to project management and work within a practice area that helps teams deliver value to their customers more quickly and with fewer hurdles. Instead of betting everything on one large launch, an Agile team delivers work in small but consumable increments. Requirements, plans, and results are evaluated continuously so that teams have a natural mechanism for responding to change quickly.

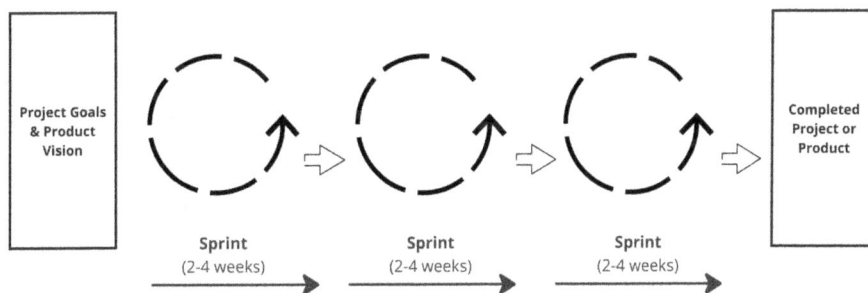

**FIGURE 1.1** The scrum sprint process.

Figure 1.1 shows that project goals are set at the start of the project, as shown on the left side of the screen. Several iterations, called "sprints" in scrum (a set of practices based on Agile principles) terminology, are used to complete portions of the project iteratively. With each sprint completed, the project is closer to achieving its goals. The other benefit of this approach is that the method for achieving the goals can be modified after each sprint if new or better ways of reaching the goals are uncovered.

## WATERFALL

An alternative to Agile methods is referred to as the *waterfall method* (Figure 1.2), named so because one task or phase follows another sequentially, most often with "gates" preventing movement back and forth between phases or steps in the process. Waterfall approaches can trace their roots back to the manufacturing assembly line, which was refined and made popular by Henry Ford in the 1910s. Additionally the waterfall methodology, also almost synonymous with the software development life cycle (SDLC) was the "gold standard" of how software was created, and how manufacturing was approached.[1]

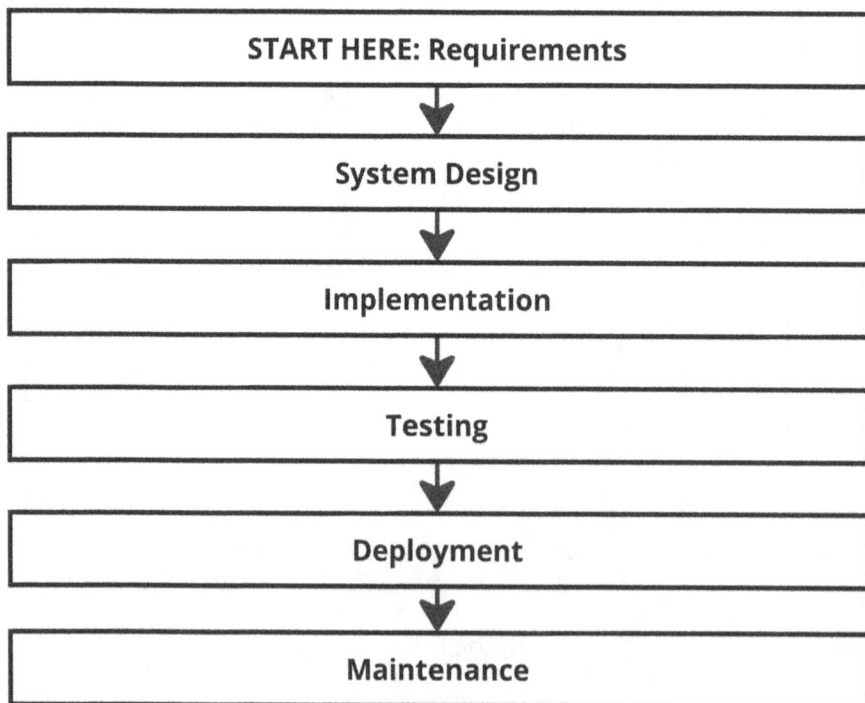

```
┌──────────────────────────────────────┐
│      START HERE: Requirements        │
└──────────────────────────────────────┘
                   ↓
┌──────────────────────────────────────┐
│           System Design              │
└──────────────────────────────────────┘
                   ↓
┌──────────────────────────────────────┐
│           Implementation             │
└──────────────────────────────────────┘
                   ↓
┌──────────────────────────────────────┐
│              Testing                 │
└──────────────────────────────────────┘
                   ↓
┌──────────────────────────────────────┐
│             Deployment               │
└──────────────────────────────────────┘
                   ↓
┌──────────────────────────────────────┐
│             Maintenance              │
└──────────────────────────────────────┘
```

*FIGURE 1.2* The waterfall method.

In a waterfall project, not only are goals defined from the start of the project, but requirements are tightly defined throughout the project. While this detail is helpful to those budgeting costs and timing at the onset of a project, they can often be inaccurate once a project is underway due to unforeseen circumstances or findings throughout the process. Because a lot of time and effort is spent creating requirements and timelines from the start, this can also prove costly if and when a project needs to undergo a change after initial requirements have been finalized.

The longer a project is estimated to take, the riskier and costlier this can be. Even smaller projects or campaigns can often create challenges because markets, customers, and competition change rapidly. Because of this, according to a recent Simform research study, waterfall projects have a 58% success rate versus a 70% success rate for ones using Agile approaches.[2]

## A BRIEF HISTORY OF AGILE

While the purpose of this book isn't to provide a full-featured history of Agile, it is important to understand that its roots come from both software development and manufacturing.

Of course, Agile did not simply spring out of nothing, there have been trends that have been developing over many decades in related industries that resulted in Agile principles being defined.

To briefly explore Agile's origins, we need to go back to the 1930s. Several approaches were created and adopted that paved the way for Agile.

### Manufacturing Leads the Way

- **1930s**—Bell Labs enacted Plan-Do-Study-Act (PDSA) cycles that bear a resemblance to some of the steps in the scrum process, as well as the continuous improvement process, we'll discuss.

- **1940s–1970s**—The Toyota Production System, also called "The Toyota Way,"[3] was created in post-WWII Japan by Taiichi Ohno, Toyota's Chief of Production, and refined over subsequent decades, which provided a blueprint—albeit in the manufacturing industry—for how Agile approaches could be adopted in software engineering.[4]

- **1988**—The term *lean manufacturing* was coined by John Krafnick and influenced a parallel path to Agile that is Lean software development.[5]

### Origins of Agile in Software

- **1970s**—Evolutionary project management which divided projects into "meaningful evolutionary cycles" was an early precursor to Agile approaches.[6]

- **1990s**—The terminology *lightweight* software development methods (as opposed to waterfall, heavyweight methods[7]) came into popularity, and spawned several types of lightweight methods like extreme programming (XP), rapid application development (RAD) and others.

- **1993**—Scrum was first put into practice at Borland by Jeff Sutherland—known as "the father of scrum" and his team there.[8]

## THE AGILE MANIFESTO

Then, finally, at the beginning of the new millennium, Agile began its true start when a group of software developers decided to write a document that would be influential over the decades to come. In 2001, the Agile Manifesto was written by seventeen software developers[9] at what is referred to as the Snowbird meeting in Utah,[10] with the following summary:

"We are uncovering better ways of developing software by doing it and helping others do it. Through this work, we have come to value:

- Individuals and interactions over processes and tools

- Working software over comprehensive documentation

- Customer collaboration over contract negotiation

- Responding to change over following a plan

That is, while there is value in the items on the right, we value the items on the left more."[11]

The Agile Manifesto has formed the basis of several approaches and concepts that will be discussed in this book. Other applications of both The Agile Manifesto as well as the Agile Principles will be discussed in the next chapter. These applications include some marketing-specific ones, and even others for other functions. This book, however, will stick to the source, and discussions of Agile Marketing will be based on the original Agile Manifesto and Agile principles.

## AN INTRODUCTION TO THE 12 AGILE PRINCIPLES

In addition to the Agile Manifesto, the group also agreed it would be beneficial to define a set of principles to guide others in their adoption of Agile. While the next chapter explores these in more depth, the following are those principles verbatim:

1. Our highest priority is to satisfy the customer through the early and continuous delivery of valuable software.

2. Welcome changing requirements, even late in development. Agile processes harness change for the customer's competitive advantage.

3. Deliver working software frequently, from a couple of weeks to a couple of months, with a preference to the shorter timescale.

4. Business people and developers must work together daily throughout the project.

5. Build projects around motivated individuals. Give them the environment and support they need and trust them to get the job done.

6. The most efficient and effective method of conveying information to and within a development team is face-to-face conversation.

7. Working software is the primary measure of progress.

8. Agile processes promote sustainable development. The sponsors, developers, and users should be able to maintain a constant pace indefinitely.

9. Continuous attention to technical excellence and good design enhances agility.

10. Simplicity—the art of maximizing the amount of work not done—is essential.

11. The best architectures, requirements, and designs emerge from self-organizing teams.

12. At regular intervals, the team reflects on how to become more effective, then tunes and adjusts its behavior accordingly.

You'll notice that the terms *software* and development explicitly stated within the principles, making these ostensibly geared toward software engineers. Yet, as we've seen over the convening years, there are many other applications of Agile beyond this, and particularly in the area of marketing which is the focus of this book. The principles will be framed in terms of marketing when revisited.

## A DEFINITION OF AGILE

So, what exactly is Agile, then? Is it a methodology, a set of principles, or something else altogether?

Merriam-Webster defines *methodology* as "a body of methods, rules, and postulates employed by a discipline: a particular procedure or set of procedures."[12]

Agile itself does not have a specific set of ceremonies, techniques, or pre-scribed steps that must happen in sequence, meaning that it is not a meth-odology. That said, it is often referred to as a methodology, which adds to the confusion about what Agile is and is not.

The best way of thinking about Agile is that it is a philosophy guide by a set of principles—the 12 that will be reviewed next—demonstrating a com-mitment to tight feedback cycles and continuous improvement. These princi-ples don't dictate exactly how work is performed and on what timeline or by whom, but rather the spirit in which work should be planned, performed, and deemed successful or not.

That said, there are several methodologies that have been created that follow Agile principles—several of which will be explored briefly, and one (scrum) that will be explored in depth throughout the pages in this book. These methodologies, such as scrum, do contain clear prescriptions on how work should be performed, the roles needed to perform the work, and more.

Following is an exploration of the principles of Agile, which will help give a much fuller understanding of how one can apply it to marketing work.

## INTRODUCING AGILECORP

Readers will follow AgileCorp throughout this book as their marketing team takes a journey from using traditional, waterfall approaches, to optimizing their efforts using approaches that embrace Agile principles and utilize the scrum methodology.

AgileCorp is a B2B software company headquartered in San Mateo, California, in Silicon Valley. The company has had a successful track record and growth based on its SaaS platform that provides businesses with a unique set of database functionality.

Part of AgileCorp's success could be attributed to its embrace of Agile principles. But this embrace only applies to the software engineering team. Other teams in the organization follow more traditional waterfall approaches, including AgileCorp's marketing team.

Despite the company's growth, based primarily on word of mouth and the great reputation of its product and its functionality, with an initial public offering (IPO) looming, the marketing team is under increased pressure to grow even more quickly.

While the marketing team would love to help the company have a successful IPO (after all, most of the employees are also shareholders who would benefit substantially), the workload is already too much for most team members and they are often falling behind schedule on the marketing campaigns and initiatives they've planned for the year.

AgileCorp's marketing department sees how the software engineering team seems to be able to take on more work and even pivot to adjust to customer demands and rarely skips a beat. After a series of conversations between marketing team members and the software engineering team, it looks like one difference between the two teams is the marketing team's reliance on waterfall methods and the engineering team's adoption of Agile principles, and the scrum methodology.

Based on this, the AgileCorp marketing team decides to explore if or how an Agile approach to marketing might be worth considering. As readers cover key ideas about Agile and Agile marketing in the pages that follow, they'll track AgileCorp's journey toward Agile marketing adoption.

## CONCLUSION

Much has been written about and attributed to Agile, but following the definition explored in this chapter should ensure readers have the most accurate understanding of Agile to help them avoid adding to the confusion that already exists. With these definitions in hand, readers should explore the twelve Agile principles.

### Notes

1. Sacolick, Isaac. A Brief History of the Agile Methodology. April 8, 2022. InfoWorld. *https://www.infoworld.com/article/3655646/a-brief-history-of-the-agile-methodology.html* Retrieved January 7, 2023.

2. Akiwatkar, Rohit. Agile Adoption Statistics: How is Software Development Changing? November 10, 2022. Simform. *https://www.simform.com/blog/state-of-agile-adoption*. Retrieved January 7, 2023.

3. Ohno, Taiichi. (1988). *Toyota Production System: Beyond Large-Scale Production*. CRC Press..

4. Lean Enterprise Institute. (n.d.). *Toyota Production System*. Lean Enterprise Institute. *https://www.lean.org/lexicon-terms/toyota-production-system/*, Retrieved June 11, 2024,

5. Womack, James P., Daniel T. Jones, and Daniel Roos. (1990). *The Machine that Changed the World*. Rawson Associates.

6. Gilb, Tom, and Kai Gilb. Evolutionary Project Management (Original page, external archive)." Archived from the original on March 27, 2016. *https://web.archive.org/web/20160327214807/http://www.gilb.com/Project-Management*. Retrieved November 8, 2024.

7. Swamidass, P. M. (Ed.). (2000). Heavyweight Project Organization. In *Encyclopedia of Production and Manufacturing Management*. Springer. *https://doi.org/10.1007/1-4020-0612-8_400*

8. Sutherland, Jeff, and J. J. Sutherland. (2014). *Scrum: The Art of Doing Twice the Work in Half the Time*. Crown Currency.

9. Beck, Kent, Mike Beedle, Arie van Bennekum et al. (2001). The Agile Manifesto. *https://agilemanifesto.org/*. Retrieved January 7, 2023.

10. Varhol, Peter. To Agility and Beyond: The History—and Legacy—of Agile Development. Tech Beacon. *https://techbeacon.com/app-dev-testing/agility-beyond-history-legacy-agile-development*. Retrieved January 5, 2023.

11. *https://agilemanifesto.org/*

12. *https://www.merriam-webster.com/dictionary/methodology*

# 2

# *The Twelve Agile Principles*

As briefly explored in the last chapter, The Agile Manifesto was brief yet powerful. The authors of the manifesto introduce twelve principles that add a layer of depth and clarity to those principles.

## EXPLORING THE PRINCIPLES

The twelve Agile principles will more fully introduce one to incorporating Agile approaches and should guide ongoing exploration and implementation of Agile marketing beyond this book. While these were originally written from a software engineering perspective, with a few minor modifications here and there, they all have application to the realm of marketing as well.

Readers will be exploring each with some light edits to make them most directly relevant for marketers, and then explore how marketers can apply these to their thinking and approach. These principles will also be woven throughout many of the ideas explored within the book.

### 1: Our Highest Priority Is to Satisfy the Customer Through the Early and Continuous Delivery of Value

The first Agile principle emphasizes how important it is to consistently deliver value. Readers might note that the original principle states "the delivery of valuable *software*" but for our purposes here, this has been modified to simply say "value." This makes the principle apply to marketing or just about anything else.

While the term "customer" in software engineering terms often (but not always) refers to internal customers that will benefit from improvements to software features and functionality, the delivery of value

Intentionally stating that the highest priority is the continuous delivery of value sets the stage for the rest of the principles, while mandating to those adopting Agile principles that if there are questions as to what to focus on, this is the clear winner.

### How It Applies to Marketers

In marketing, this principle translates to continually delivering valuable content, campaigns, and customer experiences. The goal here is to keep external customers engaged and satisfied by providing ongoing value, and to provide internal customers supplied with the materials and initiatives that drive new customers, engage current customers, and win back lapsed ones.

Applying this principle helps marketers stay focused on what is relevant and responsive to customer needs. It ensures that marketing efforts are more aligned with what customers find valuable, leading to higher engagement and loyalty, rather than jumping between tactics with questionable value.

One thing to note, however, is that the definition of *value* is critical here. The topic will be explored further in Chapter 23, but it is worth noting here that while value may be in the eye of the beholder, a shared definition of value is required for sustainable success.

### The Risk of not Applying This Principle

First, keep in mind that the writers of the original Agile Manifesto framed this as the highest priority of the twelve. If marketing teams fail to apply this principle and are unable to continuously deliver value, they risk losing customer engagement and the results of that engagement with both end customers as well as their internal ones.

With those end customers, this can lead to decreased customer satisfaction, lower engagement rates, and ultimately, a decline in brand loyalty and revenue.

With internal teams, failing to deliver continuous value may have the unwanted effect of causing teams to find workarounds. For instance, a sales team that relies on marketing to provide assets to support their efforts may start creating their own items if a marketing team fails to deliver what is needed. This may cause materials that are off brand, don't align with the overall marketing strategy, or many other negative outcomes.

By prioritizing customer satisfaction through continuous delivery of value, marketing teams can maintain strong relationships with their audience, adapt to changing needs, and drive sustained business success. The principle highlights the importance of being proactive and consistent in delivering what customers want and need, and why they became customers in the first place.

### 2: Welcome Changing Requirements, Even Late in the Process—Agile Processes Harness Change for the Customer's Competitive Advantage

The second Agile principle highlights the importance of flexibility and adaptability in responding to business environments where changing requirements are the norm, not the exception. The principle recognizes that changes can occur at any stage and encourages leveraging these changes to create competitive advantages for customers. Also note that this principle's language has been edited slightly to say "late in the process" rather than "late in development," to make it more directly applicable to marketers and marketing teams.

*How It Applies to Marketers*

In marketing, the second Agile principle means being open to adjusting approaches—campaigns, strategies, tactics, or even the way marketing work is performed—based on new information, market shifts, and customer feedback. Thus, marketers should be ready to pivot their efforts to better meet evolving customer needs and market conditions.

By being responsive to changing conditions both externally in the market or internally within the organization, marketers can capitalize on new opportunities, address emerging challenges, and better serve their customers.

*The Risk of not Applying This Principle*

Adhering to a waterfall approach, as described in Chapter 1, is the antithesis to the ideas behind this principle. If marketing teams resist change and stick rigidly to their original plans, they risk missing out on opportunities and failing to meet customer expectations. This inflexibility can lead to wasted resources, ineffective campaigns, and a loss of competitive edge.

Instead, welcoming changing requirements, even late in the game, allows marketing teams to harness change for competitive advantage. By staying flexible and responsive, marketers can better serve their customers and achieve greater success in a dynamic market environment.

## 3: Deliver Actionable Output Frequently, from a Couple of Weeks to a Couple of Months, with a Preference to the Shorter Timescale

The third principle emphasizes the importance of frequent delivery of output or updates. The goal of adopting this principle is to provide value to internal and external customers regularly and to gather feedback for continuous improvement, rather than having long waits between updates or new materials.

It should also be noted that the original principle stated that teams should deliver "actionable *software* frequently," and this was adjusted to be more directly relevant to marketers.

### How It Applies to Marketers

In marketing, this principle translates to regularly adjusting campaigns, content, and marketing initiatives. It does not necessarily mean that marketers need to be continually *launching* new things per se, but rather the marketing output should be designed to be adjusted and optimized rather than created once and run for months on end with little adjustment. By doing so, marketers can keep their audience engaged, test different strategies, and quickly iterate based on performance data.

Frequent delivery of updates in marketing helps brands maintain relevance and adjust to changes—even small but meaningful ones—that can make the difference between continuous growth and stagnation.

### The Risk of not Applying This Principle

If marketing teams fail to embrace this principle and do not deliver valuable updates frequently, they risk losing relevance and performance with key customers, who are continually in undated with other offers from the competition. Long gaps between optimizing campaigns or content can lead to decreased engagement, missed opportunities for feedback, and a slower response to market changes.

Delivering marketing output frequently, with a preference for shorter timescales, ensures that marketers remain relevant and responsive to their audience. Regular updates and new content help maintain engagement and allow for continuous improvement based on feedback and performance data.

## 4: Stakeholders and Marketers Must Work Together Regularly Throughout the Project

The fourth Agile principle stresses the importance of continuous collaboration between business stakeholders and marketers, with the goal of ensuring alignment between business goals and customer needs.

The original principle as written stated that "business people and *developers* must work together," and stipulated that they should do so "daily." This has been edited to replace *business people* with *stakeholders* and *developers* with *marketers*, and to replace *daily* with *regularly*.

The term *stakeholders* is relevant because, with the complexity of marketing teams, there are often siloes even within an enterprise organization's marketing team (e.g., a social media team might be separate from the email marketing team, search marketing team, or Web site team), let alone between marketing and other areas of the business. So regular collaboration with relevant teams, termed *stakeholders* here, captures the spirit of the principle.

As for the daily approach, readers will explore the need for regular, daily communication and collaboration within an Agile team as they learn about scrum and see how it can be applied to marketing. For the purposes of applying these principles to marketing however, it may be true that stakeholders outside of marketing need regular involvement, but whether that is daily, weekly, or some other frequency can likely be left to the teams themselves (which we will get to shortly as well).

That said, the idea behind this principle is that any disconnect between marketing and the business is not optimal and a key way to avoid that is with regular contact, communication, and exploration of ways to optimize efforts.

### How It Applies to Marketers

In a marketing context, this principle translates to encouraging regular collaboration between marketers within siloed marketing departments, as well as between marketing teams, sales teams, product teams, and other stakeholders. This ensures that marketing strategies are aligned with business objectives, product developments, and customer insights.

Collaborative efforts are core to Agile approaches, and they lead to more cohesive and effective marketing strategies as well as marketing outcomes. When marketing teams work closely across functional areas, as well as with other departments, they can create campaigns that are well-informed, timely, and aligned with overall business goals.

### The Risk of not Applying This Principle

If marketing teams operate in silos and do not collaborate with other departments, they risk creating disjointed and ineffective campaigns. Lack of communication can lead to misaligned goals, missed opportunities, and a failure to meet customer needs effectively.

Thus, regular collaboration ensures that marketing efforts are well-coordinated and continuously aligned with broader business objectives. Daily communication helps create more integrated and impactful campaigns that drive marketing—and overall business—success.

### 5: Build Initiatives Around Motivated Individuals—Give Them the Environment and Support They Need and Trust Them to Get the Job Done

The fifth Agile principle showcases how important it is to understand and build an environment that marketing teams find engaging and where team members have the leadership and infrastructure to do their best work.

The principle specifically emphasizes the importance of having motivated and empowered individuals on the team. It highlights the need to provide a supportive environment and trust team members to execute their responsibilities effectively.

#### How it Applies to Marketers

Being surrounded by a motivated team that is aligned around common goals and given the tools to be successful can be a powerful thing. In marketing, this principle means assembling a team of passionate and skilled marketers, providing them with the resources and autonomy they need, and trusting them to deliver creative and effective campaigns, content, experiences in an environment conducive to continual improvement.

While it might seem obvious, this principle takes an intentional approach to sustain, but the rewards are well worth it. Motivated and empowered marketers are more likely to produce innovative and high-quality work. When team members feel supported and trusted, they are more engaged, proactive, and committed to achieving the marketing goals.

#### The Risk of not Applying This Principle

If team members are not motivated or lack the necessary support, it can lead to low morale, decreased productivity, and subpar results, even when leadership sets high expectations, deadlines, and incentives.

Leadership and management play critical roles here. For instance, micromanagement and lack of trust can stifle creativity and initiative, resulting in less effective marketing efforts.

Building marketing projects around motivated individuals and providing them with the right environment and support fosters creativity, innovation, and high performance. Trusting team members to get the job done leads to more effective and impactful marketing campaigns.

## 6: The Most Efficient and Effective Method of Conveying Information to and Within a Development Team Is Direct Conversations

The sixth Agile principle underscores the value of direct, personal communication. This has been updated to account for the increasingly remote and virtual world we live in, thus "face-to-face" has been edited to say "direct conversations," whether those are in-person, over a Zoom call, or otherwise. Regardless of the medium they are conducted in, these direct interactions are seen as the most efficient and effective way to share information and ideas within a team.

### How It Applies to Marketers

In marketing, this principle translates to regular, in-person or virtual meetings to discuss campaigns, strategies, and performance, rather than asynchronous methods such as sending emails, Slack messages, or otherwise. In contrast to asynchronous communication, direct conversation—when approached effectively—can help ensure that everyone is on the same page and can address issues or brainstorm ideas more effectively.

Considering the pace of change in just about any industry, and the expectation of quick turnaround times in most marketing environments, direct communication fosters clearer understanding, quicker decision-making, and stronger relationships among team members than communicating solely over asynchronous methods. It minimizes the risk of miscommunication and helps address challenges and opportunities in real-time.

### The Risk of not Applying This Principle

Relying solely on written communication or infrequent meetings can lead to misunderstandings, delays, and a lack of cohesion among team members, and can lead to goals and delivery of marketing initiatives to get out of sync. Additionally, important nuances may be lost in text, and team members might not feel as connected or engaged.

Utilizing direct communication within marketing teams enhances clarity, collaboration, and efficiency. These direct interactions help ensure that everyone is aligned and can contribute effectively to the success of marketing initiatives.

### 7: Actionable Marketing Output Is the Primary Measure of Progress

Rewritten to replace *software* with *marketing output,* this seventh principle states that the most important indicator of progress is the delivery of usable deliverables, not simply artifacts that sit on a shelf, so to speak.

It emphasizes the importance of tangible outcomes over abstract metrics or documentation, and it further reinforces the need for marketing teams to be delivering working products versus endless prototyping or building large initiatives that are months in the making.

#### How It Applies to Marketers

As discussed previously, in marketing, this principle translates to focusing teams on more frequently delivering tangible results and other deliverables as the primary measures of progress. This could include completed campaigns (or optimizations to existing ones), published content, or measurable improvements in key performance indicators (KPIs).

#### The Risk of not Applying This Principle

If marketing teams do not prioritize tangible outcomes, they may spend too much time on planning, meetings, or creating documentation that doesn't directly contribute to business goals. This leads to bloated budgets, projects that become so complex that they fail to launch or other inefficiencies, delays, and an overall lack of measurable progress toward strategic goals.

Focusing on tangible marketing outcomes as the primary measure of progress ensures that marketing efforts are effective and aligned with business objectives. It helps teams stay productive and continuously deliver value through actionable results.

### 8: Agile Processes Promote Sustainable Output—Teams Should Be Able to Maintain a Constant Pace Indefinitely

This principle emphasizes the importance of sustainable work practices and where this originally said "sustainable *development*" and mentioned sponsors and developers in the list, it has been shortened to "teams."

Embracing Agile principles doesn't just mean being quick for a short period of time to produce short-term results. Adopting processes based on Agile principles should enable all participants to work at a consistent, manageable pace without burnout or excessive stress for the long-term.

*How It Applies to Marketers*

In marketing, this principle emphasizes the need for thinking about the long-term while optimizing work in the short-term. This means creating a balanced workflow allowing the marketing team to consistently produce high-quality work without overextending themselves. Sustainable practices help maintain long-term productivity and creativity.

*The Risk of not Applying This Principle*

If marketing teams do not adhere to sustainable practices, they risk burnout, decreased productivity, and higher turnover rates. Overworking can lead to mistakes, lower quality output, and a negative work environment, which ultimately hampers the team's ability to achieve its goals.

Sustainable approaches to marketing prevent burnout and ensure that the marketing team remains motivated and effective over time, thus this principle has a good deal of alignment with the fifth principle that emphasizes the value of engaged teams. After all, Agile isn't simply a short-term fix—it is a way of working that can produce great, long-term results.

## 9: Continuous Attention to Technical Excellence and Good Design Enhances Agility

The ninth principle focuses on quality of work, and the term "technical"—while originally intended for a software engineering environment—can apply equally to the work performed by a marketing team.

The benefits of some of the Scrum rituals such as daily standups as well as retrospectives also support the concept of continuous attention, as these regularly occurring components provide consistent opportunities to focus on the design, quality, and continuous improvement of the work being performed.

*How it Applies to Marketers*

How well a marketing campaign is planned, implemented, and measured requires technical mastery, albeit of different tools and skill sets than creating a software product might.

Likewise, "good design" could refer to the creatives associated with your marketing effort. However, it could just as easily, and perhaps more appropriately in this case, apply to the processes you use to plan and launch campaigns, the way you build audience segments and the methods you use to provide attribution for your efforts across channels.

*The Risk of not Applying This Principle*

Lack of strategic design when approaching marketing efforts can become apparent at several critical points in an initiative, and almost always results in rework or refactoring some ill-informed assumptions or hastily produced requirements.

Likewise, failing to provide continuous attention to detail can, at best, result in lack of cohesion in a marketing campaign, and at worst, results in a failure to perform, inconsistent measurements, branding misalignment, or many other potential negative outcomes.

## 10: Simplicity—the Art of Maximizing the Amount of Work not Done—Is Essential

The tenth principle emphasizes the value of reducing complexity in processes and solutions. By focusing on what is truly necessary and eliminating unnecessary tasks, teams can work more efficiently and effectively.

Lean approaches will be briefly explored as well, which share some of the fundamental philosophy of Agile approaches. In lean, the reduction of waste—referred to by the Japanese word *muda*—is a key concept.

In the following Agile principles, paying attention to what work is actually contributing value and eliminating that which is not is also a key tenet, and this principle underscores that idea.

*How It Applies to Marketers*

The concept of streamlining strategies and focusing on the most impactful activities does not sound too controversial on the surface, but so much of what is a matter of day-to-day work includes wasted effort, or tasks that don't contribute meaningfully to business results. Thus, applying this principle to a team's marketing work involves cutting out redundant processes and concentrating on actions that directly contribute to marketing goals.

*The Risk of not Applying This Principle*

Failing to embrace simplicity can lead to overly complex and bureaucratic processes that slow down marketing efforts. This can result in delayed campaigns, higher costs, and decreased effectiveness due to inefficiencies and distractions from core objectives.

Simplicity and a focus on prioritizing the work that truly makes an impact helps marketers stay focused and avoid wasting resources on nonessential tasks. By simplifying their approach, marketers can be more agile, quickly adapt to changes, and deliver better results with less effort.

### 11: The Best Marketing Output Emerges from Self-Organizing Teams

The eleventh Agile principle was originally written to specify software-specific components, but this has been rewritten to simply say "marketing output." The idea behind this principle is that the most effective solutions come from teams that organize themselves and are empowered to take ownership of their work and how it is done. Approaching it this way means that teams can be more innovative and efficient because rather than being told how to do their work by a manager or leader who may be disconnected from how to do the work, the ones responsible for the output get to decide how to best approach it.

Make no mistake, this does not mean that these teams are now freed from achieving goals and objectives, nor are they given the responsibility of setting those goals. The teams are still responsible to achieve the objectives set forth by leadership and the organization, but the teams are given greater responsibility as to *how* they create the work that contributes to achieving those goals.

#### How It Applies to Marketers

This means allowing marketing teams the autonomy to organize their strategies, campaigns, and workflows, as long as their results contribute to the goals and KPIs set forth. Applying this principle with marketing teams encourages a culture where team members can make decisions, experiment, and take initiative without excessive oversight.

#### The Risk of not Applying This Principle

Without allowing teams to self-organize, marketing efforts can become rigid and slow, and when the ways of working are dictated by managers that have lost touch with how the work would best be accomplished it can introduce unnecessary steps and general frustration. Overly controlled environments can stifle creativity and innovation, leading to less effective campaigns and lower team morale. Teams might also struggle to quickly adapt to new opportunities or challenges.

Self-organizing teams are more adaptable and can respond quickly to changes in the market or customer behavior. This autonomy fosters creativity and innovation, leading to more effective and impactful marketing efforts.

### 12: At Regular Intervals, the Team Reflects on How to Become More Effective, Then Tunes and Adjusts Its Behavior Accordingly

The last Agile principle highlights the importance of continuous improvement, which is a key tenet of Agile approaches. By periodically assessing their performance, processes, and marketing results, teams can identify areas for improvement and make necessary adjustments.

By making this part of the process of doing marketing, rather than an infrequent audit or review, team members will grow to feel more comfortable sharing what is working as well as what is not.

### How It Applies to Marketers

For marketers, this means setting aside time for regular retrospectives to evaluate the effectiveness of campaigns, strategies, and workflows, and to analyze the performance from both internal efficiencies, and end results. Doing this with a regular cadence allows the marketing team to learn from their experiences, optimize their efforts, and stay agile in their approach.

### The Risk of not Applying This Principle

Without regular reflection and adjustment, marketing teams can become stagnant and miss opportunities for improvement. They may continue making the same mistakes or fail to recognize and adapt to changes in the market or customer behavior, leading to less effective campaigns and strategies.

Additionally, reflecting regularly encourages team members to speak up and build the capacity to both celebrate the wins as well as to talk constructively about areas for improvement. When this is done regularly, there is plenty of opportunity to talk about the good as well as the bad.

Continuous improvement is crucial for staying competitive and effective in a rapidly changing market. By regularly reflecting and adjusting, marketing teams can enhance their strategies, address weaknesses, and capitalize on new opportunities. The overall concept of continuous improvement is explored in more depth later in the book.

## CONCLUSION

These twelve Agile principles, adjusted slightly for a marketing audience, provide a framework for creating an adaptable, efficient, and customer-focused marketing strategy, and form the foundation for the approaches we will be discussing in the pages that follow. By applying these principles, marketing teams can enhance their agility, foster innovation, and consistently deliver value to their customers, both external and internal.

Regular optimization and improvement ensure that marketing efforts remain relevant and effective in a hyper-competitive business environment. Now that readers have been introduced to the twelve principles of Agile, the next chapter explores how to put the principles into practice and how all of this relates to *marketing*.

# WHAT IS AGILE MARKETING?

Based on everything that has been reviewed so far, the definition of *Agile marketing* is not so different from Agile software development and the process discussed in Chapter 2. While the work performed is very different between software engineering and marketing teams, the approaches to using Agile within each are the same.

*Agile marketing* can be defined as an approach to marketing that utilizes Agile principles and practices.

This includes an iterative process of continuous improvement, self-organizing teams, a focus on the end customer, and the principles we have just reviewed. It should be noted that while Agile marketing and Agile software development are similar and should be approached in similar ways, they may not always be implemented in exactly the same manner. As in all things, a common-sense approach should be taken when applying Agile software development principles to Agile marketing.

As shown in Figure 3.1, the process for Agile marketing looks much like the diagram of the Agile software approach in Figure 1.1 from Chapter 1. Instead of a project goal, one might have *campaign* goals, but the idea is still the same. Take an iterative approach toward achieving campaign goals by performing the work in a series of iterations or *sprints*.

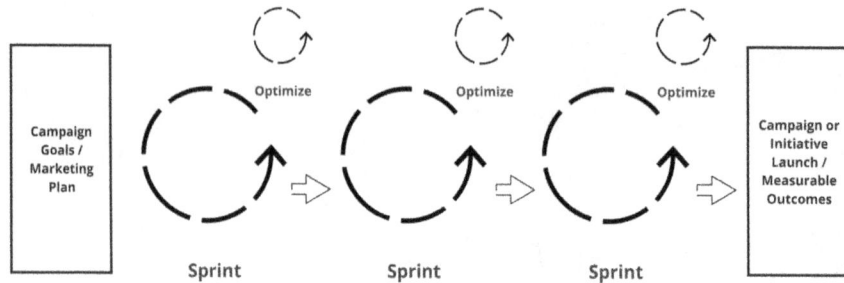

*FIGURE 3.1* Agile marketing approach.

## WHAT IS AGILE MARKETING NOT?

As important as it is to understand what Agile marketing is, it's also important to understand what it is not. Agile marketing is not a reactive approach; it is much the opposite. Agile marketing's decisions are based on a rational approach, similar to the scientific method. Agile marketing does not lack planning; it just encourages planning in shorter intervals and, in a way, encourages measuring results and incorporating feedback.

Finally, Agile marketing is not simply an excuse to continually make changes. Business goals and the definition of business value a marketing team provides will not often change, despite the need to adjust approaches. Thus, marketing teams need to balance the waste (*muda*) that switching and changing costs (in terms of time and resources) with the benefits of changing the approach using real, measurable objectives as the basis for decisions. This balanced approach helps to ensure that changes aren't happening just for change's sake.

## HOW AGILE MARKETING DIFFERS FROM TRADITIONAL MARKETING

Agile marketing differs from some of the traditional marketing methods in a few key ways.

- Agile marketing is scientific in its approach to creating hypotheses and testing them to ensure the best approaches are used to achieve the goals set at the beginning of a project or campaign.
- It embraces an iterative approach to achieving its goals. Because of this, Agile marketers are open to modifying their initial approaches if a better approach is uncovered that can more effectively achieve their goals.

▓ Finally, Agile marketing requires continuous improvement and reflection to ensure that both the marketing methods and the processes implemented are optimal. This acknowledgment that there is always room for improvement keeps Agile marketing teams motivated and engaged while continually striving for perfection.

Table 3.1 illustrates how Agile principles may be applied differently between software engineering teams and marketing teams. These distinctions can help emphasize the unique aspects of Agile in various functional areas of an organization like AgileCorp.

*TABLE 3.1* Comparison of Agile Concepts Between Software Teams and Marketing Teams

| Aspect of Agile | Application in Software Engineering | Application in Marketing |
|---|---|---|
| **Sprint Length** | Typically one–four weeks. Allows for rapid development and testing of software. | Might vary more; shorter sprints could be used for quick campaigns or adjustments based on market feedback. |
| **Product Backlog** | Composed of technical features and requirements. | Filled with creative ideas, campaigns, content needs, and market research tasks. |
| **Definition of *Done*** | Software feature is fully developed, tested, and ready to deploy. | Campaign is launched, and initial results or analytics are reviewed. |
| **Daily Standups** | Focus on development progress, technical challenges, and immediate tasks. | Focus on content creation status, campaign metrics, and shifting market dynamics. |
| **User Stories** | Often technical, focused on user functionality and system interactions. | Centered around customer personas, buyer journeys, and engagement metrics. |
| **Sprint Reviews** | Review completed software features and functionality. | Review campaign performance, creative output, and ROI. |
| **Sprint Retrospectives** | Aim to improve code quality and development processes. | Aim to enhance creative processes, campaign timing, and team collaboration. |
| **Stakeholder Collaboration** | Regular interaction with product managers, testers, and sometimes customers. | Often involves broader interactions, including sales teams, customers, and media partners. |
| **Continuous Integration/ Deployment** | Frequent code commits, automated testing, and regular deployments. | Frequent updates to campaign strategies and marketing materials based on analytics and feedback. |
| **Team Roles** | Roles are often highly specialized (developer, tester, scrum master). | Roles can be more fluid, with team members often switching between creative, strategic, and analytic tasks. |

## WHY AN AGILE APPROACH IS NEEDED IN MARKETING

Many factors contribute to the need for organizations to take an Agile approach to their marketing. The pace of change in customer preferences, competitive forces, technology, and external dependencies, such as the economy, societal impacts, data/privacy concerns and others. There is also the cost of deliberation within organizations and having to redo or undo work done on long-term initiatives.

Some immediate benefits of taking an Agile marketing approach include the following:

- The ability to optimize existing marketing efforts more quickly without waiting for lengthy review periods and cycles

- Enabling a culture of transparency, collaboration, and continuous improvement that are applied directly to marketing work being performed

- Anticipating change, even if the details are unknown or unknowable

- A quicker time to better marketing results

- An increased and continual focus on observable and measurable results and a commitment to improving them

All of this adds up to both short- and long-term gains for marketing teams and the companies they represent.

## AGILECORP'S MARKETING CHALLENGE

At AgileCorp, a B2B software company in San Mateo, California, in the heart of Silicon Valley, the marketing team has traditionally operated under a waterfall approach, planning extensive campaigns months in advance with rigid, sequential project milestones. Recently, they encountered significant challenges with this method, particularly during a major product launch. The campaign was meticulously planned; however, halfway through, a competitor released a similar product, rendering AgileCorp's original marketing strategy less effective. The marketing team found themselves struggling to adapt quickly. Significant time and resources had already been invested based on initial plans, and the team's ability to pivot was severely constrained by the waterfall method's linear and inflexible nature.

Frustrated by these limitations, the marketing team convened a meeting with AgileCorp's software engineering team, which had been successfully using scrum for the past five years. The engineers shared insights into how

Agile methodologies, particularly scrum, had enabled them to be more adaptable and responsive to changes. They highlighted several key benefits:

- Flexibility: The ability to adjust priorities in real-time based on the most current business needs and market conditions.
- Speed: Shorter development cycles (sprints) allowed for rapid iterations and quicker feedback loops.
- Collaboration: Daily stand-ups and regular sprint reviews fostered a highly collaborative environment where issues were quickly communicated and resolved.

The marketing team at AgileCorp was intrigued by these benefits, and saw a potential solution to their challenges. They recognized that adopting a scrum-based approach could allow them more flexibility to adjust campaign tactics on the fly and better align their activities with real-time market dynamics and customer feedback. The prospect of having shorter, iterative cycles with more frequent opportunities to evaluate success points seemed like a promising way to enhance their responsiveness and effectiveness in a competitive market.

Convinced by the engineering team's successful application of scrum in software development and motivated by their own recent struggles with the waterfall approach, the marketing team decided they would explore what Agile approaches might look like for their team and the work they do to support the company's growth.

This decision marked the beginning of their journey toward Agile Marketing, aiming to transform their traditional, plan-driven approach into one that is more dynamic and adaptive. In the chapters that follow, we will track their progress toward being an Agile marketing team.

## CONCLUSION

The book has looked at Agile principles in general, and then explored how each of those principles as well as the overall philosophy of Agile can be applied to marketing at a high level.

The next chapter will dive a little deeper and explore some further nuances between Agile when applied to marketing versus its original application in software engineering. All of this sets us up to learn more about several methods of approaching Agile in marketing.

# 4

# *Agile in Marketing versus Software*

Chapter 3 explored Agile principles and approaches that originated in software development and have been increasingly applied to other fields such as marketing. While the core principles of agile remain the same across different domains, there are some key differences in how Agile is applied in software engineering versus marketing, as shown in Figure 4.1.

Many marketers' first introduction to Agile principles and practices are often based on exposure from working with technology or software engineering teams that use scrum, kanban, or other approaches.

## COMPARING ENGINEERING AND MARKETING

Table 4.1 shows some differences and similarities between how software engineering teams and marketing teams approach the use of Agile methods.

### Iterative Development versus Iterative Campaigns

In software engineering, Agile focuses on developing and delivering software in short iterations, with frequent feedback and adaptation to changing requirements.

In contrast, marketing teams use agile to plan and execute campaigns in shorter cycles, with a focus on rapid experimentation, feedback, and adaptation to changing customer preferences.

*TABLE 4.1* Comparison between software engineering teams and marketing teams approach to the use of Agile methods.

| Aspect of Agile | Application in Software Engineering | Application in Marketing |
|---|---|---|
| Iterative Development | Focuses on developing and delivering software in short iterations, emphasizing frequent feedback and adaptation to changing requirements. | Plans and executes campaigns in shorter cycles, emphasizing rapid experimentation, feedback, and adaptation to changing customer preferences. |
| Nature of Work | Requires technical expertise, emphasizes collaboration, automated testing, and continuous integration. | Involves creative work, emphasizes collaborative brainstorming, rapid prototyping, and frequent customer feedback. |
| Measurable Outcomes | Success measured by functionality and reliability of software, using metrics like system performance and bug counts. | Success is often measured by customer engagement metrics such as Web site traffic, social media engagement, or sales conversions. |
| Team Composition | Consists of specialized roles like developers, testers, and product managers. | More cross-functional, with roles spanning creative, media, analytics, and sales departments. |
| Flexibility vs. Adaptability | High degree of flexibility needed to accommodate technical changes and complexities. | Needs adaptability to align with shifting customer preferences and market conditions. |
| Sprint vs. Campaign Planning | Sprint planning involves setting specific goals and tasks for short, defined periods. | Campaign planning focuses on defining objectives, strategies, and tactics for specific marketing initiatives. |
| Retrospectives vs. Debriefings | Retrospectives are held to reflect on the past sprint and plan improvements for the next. | Debriefings are used to review campaign effectiveness, gather lessons learned, and plan future strategies. |
| Prioritization Criteria | Tasks are prioritized based on technical complexity, risk, and business value. | Campaigns are prioritized based on customer needs, competitive landscape, and strategic alignment to maximize return on investment (ROI). |

When transitioning to Agile marketing, teams should embrace iterative campaign planning and execution. They should start small with pilot campaigns that allow for quick feedback loops and adjustments. This approach not only reduces the risk associated with large-scale campaigns but also enables the team to adapt to consumer reactions in real time. By learning from each iteration, marketing teams can more effectively refine their strategies and tactics, enhancing overall campaign effectiveness.

## Technical versus Creative Work

Software engineering often requires a higher degree of technical expertise, while marketing involves more creative work including copywriting, campaign imagery. Agile methods in software engineering emphasize collaboration, automated testing, and continuous integration, whereas agile marketing focuses on collaborative brainstorming, rapid prototyping, and frequent customer feedback.

In an increasingly digital marketing environment, there are numerous technical components, from analytics integration to features and functionality required to make a campaign successful. This can be where collaborations between marketing and technology teams are needed and where technical versus creative work come together in a single Agile process.

In Agile marketing, teams should foster an environment that encourages creative brainstorming and rapid prototyping. Teams should focus on collaborative efforts to generate ideas and quickly transform them into testable concepts. This could involve using tools like digital mock-ups or A/B testing platforms to experiment with different creative approaches and immediately gauge audience response, ensuring that final outputs are both innovative and aligned with consumer preferences.

## Specification Matching versus Measurable Outcomes

In software engineering, success is often measured by the functionality of the product and how it maps back to requirements specifications, while in marketing, success is increasingly tied to predefined marketing goals and key performance indicators (KPIs), although in some cases there may be more subjective requirements that depends on customer preferences.

Agile methods in software engineering emphasize measuring progress through working software and customer feedback, while agile marketing focuses on measuring campaign effectiveness through metrics such as Web site traffic, social media engagement, or sales conversions.

Define clear, measurable objectives for marketing campaigns to evaluate their success. Agile marketing should focus on key performance indicators (KPIs) such as conversion rates, engagement levels, and return on investment (ROI). Regularly collecting and analyzing data will help the team understand what works and what doesn't, allowing for timely adjustments to maximize campaign impact.

## Cross-Functional Teams versus Specialized Roles

Software engineering teams typically consist of specialized roles such as developers, testers, and product managers, all fitting within the realm of software development. In contrast, marketing teams are often more cross-functional, with members from various departments such as creative, media, and analytics.

Thus, Agile methods in software engineering emphasize collaboration across specialized roles, while agile marketing focuses on collaboration across cross-functional teams.

As marketing teams adopt Agile, it's beneficial to encourage cross-functional collaboration. This could involve integrating members from different departments—such as creative, media buying, and analytics—to work together in dynamic teams. This diversity fosters unique perspectives and skill sets, driving innovation and allowing the team to respond swiftly to changing market conditions and customer needs.

## Flexibility versus Adaptability

Software engineering requires a high degree of flexibility to accommodate changing requirements and technical complexities. In contrast, marketing campaigns need to be adaptable to changing customer preferences and market conditions.

Agile methods in software engineering emphasize flexibility through continuous integration and automated testing, while agile marketing focuses on adaptability through rapid experimentation, monitoring campaign analytics, and customer feedback.

Marketing teams should prioritize adaptability by remaining open to changing customer preferences and market trends. This involves being prepared to pivot or alter campaign strategies quickly based on real-time feedback and emerging data. Adopting tools that facilitate rapid response, such as digital marketing platforms that can adjust targeting or messaging on the fly, will empower teams to remain competitive and relevant.

### Sprint Planning versus Campaign Planning

In software engineering, sprint planning involves setting specific goals and tasks for a short period of time (usually two to four weeks). In contrast, marketing teams use campaign planning to define objectives, strategies, and tactics for a specific marketing initiative.

Agile methods in software engineering emphasize sprint planning to ensure progress and delivery, while Agile marketing focuses on campaign planning to ensure effective execution and measurement of results.

Because of the nature of marketing campaigns and their need to often run for weeks or months at a time, many Agile marketing teams treat prelaunch campaign work differently from postlaunch campaign sprints. This will be explored in Chapter 21.

Implementing sprint planning in marketing involves breaking down larger campaigns into smaller, manageable chunks with specific, short-term goals. Each sprint should end with a tangible deliverable, whether it's a piece of content, a digital ad, or a set of customer insights. This structured approach helps keep the team focused and accountable, while also allowing for regular reflection and adjustment.

### Retrospectives versus Debriefings

In software engineering, retrospectives are used to reflect on the previous sprint, identify areas for improvement, and plan for the next sprint. In contrast, marketing teams use retrospectives that serve as debriefings to review the effectiveness of a campaign, identify lessons learned, and plan for future campaigns.

Agile methods in software engineering emphasize retrospectives to improve processes and delivery, while agile marketing focuses on debriefings to improve campaign effectiveness and alignment with predicted outcomes, and adapt to changing customer preferences.

Even though they can still be *called* retrospective, these regular debriefings should be incorporated into the marketing process, where the team reflects on the success of each campaign or sprint. These sessions should focus on what was learned, what can be improved, and how to apply these lessons to future initiatives. By institutionalizing this reflective practice, marketing teams can continually enhance their strategies and operations.

### Prioritization of Features versus Prioritization of ROI

This section looks at how prioritization is performed in each method. Software engineering teams prioritize tasks based on technical complexity, risk, and business value. In contrast, marketing teams prioritize campaigns based on customer needs, competitive landscape, and strategic alignment.

Agile methods in software engineering emphasize prioritization to ensure delivery of high-value features, while agile marketing focuses on prioritization to ensure effective allocation of resources and maximize ROI.

When adopting Agile in marketing, prioritize tasks and campaigns not only based on potential ROI but also consider factors like customer value and strategic alignment. Use a weighted scoring system or a prioritization matrix to evaluate and select projects, ensuring resources are allocated to high-impact activities that align closely with business goals and customer demands.

## LEARNING FROM AGILECORP'S SOFTWARE TEAM

AgileCorp's marketing team was convinced that there was potential in a more Agile approach to their work, so they sought insights from their company's software engineering team, renowned for their effective use of Agile methodologies. One afternoon in their San Mateo headquarters, the marketing team organized a workshop, inviting the lead engineers to explain their Agile processes. The room buzzed with anticipation as marketing specialists, armed with notepads and laptops, prepared to take notes and see how the software engineering team's approach could be applied to their own work.

The lead engineer, Tobias, started by detailing their sprints, which last two weeks, within which specific features were developed, tested, and deployed. "Each sprint ends with a working software increment," he explained, emphasizing the importance of tangible outcomes at every stage. Contrastingly, the marketing team's campaigns often stretched over months with results only visible postlaunch, leading to missed opportunities for midcourse corrections. Inspired, the marketing director, Luisa, realized the potential in adopting shorter, iterative cycles for marketing campaigns, allowing for rapid adjustments based on consumer feedback and emerging trends.

Tobias also highlighted how their teams were structured around specific roles—developers, testers, and product managers—all collaborating closely and communicating regularly. This specialization ensured deep expertise in each task but was bound by flexibility to adapt to new information or project shifts. Luisa found this quite different from her own team's structure, which was more fluid, with individuals frequently juggling multiple roles across creative and analytic spectrums. She saw an opportunity to foster even more cross-functional teamwork, blending creative and analytical skills to enrich campaign strategies from multiple perspectives.

The afternoon session concluded with a discussion on retrospectives, a key ritual from scrum that the engineers had come to look forward to at the end of each sprint. Tobias shared how these meetings helped them continuously refine their methods and outputs. Marketing's campaign debriefings, although similar, often lacked the structured feedback loops that retrospectives offered. Energized by these revelations, Luisa proposed a pilot project to adopt a scrum framework for an upcoming product launch campaign, aiming to incorporate sprint planning, cross-functional collaboration, and structured retrospectives into their workflow.

This afternoon exchange marked a shift in AgileCorp's marketing approach and set the stage for a transformation that readers will continue to explore in the pages that follow.

## CONCLUSION

While the core principles of Agile remain the same across different domains, there are significant differences in how agile is applied in software engineering versus marketing, and similarly, when applied in other areas of the business there can be large or subtle differences as well.

Because Agile practices often start in one area of the business and spread throughout, understanding these differences is essential for organizations to successfully adopt agile methodologies in both areas and achieve their business objectives.

# 5

# METHODS OF IMPLEMENTING AGILE PRINCIPLES

The Agile manifesto and the related twelve Agile principles that were drafted back in 2001 have inspired many companies, teams, and individuals, and spawned numerous interpretations and usages. While there are a variety of methods that a team can use to incorporate these principles into their work, there are generally a handful of approaches that have gained a significant amount of popularity and adoption in companies both small and large.

A good deal of the remainder of this book will be spent exploring scrum, the first approach outlined here, but it can be helpful to have a good understanding of some of the other methodologies built on an Agile foundation. For instance, it is good to understand when to apply each type of Agile approach, and in some cases—as will be seen in the case of scrumban—it can make sense to combine multiple methods together to get the desired outcomes.

## SCRUM

Scrum project management is the maintenance, development, and optimization of work within specific periods and created within complex environments and was first used prior to the Agile Manifesto being written. Usage of the term in project management dates back to a 1986 Harvard Business Review article by Hirotaka Takeuchi and Ikujiro Nonaka that refers to the "rugby method," and those authors would later develop the concept further.[1]

---

[1] Takeuchi, Hirotaka and Nonaka, Ikujiro (January 1, 1986). "The New New Product Development Game." *Harvard Business Review*.

Others would also incorporate methods that would become scrum in the 1990s, including Ken Schwaber and Jeff Sutherland, who would go on to help draft The Agile Manifesto in 2001.

Thus, while scrum in some ways predated Agile, the two are linked and since with the codification of Agile principles at the beginning of the 2000s, scrum has often been synonymous with Agile, although as discussed in previous chapters, the former is a methodology and the latter a set of principles.

Scrum is a project management methodology that is executed through sequential iterations known as sprints, most often two or four-week periods. Teams set collective goals rather than individual ones. The twelve Agile principles are followed by scrum teams.

This idea of iterative improvement and self-organizing teams reinforces some of the Agile principles that have already been explored.

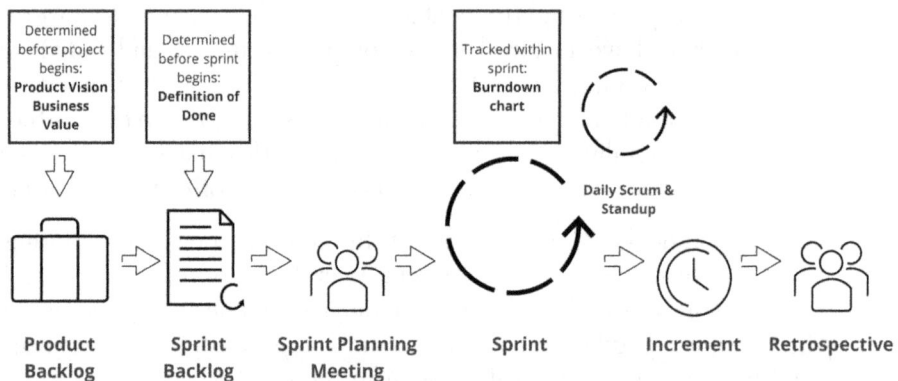

*FIGURE 5.1* Elements of scrum.

As seen in Figure 5.1, there are several key elements of scrum, including a backlog of features that are prioritized by business value and planned with the guidance of a product owner to be executed in sprints that are viewed as incremental improvements and reviewed in retrospectives to ensure that both the product produced as well as the way of working are continuously improving. The chapters that follow will be looking at each of these elements in more depth.

## SCALED AGILE FRAMEWORK (SAFe)

The second method, briefly introduced here, is called the scaled agile framework, or SAFe, methodology, and it was originally introduced in 2011, coming a decade after the Agile Manifesto.[2] It is an adaptation of scrum and focuses more on an Agile team's relationship with the rest of their organization.

SAFe was created with the intention to guide large enterprises in scaling Agile and lean practices, because at scale across a multinational organization, Scrum can have challenges. SAFe promotes alignment, collaboration, and delivery across large numbers of Agile teams while adhering to Agile principles.

### A Brief Comparison of Scrum and SAFe

While the two approaches of scrum and SAFe share roots in the Agile Manifesto, there are some key differences in their implementation. See Table 5.2 for a brief comparison.

*TABLE 5.1* A Comparison of Scrum and SAFe

| Aspect | Scrum | SAFe |
|---|---|---|
| **Focus** | Focuses on small, self-organizing teams working on small-scale projects or components of larger projects. | Designed to scale Agile across larger organizations and complex projects involving multiple teams. |
| **Scale** | Ideal for single teams or a small number of teams working independently. | Intended for large-scale implementations involving multiple teams and potentially hundreds of practitioners. |
| **Structure** | Less formal structure beyond the basic roles (product owner, scrum master, team members) and ceremonies (sprint planning, daily standup, sprint review, retrospective). | Comprehensive structure including multiple roles at team, program, and portfolio levels; extensive set of practices and workflows designed to coordinate large initiatives. |
| **Implementation Complexity** | Relatively simple and quick to implement due to minimal overhead and roles. | More complex and requires careful planning and coordination due to its comprehensive nature. |
| **Flexibility** | Highly flexible with few prescribed roles and processes, allowing teams to adapt the framework to their needs. | Structured, with specific roles, artifacts, and processes that must be followed to ensure alignment across teams. |

*(Continued)*

---

[2] "About Scaled Agile Framework—A Brief History of SAFe." Scaled Agile Inc. *https://www.scaledagileframework.com/about/*. Retrieved June 18, 2024.

| Aspect | Scrum | SAFe |
|---|---|---|
| **Control** | Emphasizes team autonomy and self-organization. Decision-making is decentralized. | Emphasizes alignment and execution across multiple teams, requiring more centralized decision-making. |
| **Planning** | Sprint-based planning limited to the duration of a sprint (typically two–four weeks). | Involves multiple levels of planning, including program increment (PI) planning, which spans eight–twelve weeks and aligns all teams within the SAFe framework. |
| **Feedback Loops** | Short feedback loops focused on the team and its immediate stakeholders. | Longer feedback loops that consider the broader program or portfolio objectives, involving more stakeholders. |
| **Primary Artifacts** | Product backlog, sprint Backlog, increment (product increment). | In addition to scrum artifacts, SAFe includes PI objectives, program board, and portfolio canvas. |
| **Suitability** | Best suited for small to medium-sized projects where rapid delivery and frequent changes are common. | Best suited for large, complex environments where interteam coordination and alignment to a broader strategic vision are necessary. |

As shown in Table 5.1, scrum generally deals with smaller, cross-functional teams that work closely together regularly, while SAFe deals with large teams that are spread out globally and don't necessarily always work closely together.

Scrum is adopted by Agile teams within an organization, while SAFe is adopted at the enterprise level. Scrum allows quick speed to market and project completion, while SAFe is generally slower to market, although still quicker than more traditional waterfall methods. Finally, scrum is relatively easy to implement, while SAFe is more difficult.

While it can be beneficial for organizations to adopt SAFe, the remaining portion of this lesson will be spent on the scrum methodology because it is more directly applicable to the Agile marketing approach being discussed. It is also possible you're a marketing team to implement scrum without requiring the rest of their organization to adopt Agile principles.

## LEAN

Inspired by lean manufacturing techniques that helped companies like Toyota pioneer new and better ways of creating quality products at scale, this methodology focuses on the creation of easily changeable software and the elimination of waste throughout the development process.

Lean principles include optimizing the whole, eliminating waste, empowering the team, delivering as fast as possible, building integrity in, and seeing the whole. There are five key principles of lean:

1. Define Value

   In lean, value is defined as what a customer would be willing to pay for, and a key part of success with this approach is finding ways to discover what customers truly find valuable as they are sometimes unable to clearly articulate it.

2. Map the Value Stream

   Having defined value in the first principle, lean's second principle is to identify all of the activities that help create and contribute to that value and reducing and eliminating anything that does not. These items to be eliminated are referred to as *muda* or waste, and that concept will be explored in a subsequent section.

3. Create Flow

   Once waste is removed from the value stream, the focus is then to ensure things run as smoothly as possible, reducing delays or interruptions.

4. Establish Pull

   Because lean was created in a manufacturing environment, the concept of inventory is key. Establishing pull means that inventory and assets are available when needed, but *only* when needed and in the quantities needed, thus reducing excess inventory which often takes up unnecessary space and resources.

5. Pursue Perfection While perfection is a North Star and not actually possible, lean emphasizes continuous improvement, referred to as *kaizen,* to push teams *toward* the most perfect state.

### A Brief Comparison of Scrum and Lean

The previous table described a comparison between scrum and SAFe. See Table 5.2 for a comparison of scrum and lean.

*TABLE 5.2* Comparison Between Scrum and Lean

| Aspect | Scrum | Lean |
|---|---|---|
| **Primary Focus** | Emphasizes iterative development with a focus on managing complex software and product development. | Focuses on maximizing value by eliminating waste throughout the manufacturing or software development process. |

*(Continued)*

| Aspect | Scrum | Lean |
|---|---|---|
| **Core Philosophy** | Based on empirical process control theory, emphasizing transparency, inspection, and adaptation. | Originates from the Toyota production system, emphasizing efficiency, continuous improvement, and respect for people. |
| **Process Structure** | Structured around sprints, fixed-length iterations where work is completed and reviewed. | Continuous flow, aiming to deliver products incrementally without the rigid structure of sprints. |
| **Roles Defined** | Clearly defined roles of product owner, scrum master, and development team. | Less emphasis on defined roles; focuses more on the process and principles like just-in-time production and worker empowerment. |
| **Feedback Loops** | Short feedback loops through daily scrums, sprint reviews, and retrospectives. | Emphasizes continuous improvement (kaizen) and quick adaptation to changes without formalized feedback sessions. |
| **Planning Approach** | Sprint planning for short cycles (typically two–four weeks) focusing on delivery of specific features or products. | Just-in-time planning, focusing on pulling work as needed to minimize inventory and work in progress (WIP). |
| **Metrics** | Focus on sprint goals, velocity, and burndown charts to track progress. | Focus on cycle time, lead time, and throughput to measure flow and efficiency. |
| **Waste Reduction** | Indirectly addresses waste by encouraging sustainable work practices and minimizing documentation. | Directly targets waste elimination in all forms (overproduction, waiting, transport, excess processing, inventory, motion, defects) as a core objective. |
| **Customer Involvement** | Regular interaction with stakeholders during sprint reviews and planning sessions. | Continuous engagement with the customer to ensure the product meets their needs and to receive immediate feedback. |
| **Cultural Impact** | Promotes a collaborative team environment with a focus on self-management. | Promotes a culture of continuous improvement, efficiency, and respect for the workforce's skills and knowledge. |

### A Related Concept: Muda

The muda principle is closely related to lean principles, which often complement Agile ones. Lean principles refer to the Japanese word *mluda*, which means "futility, uselessness, or wastefulness."

There are seven types of *muda* as defined in the lean methodology. The following list defines each one briefly.

1.  The first is the waste of overproduction or creating too much of something that cannot be used. This is often referred to as the largest waste of the seven types of *muda*. In marketing, this may include making too many variations of creative assets that won't be used, creating too much documentation, or creating other elements that fail to be used in a marketing campaign or project.

2. The second principle refers to the waste of time on hand, including idle time, waiting for others to complete their tasks, or any downtime between tasks.

3. The third type of *muda* is the waste of transportation or unnecessary movement of people or equipment. In a largely virtual environment, a marketing team may not have as many issues with this, although requiring physical assets to be shipped or requiring people to travel unnecessarily may cause this.

4. Next is the waste of processing, or perhaps more accurately, *overprocessing*, which includes any unnecessary steps in the production process. This may include unnecessary tasks and meetings that waste a large group of people's time without positively contributing to the outcomes of the project or campaign.

5. The fifth type of *muda* is the waste of inventory, which can include storing items, clutter, or continuing to use obsolete equipment, software, or even processes. While lean's origins in manufacturing draw a direct line to a physical inventory, using obsolete tools or processes may be more likely.

6. Next, is the waste of movement or the unnecessary movement of people and equipment. Again, this directly pertains to the manufacturing process, although in the marketing world, this may include requiring an individual to take too many steps to complete an otherwise simple process or even requiring too much back and forth between individuals to complete a task.

7. The final type of *muda* is the waste of defects and, with it, the waste of having to *fix* those defects and retest them.

While the seven *muda* principles originated in the world of manufacturing and the assembly line, they can also be applied to work performed in marketing.

## OTHER APPROACHES AND CONCEPTS

### Kanban

This is a visual approach to managing work as it moves through a process. *Kanban* visualizes both the process (usually as columns on a board) and the actual work passing through that process. The goal is to identify potential bottlenecks in the process and fix them so work can flow through it cost-effectively at an optimal speed or throughput.

Originally used in lean manufacturing, which has strong ties to Agile processes, kanban, the Japanese word for *sign*, originated in Japan as a method of using visual cues to keep a process flowing.

Agile teams often use kanban or kanban boards (see Figure 5.2) to visualize the relationship between the product backlog, the sprint backlog, and the work completed.

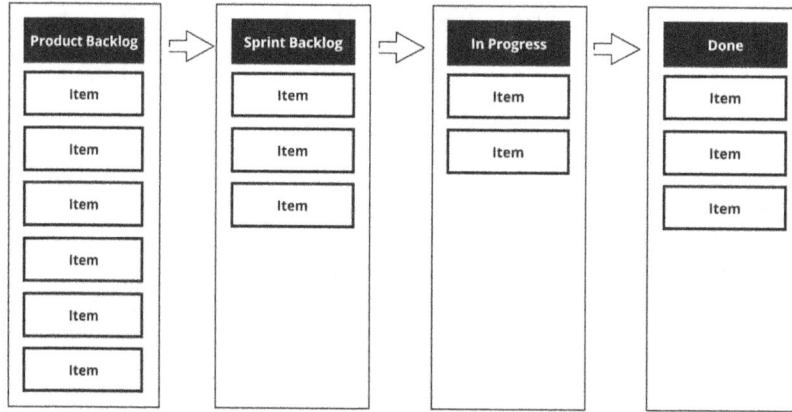

| Product Backlog | | Sprint Backlog | | In Progress | | Done |
|---|---|---|---|---|---|---|
| Item | | Item | | Item | | Item |
| Item | | Item | | Item | | Item |
| Item | | Item | | | | Item |
| Item | | | | | | |
| Item | | | | | | |
| Item | | | | | | |

**FIGURE 5.2** An example of a kanban board.

As seen in Figure 5.2, a scrum team can easily use kanban boards" to visually illustrate items in the various stages of development. Kanban boards are used in several software tools, and for teams that work in proximity to each other, they are sometimes created on whiteboards and changed manually.

## Scrumban

There are cases where strictly following scrum, kanban, or other implementations of Agile principles that are clearly defined is not optimal for a team or organization.

For instance, many teams like the visual approach of the kanban board but also want to incorporate the rituals of scrum into their work. This is not uncommon at all and is often referred to as "scrum-ban" because it combines the best parts of both scrum and kanban into one.

An organization or team may, after evaluating scrum further, decide to do something similar as well, and while the Agile principles can be a good guide to rely on, there is no right or wrong way to do it. Regardless of the eventual approach, it is important to understand the rules behind something like scrum to determine what elements teams find valuable and which elements they may want to modify to work better. This approach is, in fact, very Agile in that it relies on continuously improving how things are done instead of rigidly sticking with practices that don't work in reality.

Of course, there are many others, and if this book were more focused on software development not Agile marketing it might be appropriate to explore a few more. Readers should do their homework and explore different options to make sure they choose the right fit for their specific needs.

Each of these methods brings a different perspective to Agile implementation, focusing on various aspects of the development process to enhance flexibility, collaboration, and efficiency. The choice of method depends largely on the specific project needs, team size, organizational goals, and existing processes.

## CHOOSING THE RIGHT APPROACH FOR AGILECORP'S MARKETING TEAM

After their conversation with the software engineering team, AgileCorp's marketing team was preparing to begin their Agile journey using scrum. The team began reading more about Agile approaches to get a head start. Sarah, a marketing strategist, had been researching various implementations of Agile principles and suggested that the team also consider lean, kanban, and SAFe in addition to scrum. Eager to find the best fit for their dynamic environment, the team decided to hold a series of workshops to explore each methodology.

### Lean

The first workshop focused on lean, known for its emphasis on waste reduction and efficiency. The team was attracted to lean's principles of maximizing customer value while minimizing waste. However, after thorough discussion, they realized that lean's continuous flow model lacked the structured timeboxes they preferred for their projects with tight turnarounds, and which scrum provided. The team valued the rhythm and predictability of sprints, as it helped them plan and execute complex marketing campaigns more effectively. They decided that while lean's principles were admirable, the lack of structured iterations made it less suitable for their current needs.

### Kanban

Next, the team explored kanban, and several members were immediately drawn to its visualization of the workflow. They appreciated kanban's flexibility and the ability to visualize their work on kanban boards. However, they found that the continuous delivery approach might lead to prioritization issues without the fixed iterations to anchor their diverse projects that range from larger campaigns to quick marketing assets for sales team. The team also feared that the absence of sprint reviews and retrospectives, which seemed valuable in their initial conversations with the software team, would reduce the opportunity for reflection and iterative improvement. Thus, the team decided kanban alone might not fully support their goal of structured adaptability.

### SAFe

The third workshop that AgileCorp's marketing team held was focused on the scaled agile framework (SAFe), which appeared to offer a way to manage their often complex work. The extensive structure and roles defined in SAFe were appealing, yet the team felt it was overly complex for their department's size. The SAFe model was designed for larger groups and multiple interrelated projects, which surpassed the marketing team's current scale and needs. They concluded that SAFe would potentially introduce unnecessary overhead and complexity, diverting their focus from campaign execution to process management.

### Scrum

After evaluating all three methodologies, the marketing team convened to share insights and reflections. They agreed that scrum's framework—with its sprints, defined roles, and regular ceremonies—offered the best mix of structure and flexibility for their purposes. Scrum's iterative process allowed for adaptability within a predictable framework, which suited the fast-paced, creative nature of their work. The team felt confident that scrum provided the right balance of discipline and agility needed to enhance their marketing efforts.

After this constructive exploration of other potential options, AgileCorp's marketing team decided to fully adopt scrum. They were excited to embark on this journey, convinced that it would enhance their capability to innovate and respond swiftly to the ever-changing market landscape. Having explored these options, in fact, made them even more convinced that scrum would be the best fit for their needs.

## CONCLUSION

It should be stressed that there is no one right approach to implementing Agile principles, and each team and organization should evaluate approaches and find a way that works for them.

There is value in understanding the fundamentals and in knowing the "rules," so to speak, so that teams can then modify and interpret them in a way that best suits their needs.

The next part of the book will dive deep into scrum because, as the AgileCorp marketing team found as well, there are a number of aspects of this approach that work well in a marketing environment.

# THE ELEMENTS AND ROLES OF SCRUM IN AGILE MARKETING

The previous section explored the fundamentals of Agile, including the tenets of the Agile Manifesto and the twelve Agile principles. Also discovered were several interpretations of Agile principles including scrum, SAFe, kanban, and more.

With the fundamentals in place, it is time to review the core elements of scrum, including the meetings and processes, as well as the roles that team members will play on the Agile marketing team. Understanding these details will form the foundation of how to implement scrum in one's organization, so it is important to pay attention to these details.

While there may be some elements that readers agree need slight adjustments to better fit their work environment, it is best to understand the fundamentals and the "rules" so to speak, so that it can understood how and why they either apply verbatim or need adjustment. Many organizations follow these processes and roles exactly as prescribed, and others still have made slight modifications quite successfully. Either way, they rely on an understanding of the baseline that will be explored in Part II of the book.

Let's keep going!

# 6

# THE CORE ELEMENTS OF SCRUM

Readers now have an introduction to several different ways Agile principles can be implemented, and they should also have a good understanding of why scrum is a methodology, but Agile is not (see Chapter 1 and Chapter 2).

Scrum is one of the most popular Agile frameworks globally. Its influence extends beyond IT and software development, reaching into other sectors such as marketing, research and development, and product management. Organizations adopt scrum not only for its effectiveness in managing complex projects but also for its ability to foster a culture of innovation, flexibility, and responsiveness to change. This widespread adoption is supported by a robust community of practitioners, trainers, and coaches who ensure that the framework continues to evolve while staying true to its Agile roots.

Although other approaches utilizing Agile principles such as kanban, SAFe, and lean, others have applications for many types of work, scrum is the method most focused on in this book, and it is one that has proven effective in a marketing environment.

## THE CORE ELEMENTS OF SCRUM

The conversation will start by talking about several elements of scrum, and then they will be divided into two categories:

- The first category, the core items, includes the product backlog, the sprint backlog, the sprint planning meeting, the sprint, the daily scrum and standup, the increment, and the sprint retrospective.

▪ And the second category, consisting of additional items, includes the sprint goal(s), the definition of done, the product vision, the burndown chart, and the business value.

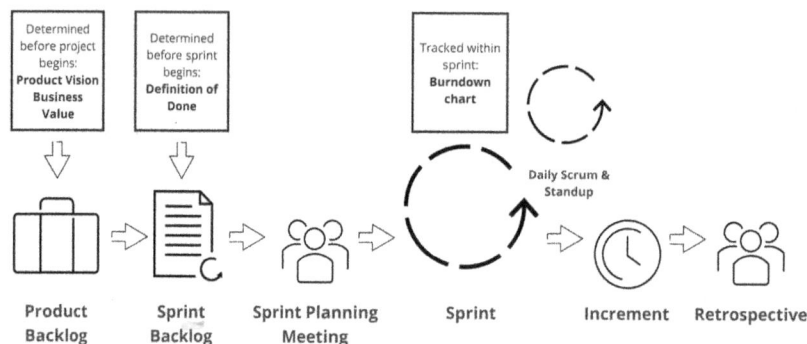

**FIGURE 6.1** Elements of scrum.

The following section reviews core items with the product backlog.

## PRODUCT BACKLOG

The product backlog is a large list of many ideas, items, and proposed work that are accumulated and compiled into a list. Some of these items may be well-defined, and others more vaguely defined.

Because of this, the product backlog is often a collection of ideas in various states of being defined and doesn't necessarily reflect all of the work that will actually be performed. It is, instead, a way to ensure that all ideas are captured and that they can be more clearly defined and prioritized when they are most likely to create business value.

In a marketing context, the product backlog represents all the campaigns, content ideas, market research initiatives, and strategic projects that the marketing team identifies as necessary to achieve their goals. It is continuously updated and prioritized based on market dynamics, customer feedback, and business objectives. The marketing product owner, who understands both the market's needs and the business's goals, manages this backlog. They prioritize items based on their potential impact on customer engagement, brand visibility, and overall return on investment (ROI).

The product backlog for the marketing team should be flexible and responsive, allowing the team to adapt to new insights and changes in the market environment rapidly. Each item in the backlog is described in enough detail so that the team can understand the expected outcomes and the value it adds to the business. This ensures that during the sprint planning, the team can select the most impactful tasks to focus on for the upcoming sprint.

Examples of Elements in a Marketing Product Backlog:

- *Campaign development*: Items might include launching a new product campaign, rebranding efforts, or seasonal promotions.
- *Content creation*: This could include blog posts, white papers, videos, or infographics aimed at different stages of the customer journey.
- *Market research*: Tasks to gather insights about competitors, customer satisfaction surveys, or exploring new market segments.
- *Digital marketing enhancements*: Optimization of SEO strategies, revamping the company Web site, or improving user experience (UX) on digital platforms.
- *Social media initiatives*: Planning and executing social media campaigns, increasing engagement on existing channels, or exploring new platforms for brand presence.
- *Email marketing campaigns*: Designing targeted email marketing strategies for different customer segments to improve conversions.
- *Event planning*: Organizing webinars, workshops, or participation in industry conferences.
- *Customer retention strategies*: Developing loyalty programs or personalized marketing tactics to increase customer retention.
- *Analytics and reporting*: Implementing new analytics tools to better understand campaign effectiveness and customer behavior.
- *Brand partnerships*: Identifying and initiating cobranding or partnership opportunities for cross-promotion.

Each of these items, once prioritized, moves into the sprint backlog where it can be broken down into smaller, manageable tasks and executed by the marketing team. This structured yet flexible approach helps ensure that marketing efforts are always aligned with the most current business objectives and market needs.

## SPRINT BACKLOG

The next item we will discuss is the sprint backlog. As compared to the product backlog, the sprint backlog is a more orderly work or task list that is a subset of that larger product backlog.

The sprint backlog only contains the items that will be completed within the current sprint, thus it is a subset of the product backlog. The elements within a sprint backlog are called items, and their form can be very different, depending on the type of work performed and the nature of the project being worked on. For example, these can be ideas, defects, improvements, and user stories.

This sprint backlog is more than just a to-do list; it is a planned set of marketing activities that are derived from the higher level objectives identified in the product backlog. It is also dynamic and can be updated and reprioritized by the team during the sprint as needed, but the goals set during the sprint planning meeting should remain stable to maintain focus.

### Relationship with the Product Backlog

For marketing teams, the product backlog might include a wide range of projects, such as new campaign ideas, content creation for different platforms, customer engagement strategies, and digital marketing enhancements. During the sprint planning meeting, the team—led by the product owner and including all team members—reviews this backlog to determine which items are the highest priority based on current business needs, customer feedback, and market trends.

The selected items are then moved to the sprint backlog. This process involves breaking down large tasks into smaller, more manageable pieces that can be completed within the sprint's timeframe. This decomposition is critical as it ensures that each task is well understood and actionable, with clear criteria for completion, known as the "definition of done."

Although some of these terms are not familiar just yet, they will be defined in due time.

## SPRINT PLANNING MEETING

The kickoff to each new sprint includes a planning meeting in which items from the product backlog are moved into the sprint backlog to be worked on within the current sprint. This meeting works best when the full scrum team is involved and works collaboratively.

A draft sprint planning meeting agenda has been provided with the supplemental materials for this book.

Sprint planning is the meeting where the transformation of items from the product backlog into the sprint backlog occurs. This meeting has two main goals:

- *What will be done?*: The team selects which tasks from the product backlog are most urgent and feasible to achieve in the upcoming sprint. This decision is heavily influenced by the product owner's insights into business priorities and the team's capacity.
- *How it will be done?*: Once the tasks are selected, the team discusses and plans how these tasks will be executed. This involves assigning responsibilities, estimating efforts, and possibly, identifying any dependencies or requirements for external resources.

### Example: Product Launch Campaign

Imagine a marketing team is preparing for a product launch. The product backlog might include tasks such as "develop launch campaign," "create promotional videos," "organize a launch event," and "coordinate social media campaign with influencers." During the sprint planning, the team decides to focus on the launch campaign and promotional videos for the next sprint. These items are then detailed in the sprint backlog with specific tasks like "design email campaign templates," "draft script for promo videos," and "book venue for the launch event."

The sprint backlog focuses the team's efforts for the sprint and provides a clear, tactical action plan derived from the strategic goals listed in the product backlog. It is the blueprint the marketing team follows daily, ensuring they are not only productive but also aligned with the overall marketing strategy. This alignment is maintained through daily stand-ups where the team reviews progress against the sprint backlog, making adjustments as necessary to stay on track toward the sprint goals.

The sprint planning meeting allows the team to focus their efforts on the most appropriate items from the sprint backlog within the sprint, which will be explored next.

## THE SPRINT

Because the sprint backlog has just been discussed, it's time to discuss what exactly a sprint is within scrum. A sprint is a predefined period—usually two or four weeks—in which a specific set of items is completed. This set of items is what was just looked at—the sprint backlog.

The sprint is a "container" of sorts that includes all of the work done within that time period. It includes meetings like the daily scrum and standup, which will be discussed next, as well as any work that is done within that period.

Agile marketing teams can potentially be working on many different types of items within a sprint. For instance, a team could be organized around a campaign, such as a product launch. Or, they could be organized around an ongoing set of work, such as creating and posting social media content.

Projects with more definite start and end points, such as the launch of a new Web site might also be approached in a scrum environment. While a Web site might have areas—such as UX design and coding—that fall outside the specific areas of marketing, the marketing team might be responsible for key areas such as content development and analytics which run in a parallel path to the design and development of the Web site. These efforts could be approached in a separate sprint-based workstream, or they might be incorporated into a larger cross-team collaborative effort. Some collaborative approaches to this are discussed later in the book as well.

Additionally, every sprint begins with the sprint planning session and ends with the retrospective, at which point a new sprint begins.

## DAILY SCRUM AND STANDUP

The daily scrum is a more formal meeting of the working team within a sprint, led by the scrum master, a role explored shortly, and follows a fifteen-minute time frame.

By contrast, the standup meeting is a little less formal and includes a larger team, including stakeholders like the product owner. The standup meeting gets its name because it is a short meeting in which the team members shouldn't have time to sit down and get comfortable; if people are standing, they will want to keep the meeting brief.

The standup is not intended to be a full report-out of everything happening. Instead, it is a chance for team members to answer three questions:

- What did you accomplish yesterday?
- What will you work on today?
- Are there any blockers in your way?

It is also important that the entire team can attend because direct communication is essential and one of the core principles of the Agile approach.

A draft standup meeting agenda has been provided with the supplemental materials for this book.

## THE INCREMENT

The increment is how teams refer to the current version or portion of the set of work they are performing. In software engineering, it is the current version of the product under development, however, in a marketing context, it could be a phase of a campaign or a version of a measurement initiative. The increment includes all of the work previously completed and the items within the sprint backlog that the team is currently working on.

Marketing teams may struggle with this item because they often can't deliver *part* of one of their deliverables. For instance, if the goal is to deliver a white paper, it is not desirable to release half of the white paper. Instead, the increment would need to include the entire white paper.

A move to a more iterative process in which campaigns or other initiatives can roll out incrementally can lead to better outcomes because what was learned from initial tests can be fed back into subsequent iterations and components.

## THE SPRINT RETROSPECTIVE

A critical part of the Agile approach is having an opportunity to reflect on the work performed and to find a way to optimize and improve upon it. The sprint retrospective provides this opportunity and should include the full team and stakeholders, and it is usually run by the scrum master. The retrospective is a meeting that should be time-limited and should occur after one sprint ends and before the next one starts.

Its purpose is to provide a constructive forum to answer three primary questions:

- What was done well in this sprint?
- What wasn't done well?
- What improvements can be made?

The answer to these questions should then be incorporated into the planning and execution of the next sprint.

A draft retrospective meeting agenda has been provided with the supplemental materials for this book to assist with running this meeting effectively. The ins and outs of how to run an effective retrospective meeting will be discussed later in the book.

## CONCLUSION

This has been an introduction to the core elements of scrum. Of course, with only these elements there are still some pieces missing that will likely be used on a daily basis in Agile marketing work. The next chapter will explore these, and then walk through a full example of using scrum in practice in a marketing environment.

# 7

# ADDITIONAL ELEMENTS OF SCRUM

Having explored the core elements, the discussion turns to some of the additional elements of scrum. These are all very important items, although their definition, adoption, and usage can vary widely depending on the organization and team.

## THE SPRINT GOAL

The sprint goal is how the common goal for the current sprint is defined. While it contains many items, or tasks, from the sprint backlog, the sprint goal itself is the summary of them all.

The sprint goal is often defined as descriptive prose, as opposed to a complex or technical language that might require understanding marketing jargon or software terminology. The purpose of writing the sprint goal is to give the team a shared understanding of what should be accomplished within the iteration currently being worked on in the current sprint, including the sprint backlog.

In short, the sprint goal is a concise statement of what the scrum team plans to achieve during the sprint. It serves as the overarching objective that guides the development work, provides a framework for making decisions during the sprint, and offers the team a clear focus. The goal is crucial for aligning the team's efforts and enhancing cohesiveness and motivation throughout the sprint.

### Creation of the Sprint Goal

The sprint goal is formulated during the sprint planning meeting, which involves the entire scrum team: the product owner, the scrum master, and the development team. The process includes the following steps:

- *Review the product backlog*: The product owner presents the high-priority items from the product backlog that they believe will bring the most value to the project.
- *Collaborative discussion*: The team discusses the presented items, and considers their complexity, dependencies, and the team's capacity.
- *Formulating the goal*: Based on the discussion and selected backlog items, the team collaboratively formulates a sprint goal. This goal should be an achievable outcome that can be reached by implementing the selected backlog items.

### *Best Practices*

To be successful at setting a sprint goal, here are some tips:

- *Be specific and clear*: The sprint goal should be specific enough to provide a clear direction and also allow for flexibility in how it is achieved.
- *Measurable*: It should be articulated in a way that makes it easy to measure progress and success.
- *Relevant*: Ensure the goal aligns with larger project objectives and holds significance for stakeholders.
- *Attainable*: The goal should be realistically achievable within the sprint, considering the team's resources and capabilities.
- *Time-bound*: The goal must be attainable within the sprint's time frame, which is typically two to four weeks.

Table 7.1 offers more insight into setting a sprint goal.

**TABLE 7.1** What to Do and What Not to Do with the Sprint Goal

| What to Do | What Not to Do |
|---|---|
| Align the goal with business objectives. | Set a goal without stakeholder input or alignment. |
| Make it inspiring to motivate the team. | Use technical jargon or details that may not be universally understood. |

*(Continued)*

| What to Do | What Not to Do |
|---|---|
| Keep it flexible enough to accommodate changes without losing focus. | Create a rigid goal that doesn't allow for adaptation as work progresses. |
| Communicate the goal clearly to all stakeholders. | Leave ambiguity in its interpretation or purpose. |
| Review and reference the goal daily to guide decisions and work. | Ignore the goal post planning or fail to use it as a reference during the sprint. |
| Adjust the goal in subsequent sprints based on learning and feedback. | Stick with a formulated goal that is repeatedly not achievable. |

By following these practices and being mindful of the do's and don'ts, the scrum team can ensure that the sprint goal effectively guides their efforts, keeps them focused and motivated, and aligns their work with the broader project and business objectives.

## The Definition of Done

The *definition of done* (DoD) is the criteria that must be met by an item added from the product backlog and into the sprint backlog for it to be considered complete and part of the current Increment.

It is important that these definitions are short and understandable by all so that it is easy to determine whether their requirements have been met and the items can be considered "done." While the definition of done can be overlooked as unnecessary or obvious, the exercise of outlining exactly what it is can often be more enlightening than one might imagine at first glance.

This ensures that everyone on the scrum team understands exactly what is required for work to be potentially shippable or deliverable, promoting transparency and alignment within the team.

### Purpose and Usage

- *Consistency*: The DoD ensures that all team members have a consistent understanding of what "done" means, reducing discrepancies in quality and completeness.
- *Quality assurance*: It serves as a checklist that guarantees all necessary steps (like testing, documentation, and code review) are completed before a task is marked as done, maintaining the quality of the deliverable.
- *Transparency*: Having a clear DoD makes the progress of tasks more transparent to stakeholders and team members, facilitating better communication and expectation management.

The DoD is typically established during the initial sprints and can evolve as the team gains more understanding of their workflow and project needs. It is revisited and possibly revised during sprint retrospectives as the team identifies areas for improvement.

Table 7.2 lines up good DoDs to bad DoDs with some descriptive definitions.

*TABLE 7.2* Good Definition of Done versus Bad Definition of Done

| Good Definition of Done | Bad Definition of Done |
|---|---|
| *Specific*: Clearly states what tests must pass, what documentation must be completed, and any other criteria relevant to the project. | *Vague*: Uses ambiguous terms like *adequately tested* or *sufficient documentation* without specifying what these entail. |
| *Achievable*: All criteria can realistically be completed by the team within a sprint. | *Unrealistic*: Includes criteria that are beyond the team's current capabilities or resources, setting them up for failure. |
| *Measurable*: Each item in the DoD can be objectively measured or checked off, leaving no room for interpretation. | *Subjective*: Criteria are open to individual interpretation, leading to inconsistent outputs. |
| *Relevant*: Directly relates to the quality and completeness of the product, ensuring it meets customer and stakeholder expectations. | *Irrelevant*: Contains items that do not directly impact the quality or delivery of the product. |
| *Agreed upon*: Formulated and accepted by the entire team, ensuring collective responsibility and buy-in. | *Imposed*: Created without team input, potentially ignoring their insights and leading to resistance or confusion. |

The DoDis is a foundational element in maintaining the integrity and quality of the work delivered in each sprint. It acts as both a guideline and a benchmark for the team, ensuring that every completed task truly meets the necessary standards to be considered done.

## The Product Vision

The *product vision* is defined as a description of the product, project, or campaign being worked on. It should contain a set of information that gives a full picture of the initiative, including audience, competitors, advantages, promotion methods, channels to be used, measures of success, and more.

The product vision is defined before work begins, that is, at the earliest stages, and it helps inform the team on prioritization and other decisions to make. Marketers can often replace the word "product" in product vision with something like "campaign" or "project."

## The Burndown Chart

The burndown chart (Figure 7.1) is a visual representation of the items completed from the sprint backlog, and for many in-person teams, this might be captured on a wall or whiteboard. For virtual teams, this might be captured in a commonly-used charting, spreadsheet, or project management application.

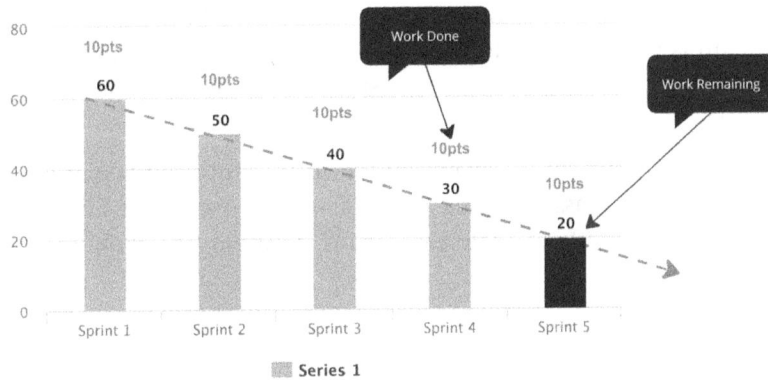

*FIGURE 7.1* Burndown chart.

The chart is intended to be a quick and easy way to view the progress of a team on the progress at a glance. The burndown chart rarely encompasses items from beyond the current sprint backlog, although it might also include a view of the larger product backlog list in some cases.

## Story Points

How does a scrum team determine how much work can be done within a sprint? A key component is having a method to estimate the level of effort required by a task. This is where story points enter the picture. Story points are a unit of measurement used by scrum teams to estimate the level of effort it will take to complete an item in the product or sprint backlogs.

While many teams give time estimates such as hours, days, or weeks, Agile teams using scrum often transition to using story points instead. These allow a relative measure of effort without getting bogged down with minutes and hours. Using story points can also help abstract away a focus on keeping busy (e.g., how many hours were spent working?) versus working on what is valuable (e.g., what is the general level of effort used to accomplish something?).

Common increments for story points are 1, 2, 3, 5, 8, 13, and 21, for instance, with 21 being the highest allowable number of points before a task must be broken down into smaller pieces. In fact, using those numbers just mentioned, it would be advisable to rarely have an item worth 13 or 21 points as it would likely tie up one or more individuals completely during the sprint.

Story points are also used differently between different scrum teams, and thus they help organizations avoid competition between teams. Thus, a scrum team is only competing with themselves to complete more story points in a sprint versus competing with outside teams since everyone's definition of a "1" or a "13" might be a little different.

Teams that are brand new to scrum and story points may need to start with some baseline assumptions and evolve them over time. But remember, that is the whole beauty of Agile and scrum; iteration and continuous improvement are all part of the process!

## Business Value

While many references on Agile and scrum don't go into as much detail about this, it is important that we introduce the concept because it is a core driver of prioritization in scrum. Without understanding what is meant by "business value," it is hard to prioritize what gets done and when.

For instance, the items that get prioritized from the product backlog into the sprint backlog, and then which get prioritized from the sprint backlog into each sprint need a method of determining which are the highest value.

Business value is the key driver in this determination, and more time will be spent on this topic later in the book. For now, the definition of *business value* will be that which is deriving the most benefit to the customer. This may be a direct financial benefit, or it may be a benefit such as improving effectiveness of a marketing campaign, reducing the time it takes a customer to solve a challenge, or many other potential outcomes.

As readers can likely already see, one aspect that makes business value difficult to define and agree upon is that it can vary widely depending on the organization, and even depending on the team within the organization. While some companies may prioritize sales, others may prioritize efficiency, customer satisfaction, or other factors. It is ultimately the product owner's responsibility to determine the definition of business value, although it is almost always tied to an organization key performance indicator (KPI).

## CONCLUSION

There are many elements of scrum to remember, and one needs to remember what order they fall within implementation of sprints within a project team. Thus, it can be helpful to keep a visual handy, particularly when first adopting scrum.

This also becomes second nature after working within the scrum framework a few times. The following chapter looks at a practical example of how the scrum methods explored here can be applied in a marketing setting.

# 8

# SCRUM IN PRACTICE

With a better understanding of each element of scrum, it's time to talk through two real-life examples. This chapter walks through examples of how a marketing team might use the scrum process from start to finish.

The AgileCorp marketing team decided to use an email marketing campaign as their first project to run through their new Agile processes. The elements of scrum (Figure 8.1) present in the following example.

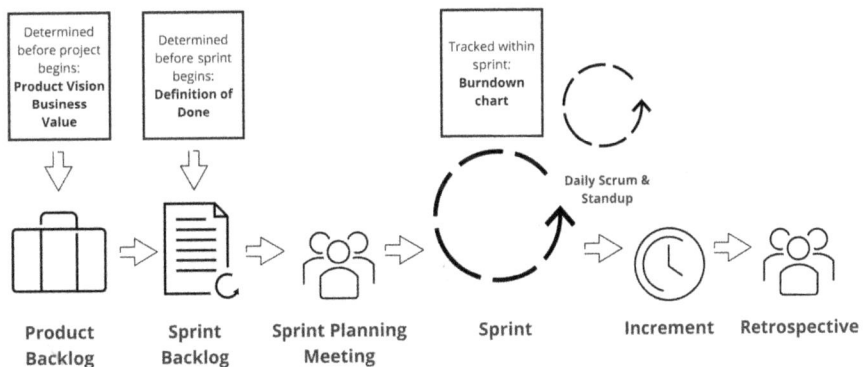

**FIGURE 8.1** The elements of scrum.

## EXAMPLE 1: EMAIL MARKETING CAMPAIGN USING SCRUM

The discussion in this example describes how an email marketing campaign would be performed using the scrum process. The AgileCorp marketing team has just been tasked with creating a campaign for AgileCorp 365, a new subscription feature that bundles several of their most popular features together. They believe that an email campaign will be the best place to start for this initiative.

### Establishing the Product Vision and Definition of Business Value

Prior to beginning the project, the product vision must be established and the business value must be understood. For this example, the product vision for the AgileCorp marketing effort will be to educate and inform current customers about the new subscription service that will help them use the product suite more effectively.

The goal of the effort and the business value it will create will be to add customers for a monthly subscription service.

### Creating the Product Backlog

With the product vision and business value defined, it is now time to create the product backlog. What are all of the elements that are needed for an effective email campaign? The following list breaks it down into pieces that can be accomplished in a series of steps.

- The team needs to know the exact audience they are sending the email to, which may need to be pulled from their customer relationship management (CRM) system.
- The team will need the creative elements, such as the copywriting and graphics that will go in the email.
- The graphics may include photography that will either need to be sourced from existing assets or potentially new photography or images that need to be created.
- The team may need tracking codes to see where users go when they click a link in the email.
- The team may need to create a specific landing page that users are directed toward from a call to action in the email.
- The email will need to be tested to ensure that it works well across mobile and desktop devices and on a variety of email clients.

As one can see, there are many elements, and there are likely many more that could be included here. These items will all go into the product backlog as items that will eventually need to be accomplished.

### Creating the Sprint Backlog and Individual Sprints

The items from the product backlog are then grouped in sprints, with each sprint including both a goal, such as completing all the creative elements and a definition of done for each item. These items exist in the sprint backlog until they are moved into an individual sprint.

A definition of done for copy in an email might include approval from a senior marketing leader and approval from the legal team.

The scrum team will collaborate on how to approach the items within the sprint backlog and update the burndown chart that we explored in Chapter 7 as items are completed. The team has a daily scrum meeting to talk about what they accomplished, what they are working on, and any potential blockers to completing the tasks they are working on. For instance, if they are working on the creative assets and relying on an outside vendor to create graphics, the scrum team member can communicate this to brainstorm on ways to either create a workaround or adjust their work to accommodate a delay.

In reviewing their work, the team is able to see the current iteration, which includes the work already performed and the work in progress.

### The Retrospective

Finally, once they complete the current sprint, the marketing scrum team will have a retrospective meeting to discuss what went well, what could be improved, and if any process improvements can be made. These suggested improvements can then be implemented when the next sprint begins.

And there you have it. A completed scrum process from start to finish. Thanks to the team at AgileCorp, readers have now gone through one entire cycle.

## EXAMPLE 2: DIGITAL ADVERTISING CAMPAIGN

This example explores how a digital advertising campaign on social media would be orchestrated using the scrum process. Imagine the AgileCorp marketing team is tasked with promoting a new software release via a targeted social media campaign. The aim is to increase software downloads through engaging ads on platforms like Facebook and Instagram.

### Establishing the Product Vision and Definition of Business Value

Before launching into tasks, it's crucial to define the product vision and the associated business value. In this scenario, the vision for AgileCorp's marketing effort is to engage potential customers with compelling content that highlights the unique features and benefits of the new software, encouraging them to download it. The business value is clear: Increase the number of software users, which in turn raises the customer base and potential revenue.

### Creating the Product Backlog

Once the vision and value are set, the next step is to build the product backlog, listing all elements needed for a successful digital advertising campaign:

- *Target audience identification*: Analyzing data to identify which segments of the social media audience are most likely to be interested in the software.

- *Ad creative elements*: Designing visually appealing ad graphics and writing persuasive copy that resonates with the target audience.

- *A/B testing elements*: Creating variations of ad visuals and copy to test their effectiveness in different segments.

- *Ad placement strategy*: Deciding on which platforms ads will be placed and the timing/frequency of ads.

- *Conversion tracking setup*: Implementing tools and codes for tracking ad performance and user actions post click.

- *Landing page development*: Crafting specific landing pages that visitors will be directed to after clicking the ads, optimized for conversion.

These tasks are detailed in the product backlog as individual items that need to be addressed through a series of sprint cycles.

### Creating the Sprint Backlog and Individual Sprints

From the product backlog, tasks are organized into sprints. Each sprint might focus on a specific aspect of the campaign—for example, one sprint could be dedicated to creating and approving all ad creative elements, while another might focus on setting up and testing conversion tracking.

- *Definition of done for ad creatives*: This could include final approval from the marketing director and compliance checks by the legal team.

▪ *Daily scrums*: The team meets to discuss progress, including what has been done, what's next, and any impediments they encountered. For example, if there is a delay in ad approval from a platform, the team can discuss alternatives or solutions to keep the timeline on track.

### Retrospective

After each sprint, the team conducts a retrospective to reflect on what went well and what could be improved. This might reveal insights like the need for faster content approval processes or better communication with the platform representatives to speed up ad approvals.

Using scrum for a digital advertising campaign on social media enables the AgileCorp marketing team to be nimble and responsive in their approach. By breaking down the campaign into manageable sprints, focusing on specific tasks, and continuously improving through retrospectives, the team can effectively increase software downloads while adapting to insights gained from ongoing analytics. This structured yet flexible approach ensures that every element of the campaign is optimized to meet the defined business goals.

## CONCLUSION

While some scrum approaches may seem more natural in a software engineering environment (because that is where they originated), the principles, elements, and roles involved in Agile and scrum can be applied to any type of work, including marketing. Although some minor revisions may be required, overall, scrum and Agile work great with marketing teams, campaigns, and projects.

# ROLES OF A SCRUM TEAM

At this point, readers should have a good understanding of the elements of scrum and how they work together to ensure that the requirements of a marketing initiative can start as requirements and be completed in a series of sprints, ultimately completing the work.

The elements of scrum and an Agile marketing project have been defined, and this chapter will review the roles of an Agile team.

- the product owner
- the scrum master
- the product team

Additionally, this chapter will also discuss some optional and related roles, such as stakeholders, domain experts and auditors, and integrators.

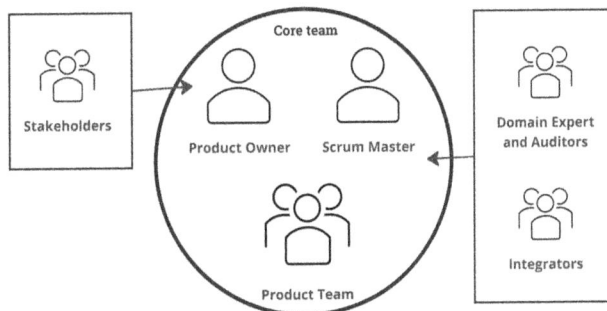

**FIGURE 9.1** Roles of a scrum team.

## THE PRODUCT OWNER

The first role of an Agile team this chapter will discuss is the *product owner*. It is the product owner's function to oversee the scrum master and the product team. The product owner is most often the product expert, representing the customer and the internal stakeholders.

The product owner is responsible for managing the backlog and other production elements. Most importantly, the product owner uses their understanding of the product vision to help prioritize the backlog in order to drive the most business value. In fact, it is the product owner's responsibility to understand and interpret the business value most needed and the amount of business value a feature or set of features will create.

## SCRUM MASTER

The *scrum master* has two primary responsibilities: leading and managing the project. They ensure the successful execution of the project or initiative using Agile practices and the scrum methodology.

The scrum master makes decisions on how a project is implemented, work to resolve any blockers or issues that could potentially delay delivery, and is responsible for securing the necessary resources to meet deadlines and commitments.

## THE PRODUCT TEAM

The third element of the Agile team is the *product team*, consisting of several people across various roles to successfully complete the project or initiative.

The product team is cross-functional, meaning that it comprises all roles with different skill sets and capabilities necessary to do the work and complete the objectives.

The product team is responsible for completing the items in the sprint backlog, which is pulled from the longer list of items, the product backlog.

To clarify, see Table 9.1 for a comparison of the three core roles on a scrum team.

TABLE 9.1 Comparison of scrum team roles.

| Role | Chief Responsibilities | Basis for Decisions | Characteristic of Success |
|---|---|---|---|
| Product Owner | - Prioritizes the product backlog to align with business goals and market demands.<br>- Clarifies requirements and communicates the vision to the team.<br>- Acts as the liaison between the marketing team and stakeholders to ensure needs and expectations are met. | - Business objectives<br>- Customer feedback<br>- Market trends | - Delivers campaigns and projects that drive significant market impact and align with strategic goals.<br>- Maintains a clear, prioritized backlog that guides the team effectively. |
| Scrum Master | - Facilitates scrum ceremonies (daily standups, sprint planning, reviews, and retrospectives).<br>- Supports the product team by removing impediments and ensuring a smooth workflow.<br>- Promotes Agile practices and ensures the team adheres to scrum principles. | - Scrum principles and practices<br>- Team feedback<br>- Efficiency and effectiveness of processes | - Fosters a collaborative and productive team environment.<br>- Enhances team performance and ensures continuous process improvement. |
| **Product Team** | - Executes tasks from the sprint backlog to create marketing materials and campaigns.<br>- Collaborates to solve problems and innovate solutions.<br>- Provides feedback on what is working and what is not during the sprint reviews and retrospectives. | - Priorities set in the sprint backlog<br>- Creative and strategic insights<br>- Collaborative discussions within the team | - Produces high-quality, creative, and effective marketing outputs consistently.<br>- Adapts quickly to changes and continuously improves their deliverables. |

While each role is distinct, they each play a pivotal part in ensuring that the team's workflow remains agile, focused, and aligned with overarching business goals.

## ADDITIONAL ROLES

In addition, several other roles may or may not be included in an Agile team. This is dependent on the exact needs of the work being performed.

### Stakeholders

It can be said that the stakeholder role is never truly optional, although their involvement in a particular task may be significant or not, depending on certain variables. These include the stakeholders, who are the ultimate owners of the project or initiative. The product owner is appointed by the stakeholders to ensure the project succeeds, although, at some points, stakeholders may be more involved in the process.

On high-impact projects, stakeholders will likely play a bigger role than on a small, short-term initiative, although it is the job of the product owner to always keep the needs and priorities of the stakeholders in mind when prioritizing and making decisions.

### Domain Experts and Auditors

Domain experts and auditors may be brought in from time to time to confirm and test hypotheses and shed light on tough challenges that require outside expertise.

These experts do not have as regular a presence as the other members of the product team, so they are brought in and out as needed to either provide guidance or to check that work has been done in the correct or compliant way.

The product team might already have domain experts on it, so this component's need varies depending on the specifics of any initiative

### Integrators

Integrators, who may not be needed consistently throughout the project or initiative, are brought in to ensure the completed work can be implemented and works with existing people, processes, and platforms.

Going back to our example of creating an email campaign, an integrator, in this case, might be the Web development team that is not part of the core marketing team involved in the sprint but is required to create a landing page and install tracking codes necessary to ensure measurement of the campaign. Integrators are not part of the core team working within the sprint but are often critical to ensure the project is a success.

## HOW AGILECORP CREATED IS FIRST AGILE MARKETING TEAM

AgileCorp's marketing team recently embarked on their journey to adopt scrum and had a successful first run with their email campaign that discussed in Chapter 8. Their next effort was to create a landing page for their new subscription service. The team gathered in a conference room with walls adorned with colorful sticky notes and whiteboards filled with ideas, ready to map out their new scrum roles.

### Choosing the Product Owner

The first role to fill was that of the product owner. After some discussion, the team agreed that Jenna, a senior marketing manager known for her deep understanding of AgileCorp's business strategy and customer base, including their potential motivation to sign up for a subscription service, would be ideal for the role. Jenna had a knack for prioritizing tasks based on impact and was adept at communicating complex ideas clearly. Her new role would involve prioritizing the product backlog to ensure that every sprint was aligned with AgileCorp's broader business objectives and meeting the market's demands.

### Selecting the Scrum Master

The next role to cover was the scrum master. The team chose Alex, who had previously facilitated cross-departmental projects and was enthusiastic about promoting Agile practices. Alex's role would be to ensure that the scrum ceremonies were effectively conducted, impediments were swiftly removed, and the team's adoption of Agile principles remained on track. His leadership style focused on being a facilitator rather than a micromanager was deemed essential to help the team transition smoothly into their new scrum working style.

### Forming the Product Team

The product team would consist of various talents within the marketing department. This team included Mia and Carlos, both creative specialists with a flair for impactful campaigns, and Leah, a data-driven digital marketing analyst. Together, they would handle the execution of tasks from the srint backlog, bringing together creativity and analytics to produce innovative and effective marketing strategies.

### The Stakeholder

Nakisha, the CMO of AgileCorp, was designated the role of stakeholder. Her job was to ensure that the projects undertaken by Jenna, Alex, Mia, Carlos, and Leah were not only innovative and agile but also strategically aligned with AgileCorp's overall business goals. Nakisha would participate in key ceremonies like sprint reviews to provide executive oversight and ensure that the marketing outputs were coherent with the company's strategic direction.

### Launching the Initiative

With roles clearly defined, the AgileCorp marketing team initiated their first sprint with enthusiasm. Jenna organized the product backlog, focusing on immediate business opportunities and customer engagement strategies. Alex prepared for the first sprint planning meeting by setting up tools for task tracking and communication. Mia, Carlos, and Leah started brainstorming the creative approach to their first campaign under the new system.

As the sprint progressed, the team found their rhythm. Daily standups led by Alex became a crucial part of their routine, ensuring everyone was aligned and impediments were quickly addressed. Jenna's decisions on the backlog priorities guided the team's efforts effectively, while Nakisha's involvement in the sprint reviews provided valuable insights and adjustments ensuring strategic alignment.

The AgileCorp marketing team would still hit some bumps in the road in their Agile transformation, but with clearly defined roles and responsibilities, they were well on their way.

## CONCLUSION

Adopting a scrum-based Agile marketing approach is about more than just steps in a process. The roles and responsibilities of the people involved are key, and as demonstrated, it takes a strong team to run a successful Agile marketing project.

At this point, readers should be starting to see how the elements of scrum and the roles and responsibilities of scrum team members work together to create work within sprints. Part III of this book will dive deeper into what it's like to use scrum as an Agile marketing team.

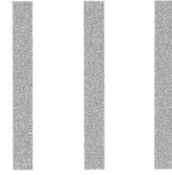

# IMPLEMENTING SCRUM IN YOUR ORGANIZATION

The next part of this book incorporates knowledge of scrum and the activities and roles it provides to teams, and it applies that knowledge to marketing work by looking at some of the elements in greater depth, as well as some of the challenges that can arise within each element.

The first thing explored will be some practical insights on how to get the most out of sprint estimation and planning, retrospectives, and other things to remember.

Then, the discussion turns to more about moving from a traditional marketing approach to an Agile one and explores some things to keep in mind that will make it easier for teams to transition to using scrum on a day-to-day basis.

Finally, time will be spent discussing some specific challenges and opportunities teams may face as they begin your Agile marketing journey.

# 10

# CREATING THE BACKLOG

Readers now have at least a basic understanding of all the elements and roles within scrum, so this chapter will start an exploration of scrum in the practice of Agile marketing by looking at some key concepts that were touched on earlier. The discussion that follows goes more in depth about how they work together.

## PRODUCT BACKLOG

Creating an effective product backlog in an agile marketing environment involves strategic organization and clear prioritization to ensure that marketing efforts are aligned with business goals and market demands.

### Steps to Create an Effective Product Backlog

This section looks at how marketers can organize and manage product backlog effectively, and introduces a new term into the mix: *epics*. As shown in Figure 10.1, epics consist of a number of tasks and can be thought of as a project that has multiple elements that need to be completed in order for it to be considered done.

| Epic Name 1 | Epic Name 2 | Epic Name 3 |
|:---:|:---:|:---:|
| Task | Task | Task |
| Task | Task | Task |
| Task | Task | |
| Task | | |

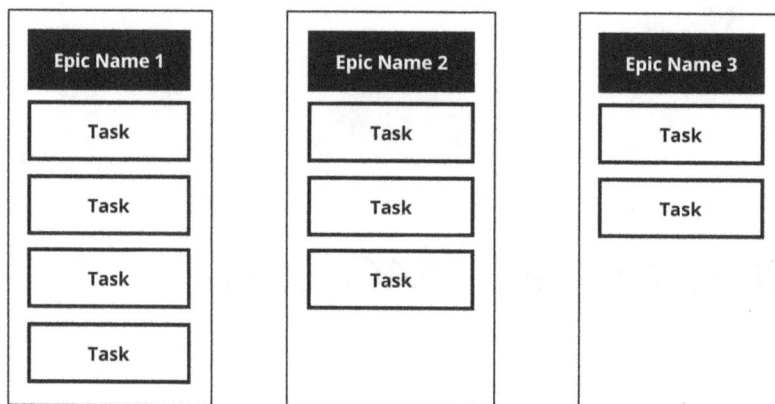

*FIGURE 10.1* Epics consist of a number of tasks.

## Identify Epics

Epics are large-scale objectives that usually extend over multiple campaigns or a series of interconnected marketing activities. These broad, overarching goals are crucial as they represent significant business or marketing outcomes that the team aims to achieve. Defining epics involves identifying key themes or major initiatives that are aligned with the organization's strategic objectives, such as increasing market share, launching a new product line, or entering a new market.

## Developing Effective Epics

When starting with epics, it's important to ensure that each one is well-defined and scoped to drive substantial value toward the business's overarching goals. An epic should be clear and concise yet comprehensive enough to encompass all related activities that contribute to the goal. For instance, an epic could be "Increase Brand Awareness in Emerging Markets," which would include a variety of campaigns and tasks like market research, localized content creation, and multichannel advertising strategies.

## Best Practices for Identifying Epics

1. *Alignment with business goals:* Ensure each epic directly contributes to strategic business objectives. This alignment helps in prioritizing resources and efforts effectively across marketing initiatives.

2. *Stakeholder engagement*: Involve key stakeholders in the epic definition process to gather insights and ensure that the epics reflect broader business perspectives. This includes discussions with senior marketing leaders, sales teams, and even customer service representatives who can provide valuable feedback on customer needs and market trends.

3. *Flexibility and adaptability*: While epics should be significant, they also need to retain some flexibility. Market conditions change, and so might the organization's strategic direction. It's crucial that epics allow for adaptation without losing sight of the end goals. This adaptability can be facilitated by regularly revisiting and revising epics based on ongoing performance data and market feedback.

Epics help organize and prioritize efforts around key business and marketing objectives. They require careful consideration and alignment with overall strategic goals, and should be broad enough to encompass related campaigns but focused enough to guide specific activities. By involving stakeholders in the creation process and maintaining flexibility in execution, marketing teams can ensure that their epics effectively drive significant business outcomes.

### Break Epics Into Tasks

This is a critical step that transforms broad, strategic objectives into actionable and measurable activities. This decomposition is essential for making the work manageable and aligning it with the team's sprint cycles. Tasks are the building blocks of the Agile process, each designed to contribute significantly to the overarching goals outlined in the epics. By subdividing epics into smaller, more specific tasks, teams can better plan, execute, and track progress while maintaining focus on the end goals.

### Creating Effective Tasks from Epics

When transforming epics into tasks, it's crucial to ensure that each task is clear and actionable. This means defining tasks in a way that they can be realistically completed within the confines of a sprint—usually a few weeks. Each task should have defined deliverables and criteria for success, making it easy for team members to understand their responsibilities. For example, if the epic is to increase brand awareness through social media, tasks might include creating specific numbers of posts, designing targeted ads, or analyzing engagement metrics from past campaigns.

### Best Practices for Breaking Down Epics

1.  *Specificity and clarity*: Each task must be well-defined with clear expectations. This includes what needs to be done, by whom, and the expected outcome. Tasks should be granular enough that they can be completed independently without ambiguity about what constitutes completion.

2.  *Contribution to the epic*: Ensure that each task has a direct line of sight to the epic. This means that every task should have a measurable impact on advancing toward the epic's goals. This alignment helps in maintaining focus and ensuring that all efforts are contributing to the strategic objectives.

3.  *Regular reviews and adjustments*: As tasks are being executed, it's important to continually assess their effectiveness and alignment with the epic. This might involve adjusting tasks based on feedback, performance data, or changes in market conditions. Agile marketing thrives on adaptability, and the task breakdown process should be dynamic to accommodate necessary pivots or enhancements.

Decomposing epics into tasks helps in managing workload effectively within the Agile framework and ensures that each piece of work is purposeful and aligned with larger marketing goals. By focusing on specificity, direct contribution to epics, and maintaining flexibility in task execution, marketing teams can enhance their productivity and strategic impact within each sprint cycle.

### Prioritize

Prioritization is a critical process that ensures the most impactful and urgent tasks are addressed first, maximizing the effectiveness of marketing efforts in alignment with business goals. The prioritization of tasks directly influences the team's ability to deliver value quickly and efficiently, and given the dynamic nature of the marketing landscape, being able to adjust priorities based on changing conditions or new insights is crucial for maintaining relevance and competitiveness.

### Methods for Effective Task Prioritization

To prioritize tasks effectively, marketing teams should consider several factors: the potential impact of each task on achieving business goals, the urgency of the tasks, and the resources available to complete them. A scoring system can be highly beneficial here, providing a structured and quantifiable method to assess each task. This system might evaluate tasks based on criteria such as expected return on investment (ROI), resource requirements, alignment with current marketing strategies, and risk factors. Tasks are then ranked according to their scores, helping to clarify which ones should be tackled first.

### Best Practices for Prioritizing Tasks

1. *Transparent and collaborative scoring*: Engage the entire team in the scoring process to ensure a comprehensive understanding of each task's benefits and requirements. This collaborative approach helps in gaining diverse perspectives, which is crucial for accurate prioritization.

2. *Dynamic prioritization*: The market conditions and organizational goals are ever evolving, and so should be the prioritization of tasks. Regularly revisit and revise the priorities based on new data, feedback from ongoing campaigns, or shifts in the business environment. This agility enables the marketing team to remain effective and responsive.

3. *Balance impact with feasibility*: While the impact on business goals is a primary factor, the prioritization process should also consider the feasibility of tasks. This includes assessing resource availability and the realistic timelines needed to achieve quality results without overburdening the team.

Effective prioritization is fundamental to scrum, ensuring that resources are allocated to tasks that provide the most significant benefit aligned with strategic goals. By employing a structured scoring system, teams can objectively assess and rank tasks, making informed decisions about what to focus on in each sprint. Regular updates to this prioritization, driven by team input and market insights, are crucial for maintaining flexibility and ensuring that the marketing efforts continually align with the highest business values. This approach not only optimizes resource utilization but also helps in achieving quicker and more impactful marketing outcomes.

### Refine Regularly

Regular refinement of the product backlog is a fundamental practice in scrum, ensuring that the marketing team's efforts remain aligned with current business objectives and market conditions. This continuous process allows the marketing team to adapt quickly to new challenges and opportunities, maintaining the relevance and effectiveness of their campaigns. By consistently updating the product backlog, the team can ensure that all tasks are reflective of the latest insights and strategic shifts, optimizing the impact of their work.

*Process of Refining the Product Backlog*

The refinement process involves several key activities: reprioritizing existing tasks to reflect new information or changes in urgency, adding new tasks that arise from evolving market conditions or new strategic initiatives, and removing tasks that are no longer relevant to the current marketing objectives. This dynamic approach to managing the backlog helps prevent stagnation and keeps the team focused on high-value activities. It also facilitates better resource allocation and planning, ensuring that the team is always working on the most impactful tasks.

## Best Practices for Regularly Refining the Backlog

1. *Scheduled review sessions*: Depending on the volume of work in a backlog, teams can hold regular backlog grooming sessions, which can be weekly, biweekly, or as needed depending on the pace of change in industry and projects. These sessions should involve key team members and stakeholders to ensure that everyone has a say in the prioritization and relevance of tasks.

2. *Responsive to change*: Stay alert to company insights and industry trends, consumer behavior, and feedback from current campaigns. Use these insights to make informed decisions about adding, removing, or reprioritizing tasks in the backlog. This responsiveness is critical to maintaining an agile and effective marketing strategy.

3. *Clear criteria for adjustment*: Develop clear criteria for why tasks might be added, removed, or reprioritized. This might include changes in strategic direction, better alignment with customer needs, or new competitive pressures. Having predefined criteria helps streamline the decision-making process and ensures consistency in how changes are implemented.

Regular refinement of the product backlog is crucial for keeping efforts efficient and aligned with the latest business goals and market conditions, which provides scrum teams with greater possibilities of success. By actively managing the backlog through scheduled reviews, responsiveness to changes, and clear criteria for adjustments, marketing teams can ensure they are always working on the most relevant and high-impact tasks. This not only maximizes the effectiveness of marketing efforts but also supports the overall agility of the organization in responding to new opportunities and challenges.

### An Example

Suppose the epic is to "Increase Brand Awareness in the 18–24 Year Old Market." Generally speaking, accomplishing something like this could be a very large effort for even a small company. Therefore, it would make sense to separate this rather expansive goal into distinct but related pieces.

Therefore, a marketing team could collaborate to determine how several tactics could be performed in parallel to accomplish this goal. This could be broken down into several tasks:

- *Task 1*: Develop a social media campaign targeting young adults with interactive content.
- *Task 2*: Collaborate with influencers who resonate with the young adult demographic to promote our products.
- *Task 3*: Create a series of educational webinars on topics relevant to young adults.
- *Task 4*: Measure the engagement and conversion rates from the campaign and adjust strategy based on analytics.

### Effective Product Backlog Management

While there are many factors that go into any Agile marketing team's product backlog, there are some best practices that any team can keep in mind:

- *Keep tasks manageable*: Ensure that each task is small enough to be completed within a sprint but large enough to deliver measurable value. This will likely require talking with the product team to understand their work better.
- *Write clear descriptions of tasks*: Each task in the backlog should have a clear description so any team member can understand what is expected without needing extensive additional explanation.
- *Regularly incorporate feedback*: Incorporate insights from previous campaigns and market research to refine and adjust the backlog items. This ties into continuous improvement efforts as well.

### What to Avoid

Additionally, it is important to avoid some behaviors and tendencies to take shortcuts. Here are a few things to stay away from:

- *Don't overload the backlog*: Avoid stuffing the backlog with too many tasks, which can overwhelm the team and dilute focus on priority initiatives.

- *Avoid vagueness*: Do not leave tasks vague or poorly defined, as this leads to confusion and inefficiencies during execution.
- *Neglecting business alignment*: Do not include tasks that do not directly contribute to strategic marketing goals or business outcomes.
- *Static prioritization*: Avoid failing to revisit and revise the priorities based on changing market conditions or business objectives.

By effectively managing the product backlog in this structured way, agile marketing teams can ensure that they are always working on the most impactful tasks that drive toward achieving strategic marketing and business goals.

## CONCLUSION

One might remember that there are two backlogs teams are tasked with maintaining: the product backlog and the sprint backlog. Although the product backlog was covered in this chapter, sprint backlog will be covered following the exploration of sprint planning in Chapter 11.

# 11

# *Sprint Planning*

Before the work begins, the important step of sprint planning sets the stage for the work to be done. This chapter looks at the process of planning work and the stages involved. First, a fundamental question needs to be answered: How long should a sprint be?

## SPRINT LENGTH

There is no single arbitrary standard for how long a sprint should be, although it is generally agreed that they should be measured in work weeks. That said, whether a sprint lasts two, three, or four weeks can depend on many factors. Also, because of the need to create a substantive amount of work, plus including the work of planning and a retrospective, a one-week sprint doesn't leave enough time for actual work to be done. Thus, the preferred amounts would be somewhere between two and four weeks.

Choosing the appropriate sprint length is crucial for the efficiency and effectiveness of an Agile marketing team. The length of the sprint impacts how quickly the team can adapt to market changes, manage workload, and maintain momentum. It is not recommended to have a sprint that is shorter than two weeks or longer than four.

There are several factors to consider when deciding whether sprints should be two, three, or four weeks in duration. It's possible that some of the characteristics that dictate a shorter sprint cycle apply, while others that dictate a longer sprint cycle apply as well. This will require teams to use judgment to determine the best approach.

### Project Complexity and Scope

Start with how many moving pieces teams are typically dealing with on a marketing campaign or initiative. Determine which of the following is most often the case:

- *Complex projects*: Longer sprints (three–four weeks) may be necessary for more complex projects for which tasks require more time to be executed properly. This additional time allows for deeper research, more detailed execution, and thorough testing before delivery.

- *Simple projects*: Simpler or less complex initiatives might benefit from shorter sprints (two weeks) as they allow for quicker iterations and faster feedback loops, which are crucial in a dynamic marketing environment.

- *Short-term projects and campaigns*: Even campaigns or marketing initiatives that have a greater complexity, yet are required to launch and run in a short timeframe might benefit from a shorter sprint cycle.

### Team Size and Composition

The number of people on a team, as well as the diversity and communication styles of team members can also have an impact on how to plan sprint timing.

- *Large teams*: Larger teams might lean toward longer sprints because coordinating and aligning the work of many team members can take more time. Longer sprints provide the necessary runway for managing communications and interdependencies within the team.

- *Widely dispersed teams*: On teams where communication is not as instantaneous as those that work closely or side by side with one another, a longer sprint cycle may work better to accommodate for delays in information reaching the right people. This could also apply to teams where there are a large amount of third party agencies or consultants and contractors.

- *Small teams*: Conversely, smaller teams that are in close communication on a regular basis may find shorter sprints more manageable and effective. They can quickly plan, execute, and review work, thus maintaining agility and responsiveness. Note that these teams don't necessarily have to physically near one another as long as they can communicate easily electronically.

### Feedback and Iteration Cycles

Another factor to take into account is the speed at which feedback can be both given and implemented. These cycles of iteration can make extremely short sprint lengths unrealistic in more complex cases. Here are a few things to keep in mind:

- *Feedback frequency*: If the campaign or project demands frequent adjustments based on consumer feedback, shorter sprints might be more suitable. This setup allows the team to rapidly iterate on marketing campaigns, adjusting strategies in response to real-time market feedback.
- *Stable requirements*: If the project has relatively stable requirements and less frequent need for adjustments, longer sprints could be a better fit, allowing for deeper focus and less frequent disruption.
- *Complex integrations*: Additionally, if a single change can have multiple upstream and downstream effects, this may also dictate a longer sprint duration.

Other factors to be considered are things like the need for stakeholder involvement, risk mitigation, and leaving time to fully think through risk implications during the sprint cycle.

Choosing the right sprint length is a strategic decision that should align with the team's goals, project needs, and operational context. It may also require some experimentation; many teams adjust their sprint lengths based on retrospective insights and evolving project demands to find the optimal rhythm that suits their specific circumstances.

## PLANNING SPRINTS

This discussion starts with the process of planning a successful sprint. There are three phases of sprint planning (Figure 11.1), which will be walked through one at a time:

- sprint design
- velocity estimation
- work allocation

```
┌──────────────┐      ┌──────────────┐      ┌──────────────┐
│              │      │              │      │              │
│ Sprint Design│ ───▶ │   Velocity   │ ───▶ │     Work     │
│              │      │  Estimation  │      │  Allocation  │
│              │      │              │      │              │
└──────────────┘      └──────────────┘      └──────────────┘
```

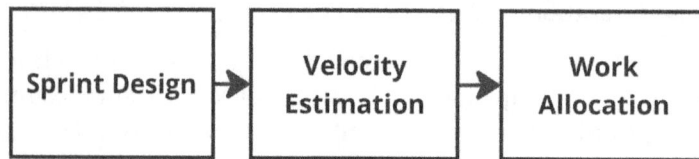

*FIGURE 11.1* Sprint planning.

## Phase 1: Sprint Design

Designing the sprint happens once at the beginning of the sprint, although the process itself can be continually improved to make it better and more efficient. Ideas for improving this process can be introduced during a retrospective, which is the best time to do so.

There are several components to designing a sprint, and these are performed differently by different teams. The following list describes some high-level recommendations:

- The first is the *sprint planning meeting*, where the product backlog is analyzed, and individual elements are pulled to become part of the current sprint backlog.
  - A key part of the sprint planning meeting is task breakdown, when tasks are identified and estimated, allowing the team to finalize the sprint backlog.
- The *daily scrum meeting* will occur and needs to be scheduled. As mentioned previously, the daily scrum meeting is when the daily progress of the sprint is reviewed with the team, and tasks are prioritized and assigned as the sprint burndown chart is referred to and adjusted.
- *Backlog grooming* refers to the process of reviewing, refining, and filling gaps in the product backlog based on the progress from sprints.
- The *sprint setrospective meeting* is when the results of a completed sprint are analyzed and compared to the goals, and when the team reviews the methods used during the sprint to identify areas for improvement in the next sprint.

There should be consensus on the design of the sprint since it may affect several other concurrent efforts within an organization. This includes things such as the length of each sprint (e.g., two weeks or four weeks) and the amount of work to be produced over time. This will be covered in the next section.

### Phase 2: Velocity Estimation

The next step in sprint planning is velocity estimation. But what exactly is meant by "velocity?" The best way to describe *velocity* in terms of a sprint is to say that it is the amount of work that can be accomplished within the time allotted for the sprint, usually either a two- or four-week timeline.

Therefore, before each sprint, the program manager and product owner need to estimate the sprint's velocity based on the product team's availability. For instance, if the team's graphic designer and copywriter are going to be busy on another marketing campaign during this next sprint, they will not be able to work full time on the items in the sprint.

Planning tools that show resource utilization and allocation often make this process easy. If a team is already using software that shows team scheduling and level of effort for tasks, they can estimate the potential velocity more reasonably. It is important not to overestimate, as this may cause work to fall behind or not be accomplished within the sprint cycle.

The advantage of creating this velocity estimate at the beginning of each sprint (as opposed to at the absolute beginning of the project) is that learnings from the previous sprints can be applied, including a more realistic estimate of how much work can be completed, to other types of learnings from sprint retrospectives.

### Phase 3: Work Allocation

After completing the sprint velocity estimate, it is time to allocate the work to the team to accomplish the work in the sprint backlog.

This process involves reviewing each item in the sprint backlog and determining who will work on each task. Often, this could be several people. For instance, if a banner ad is included in the sprint backlog, the team will need a graphic designer and a copywriter to work together, and they may need someone involved in tracking or analytics to assign a promo or tracking code for the individual banner. The velocity estimation process will help to prioritize this and will help to determine what resources are available to perform this work.

Another thing to keep in mind is that one of the key benefits of scrum teams is that they can be self-organizing to a degree. In other words, the team should have some latitude on how tasks are completed and by whom. If there is a small team with only one copywriter, there may not be a lot of choice as to who copywriting tasks fall to, but when possible, the product team should be empowered to determine how to best complete the tasks and who to include in the work being done. This also translates into a higher degree of accountability for the tasks performed and can be a motivating factor for the entire team. Once work allocation is completed, the scrum team has everything they need to begin a sprint!

Sprint planning is an important part of scrum and ensures that each sprint is successfully completed and that each successive sprint continues to improve based on learnings. There are several ways that scrum and sprint planning work together:

- Sprint planning helps each sprint run more smoothly.
- Sprint planning ensures that the amount of work required of the product team is reasonable to be completed in the sprint timeframe.
- Sprint planning allows scrum teams to self-organize to ensure the best resource is performing the task.

## EFFECTIVE SPRINT PLANNING

Even experienced Agile marketing teams can run into challenges with planning a successful sprint, but there are some best practices that teams can follow to ensure greater success as described in the following sections.

### Prepare in Advance

Ensure that the product backlog is well-groomed and prioritized before the planning meeting. This preparation allows the team to focus on discussing the most valuable tasks and how they can be accomplished during the sprint.

Teams can easily get bogged down in details if there isn't adequate preparation done ahead of time. Remember to move forward not backward during sprint planning.

### Set Clear Objectives

Begin sprint meetings meeting by clarifying the goal of the sprint. This goal should align with the business objectives and provide a focus for the team throughout the sprint.

If there are no clear objectives, it's time to work with the product owner to get clarification. For instance, when hearing about major implications of the work being done, or just hearing critical measurement criteria for the first time, there is a likely disconnect. If this is the case, it is time to have a constructive conversation about the type of information it is helpful for the scrum team to have about what they are working on together.

As important as objectives are the definition of when something is completed. Clearly define what *done* means for each task to avoid any ambiguity about what is expected to be delivered at the end of the sprint.

### Encourage Full Team Participation

Involve all team members in the planning process. This inclusion ensures diverse input and commitment, as team members are more likely to commit to the work they've helped plan.

Don't make it a solo effort. Avoid allowing one person (e.g., the scrum master or product owner) to dominate the planning. Sprint planning should be a collaborative effort where every team member's input is valued.

Remember the Agile principles, and how work as a team is so important to this way of working. Scrum works best with self-organizing teams, and that doesn't just mean one person organizing things. This means that all team members are working together and that everyone is able to hear and be heard.

### Continuously Improve Task Breakdown and Estimation

Estimation and planning take time, so it is natural that it might take some time to determine a team's velocity—or how quickly they can get a specified amount of work done.

That said, it is best to give a team enough to keep them busy, but the sprint should not be filled with more tasks than the team can handle. Overloading the sprint can degrade quality of work and reduce overall team morale.

Additionally, consider the team's capacity during the sprint, including holidays, planned absences, and other commitments that could affect productivity.

It can also help to break down large tasks into smaller ones. These more manageable actions that can be realistically completed within the sprint. This breakdown also helps in estimating more accurately and facilitates smoother execution.

## CONCLUSION

While scrum and sprint planning have several steps performed by several different roles, it's important not to get mired in the details and lose sight of the product vision or the business value a team intends to create. Incorporate user stories to simplify complex requests into easy-to-understand requirements and have a "learn by doing" mindset that means teams don't have to know everything at the start of a project.

Generally, on Agile projects, whether software or marketing, the level of knowledge and detail increases over time, which is a good thing. By the time more detail is provided, the team understands the basics. Finally, create tangible and measurable goals and focus on those as outcomes. This will help everyone stay aligned and work together to achieve those goals.

# CHAPTER 12

# DAILY STANDUPS

Marketing teams choose to adopt Agile practices such as scrum because they need to move at a greater velocity. To be successful at these greater speeds, communicating effectively is critical. Daily standups, a key practice within scrum, serve as a core way of achieving more continuous and effective communication. Originating from software development teams under the scrum framework, as discussed previously, daily standups have proven to be equally beneficial in the marketing arena, where the landscape is continually evolving and the need for rapid adaptability is crucial.

A daily *standup* is a brief meeting, typically no longer than fifteen minutes, designed to quickly align team members on current projects and identify any immediate impediments that might disrupt workflow. In fact, the name "standup" is based on the idea that everyone should be standing for the meeting, which can become uncomfortable after about fifteen minutes. Jeff Sutherland was instrumental in defining this aspect of scrum and described how a daily meeting at a previous company lasted an hour which was too long.[1] It is important to keep in mind that part of the design of the standup in scrum is to keep it brief yet impactful.

For marketing teams, this ritual fosters a culture of openness and collaboration while ensuring that every team member is aligned with the team's goals and daily tasks. The structure of these meetings encourages concise and focused discussions, making them an invaluable part of the day.

This chapter explores the standup in more detail: why it is so important, what makes a good one, some best practices, as well as what to avoid.

## THE PURPOSE OF THE DAILY STANDUP

The daily standup meeting serves several important purposes that make Agile marketing teams successful. These brief, focused gatherings are integral to maintaining the rhythm and momentum of ongoing projects, ensuring that all team members are aligned and equipped to tackle their tasks effectively each day. The following are the core purposes of the daily standup:

### Synchronization of Team Efforts

The primary goal of the daily standup is to synchronize the activities of each team member with the overall project objectives. By sharing what each person has worked on and will work on, the team can align their efforts seamlessly, ensuring that everyone is moving in the same direction. This is particularly crucial in marketing, where activities often involve multiple overlapping projects with dependencies on various team members.

### Identification of Blockers

Quick identification of blockers or impediments to work getting done, or getting done well, is another reason for the standup. The meeting's format allows each team member the opportunity to report any obstacles or challenges they are facing that might hinder their progress. Addressing these blockers promptly ensures they don't escalate into more significant issues that could derail project timelines. For Agile marketing teams, blockers could range from delays in content approval, difficulties with third-party creative vendors, or technical challenges with marketing automation tools.

### Fostering Team Communication and Collaboration

The daily standup encourages open communication and collaboration within the team. This regular touchpoint helps teams build a culture of transparency and trust, where members feel comfortable sharing their successes and struggles. It also provides a platform for spontaneous collaboration, where team members can offer help or suggest solutions to challenges mentioned by others.

### Enhancing Responsiveness to Change

The work of marketers is dynamic, whether based on external factors like market trends, competitor actions, and customer behaviors, or from internal factors like changing priorities and shifting strategies. Standups allow marketing teams to be highly responsive to these changes. By regrouping every day, teams can quickly pivot or adjust their strategies, ensuring that their marketing efforts remain effective and relevant.

### Reinforcing Accountability

When team members verbally commit to their tasks in front of their peers, it naturally enhances accountability. This regular recounting of what each person has done and what they plan to do next helps individuals stay focused on their responsibilities. It also encourages a sense of ownership and pride in their contributions, driving higher motivation and productivity.

Daily standups play a pivotal role in not just keeping the marketing projects on track but also in building a proactive, agile, and collaborative team culture.

## PARTICIPANTS

As important as *what* is discussed in a daily standup is *who* is there, and the roles that each participant plays. In the spirit of Agile principles, each contributor has a unique role and all work together to make processes as efficient and effective as possible.

Understanding these roles and their responsibilities helps ensure that the daily standups are productive and focused. Here's a breakdown of the typical participants in a marketing team's daily standup:

### Product Owner

The product owner is crucial in the daily standup, primarily to provide clarity and direction regarding the overall priorities and objectives of the marketing efforts. While they do not need to lead the standup, their presence is essential to answer any strategic questions and to help resolve priority conflicts that may arise during the discussion.

During the standup, the product owner ensures that the tasks being worked on are aligned with business goals and provides quick decisions on any priority conflicts.

### Scrum Master

The scrum master facilitates the daily standup to ensure that it stays on track and adheres to the time constraints. This role is responsible for maintaining the focus of the meeting, making sure that it does not devolve into problem-solving or stray off topic. The scrum master also notes any impediments or issues raised during the standup that require further attention or resolution outside of the meeting.

During the daily standup, the scrum master keeps the meeting within the fifteen-minute time frame, facilitates the flow from one team member to the next, and helps identify solutions or interventions for blockers that can be handled immediately.

### Team Members

All members of the marketing team actively participate in the daily standup. Each member is expected to succinctly share their updates based on the three key questions: what they accomplished since the last meeting, what they will work on today, and any obstacles they're facing. This includes content creators, search engine optimization (SEO) specialists, digital marketers, graphic designers, social media managers, and any other roles involved in the sprint.

During the standup, each team member is responsible for preparing their updates in advance, being concise in their communication, and being respectful of the time limit. They should also be ready to offer help or collaboration if they see an opportunity to assist a teammate with a blocker.

### Stakeholders

Occasionally, stakeholders or other departments might be invited to attend the standup, especially if their input or updates are crucial to the marketing team's activities. However, their involvement should be kept to a minimum to maintain the meeting's pace and focus. They are an optional attendee.

By clearly understanding the roles and responsibilities of each participant in the standup, the team can leverage these brief meetings to enhance coordination, address immediate issues, and accelerate their initiatives effectively.

## THE STRUCTURE OF THE MEETING

The daily standup is a cornerstone of the scrum approach and follows the Agile principle that teams must work together daily throughout the project. The meeting is designed to optimize the time and efficiency of the team while keeping everyone aligned on the day's priorities. To achieve this, the standup must be well structured and strictly timed. The following sections look at how to structure an effective daily standup for a marketing team:

### Duration and Timing

- *Fifteen-minute timebox*: The standup should last no longer than fifteen minutes. This constraint helps keep the discussion brief and to the point.
- *Consistent scheduling*: Conduct the standup at the same time and place every day. This regularity helps establish a routine that team members can rely on, and it minimizes disruptions to the workday.

### Format

The format of the daily standup revolves around three specific questions that each team member answers in turn. This format is designed to provide quick insights into what's been accomplished, what will be done next, and what issues might be impeding progress:

1. What did I accomplish yesterday?

   Team members briefly describe their achievements since the last standup, focusing on completed tasks that contribute directly to the sprint goals.

2. What will I work on today?

   This update gives team members the opportunity to outline their tasks for the day, linking their planned activities to the overall objectives of the sprint. It helps identify potential overlaps or dependencies between team members' tasks.

3. What obstacles are impeding my progress?

   Here, team members mention any blockers or challenges that could prevent them from completing their tasks. Highlighting these issues promptly allows the team to swiftly address potential delays.

### Participation

*Round-robin approach*: At a daily standup, each team member speaks in turn, ideally standing up to signify the brief nature of the meeting. The scrum master or a designated facilitator should help maintain the order and flow of the updates, particularly for teams that are new to the process. Even teams that are used to the process yet new to working with one another benefit from the scrum master being a facilitator, however.

*Focused content*: Each update should be succinct and relevant. This is not the time for long discussions or problem-solving, which should be taken offline and handled separately.

### Facilitation

*Lead facilitator*: The scrum master facilitates the standup to ensure it starts and ends on time and stays on track. They also note any issues that need further discussion or intervention and can schedule follow-up meetings if necessary.

*Keeping the pace*: The scrum master ensures that the discussion does not veer off into detailed problem solving or side conversations. They keep the meeting moving by gently steering team members back to the three questions if they stray.

### Tools and Visual Aids

*Use of task boards*: Whether physical (for in-person teams) or digital (for hybrid or fully remote teams), task boards are often used during the standup to visualize progress. Team members can reference the board as they discuss their tasks, making it easier for everyone to understand the current state of the sprint.

*Meeting notes*: While extensive notes are not necessary, capturing key points, especially regarding impediments and their proposed solutions, can be helpful. These notes can be briefly reviewed at the start of the next standup to ensure continuity and follow-up on unresolved issues. Individual team members should be held responsible for keeping notes that are directly relevant to their own activities. After all, fostering a culture of accountability means everyone is responsible for making sure they know what their priorities are and the directly relevant information to their own work is.

With a structured approach, the daily standup can serve as an efficient tool for synchronization and communication, keeping the team agile, informed, and ready to tackle each day's challenges effectively.

## BEST PRACTICES

In addition to the basics of roles and structure, teams that implement efficient daily standups will achieve better results more quickly. Here are several best practices that Agile marketing teams should adopt to make the most out of their daily standups:

### Start on Time, Every Time

Punctuality is crucial and sets the stage for the working dynamic of the team over time. Start the standup at the scheduled time regardless of whether all team members are present. This practice reinforces the importance of the meeting and respects the time of those who arrive promptly. This mutual respect is key to building a long-term constructive working relationship among a scrum team.

### Keep It Standing and Focused

It is important to keep the standup focused. Encourage team members to stand during the meeting. Doing so naturally keeps the energy levels high and helps maintain the brevity of the meeting. This is particularly effective in preventing the standup from turning into a longer, sit-down discussion.

Of course, knowing that many teams are now working remote or in hybrid settings makes this less realistic in some cases. That said, it is possible to still keep the *spirit* of the standup by keeping it short and focused.

An additional way to maintain focus is to adhere strictly to the three guiding questions of the standup: what was done yesterday, what will be done today, and what are the impediments. This focus prevents the conversation from drifting into detailed status updates or problem-solving discussions, which should be reserved for separate meetings.

### Limit to Team Members Only

It may be tempting to let in others who might have good ideas or strong opinions about the work being done.

Don't give into this: Only active contributors to the sprint should speak during the standup. While stakeholders and others may attend to listen, they should not participate in the discussions unless absolutely necessary. This keeps the updates quick and relevant.

Additionally, part of the job of the product owner is to manage stakeholder requests and ideas. These should be brought to the team without being vetted first.

### Use a Token or Talking Stick

While this may be particularly tricky in remote or hybrid situations, sometimes it can be difficult to manage team members talking over one another in a standup.

Thus, to manage turn-taking effectively, use a physical object as a token or talking stick. The person holding the token has the floor, which can help manage the flow of conversation, especially in larger teams.

In a virtual environment, utilize the "raised hand" icon that is present in most virtual meeting software. Team members who raise their hands can be given a chance to talk in the order they have raised their hands. The leader of the standup meeting should be able to manage this effectively.

### Address Impediments and End with a Clear Action Plan

Any blockers or impediments mentioned during the standup should be noted by the scrum master or team lead. It's crucial to address these immediately after the standup or designate a specific time to resolve these issues, ensuring they don't stall progress.

Additionally, no one likes to leave a meeting and wonder what the point of it was. While many team member may be proactive or keep active notes by habit, make sure to conclude the meeting with a quick recap of the key actions to be taken, especially regarding the resolution of impediments. This ensures everyone leaves the standup with a clear understanding of their priorities and next steps.

The leader of the standup meeting may also want to post any group takeaways or next steps in a common messaging app like Slack or Teams. Be careful not to assign new responsibilities after the meeting has already ended. The team should use the meeting time to agree on next steps.

### Keep a Positive Atmosphere

Encourage a positive, supportive environment where team members feel comfortable sharing their true progress and any challenges they're facing. This openness fosters better collaboration and problem-solving as a team.

If negativity is an issue, one first step is to remind everyone of the Agile principles of teamwork, self-organizing, and continuous improvement, not to mention others. The next section of the book further explores getting teams to work better together, but for the time being, remember that scrum teams work best when everyone is open, honest, and shares the positive as well as constructive areas for improvement.

Incorporating these best practices into a marketing team can ensure that these brief meetings are not only efficient and focused but also instrumental in driving the day-to-day progress of projects, fostering team alignment, and promoting a proactive problem-solving culture.

## THINGS TO AVOID

While the basics of a daily standup may seem straightforward, there are several common pitfalls that marketing teams should be aware of to prevent these gatherings from becoming unproductive. Avoiding these issues ensures that the standup remains a valuable part of the scrum process:

### Turning the Standup into a Detailed Discussion

Avoid using the standup for problem-solving or lengthy discussions about specific issues. Standups should focus on quick updates and identifying blockers, not resolving them on the spot. Detailed discussions should be taken offline in separate, focused meetings.

### Allowing Side Conversations

Side conversations can easily derail the focus and flow of the standup. Encourage team members to stay on topic and save unrelated discussions for after the meeting. This keeps the standup concise and on track.

### Not Preparing for the Standup

Team members should come prepared with their updates on what they accomplished yesterday, what they plan to do today, and any impediments they're facing. Lack of preparation can lead to vague or forgotten updates, which diminish the value of the standup.

### Dominating the Conversation

Ensure that no single team member dominates the standup. Each member should have equal time to speak. This balance can be facilitated by the scrum master or the team lead, who should gently guide the conversation to ensure everyone has a chance to contribute.

### Ignoring or Overlooking Blockers

Do not dismiss or overlook the blockers that are mentioned. Blockers are critical issues that can impede progress. They should be noted and addressed quickly after the standup to ensure they do not affect the sprint's success.

### Lack of Engagement

Watch out for signs of disengagement, such as team members not listening to others or showing a lack of interest in the updates. Encourage active participation and consider ways to make the standup more engaging.

### Inconsistency in Timing and Attendance

Inconsistency in the timing of the standup or frequent absenteeism can undermine the rhythm and reliability of the meeting. Strive for consistent scheduling and prompt starts to build a routine that team members can rely on.

### Failing to Act on Feedback

Avoid ignoring feedback about the standup itself. Regularly solicit and act on feedback to improve the effectiveness of the meetings. Continuous improvement should be a core aspect of not just the projects but also the processes including standups.

### Skipping Standups

Do not skip standups unless absolutely necessary. Regular standups are essential for maintaining momentum and alignment within the team. Even if some team members cannot attend, hold the standup with those who are available.

### Overformalizing the Meeting

While structure is important, over formalizing the standup can make it rigid and stilted. Keep the atmosphere light and conversational to encourage openness and collaboration.

Being aware of and actively avoiding these pitfalls allows a team to maximize the benefits of daily standups, ensuring these meetings enhance productivity, improve communications, and help identify and resolve issues swiftly. This proactive approach is essential for maintaining the agility and responsiveness of the team throughout the sprint.

## FOLLOW-UP ACTIONS

Effective follow-up actions are crucial for capitalizing on the momentum generated during daily standups. These actions ensure that the team's discussions translate into concrete steps that drive progress throughout the sprint. Here are some items that should immediately follow the standup to ensure it is effective.

### Documentation of Blockers and Decisions

Immediately after the standup, the scrum master should document any blockers or critical issues identified. This documentation should include specific details about the problem, who is responsible for addressing it, and any deadlines for resolution. Keeping a record ensures accountability and provides a reference for tracking progress on these issues.

Note that this is documentation of the blocker and does not make the scrum master responsible for making an individual team member work on those specific tasks at a specific time. The individual team members are responsible for how they resolve issues, making them ultimately accountable. The list that the scrum master makes is for documentation purposes and to make sure that nothing slips through the cracks.

### Assigning and Addressing Blockers

Assign each identified blocker to a specific team member or arrange for the necessary resources to resolve it. The assignment should be clear and agreed upon by all involved parties within the standup to prevent any confusion or delays in addressing the issue.

### Scheduling Additional Meetings

If issues arise during the standup that require more in-depth discussion or collaboration, schedule follow-up meetings or working sessions specifically for those topics. These meetings should be time-boxed to maintain efficiency and should involve only the necessary stakeholders to keep them productive.

### Updating Project Management Tools

After the standup, it's essential to update any project management tools or systems the team uses. This update might include marking tasks as completed, adjusting the timeline of ongoing tasks, or adding new tasks that were discussed during the standup. Keeping these tools updated in real-time ensures that the entire team has visibility into the project's current status and understands their responsibilities.

### Communicating Outcomes to Stakeholders

The scrum master will work with the product owner to inform relevant stakeholders of any significant updates or decisions from the standup, especially those that might impact project scope, timelines, or resources. This communication can be in the form of a brief email or a quick call, depending on the urgency and preference of the stakeholders.

### Reviewing the Day's Objectives

After addressing immediate follow-up needs, team members should review their objectives for the day to ensure alignment with the sprint goals and the updates from the standup. This review helps individuals prioritize their tasks effectively, focusing on what will drive the most value for the sprint.

### Encouraging Quick Wins

Encourage team members to identify and tackle any *quick wins*— tasks that can be completed quickly but have a significant impact. This approach can boost morale and create a sense of progress and accomplishment within the team. After all, with agility as the goal, speed is a significant component of that.

Sometimes other best practices evolve from work as well, so use these items as a guide to build upon. By effectively managing these follow-up actions and others that may be added to this list, the team can ensure that the insights and issues raised during the standup are addressed promptly, keeping the sprint on track and maintaining high levels of team productivity and engagement.

## MEASURING THE SUCCESS OF STANDUPS

Even though they only last fifteen minutes per day, a daily standup is still a considerable investment over the lifetime of a project. To ensure that these meetings are effectively contributing to the overall productivity and cohesion of the team and the initiatives they are assigned, it's essential to have a system for measuring their success. Evaluating the impact of these meetings can help identify areas for improvement and ensure that they remain a valuable tool. See Table 12.1 for a look at the key metrics and indicators to consider when assessing the success of daily standups,

**TABLE 12.1** Metrics of Success for a Daily Standup Meeting

| Area | Metric | Indicator(s) |
|------|--------|--------------|
| **Participation** | Attendance Rate | Percentage of team members attending daily standups |
| | | Consistency of attendance by key team members |
| | Engagement Level | Active participation and contribution from team members |
| | | Frequency of team members raising issues or providing updates |

*(Continued)*

| Area | Metric | Indicator(s) |
|---|---|---|
| **Communication** | Clarity of Updates | Conciseness and relevance of updates shared by team members |
| | | Understanding and retention of information by team members |
| | Information Flow | Timely sharing of critical information affecting the project |
| | | Reduction in misunderstandings or miscommunications |
| **Problem-Solving** | Issue Resolution Time | Time taken to identify and address blockers |
| | | Number of issues escalated during standups and their resolution status |
| | Proactive Identification of Risks | Frequency of potential risks or issues identified and discussed |
| | | Actions taken to mitigate identified risks |
| **Team Coordination** | Alignment on Tasks and Goals | Consistency in understanding and pursuing daily goals and tasks |
| | | Reduction in duplicate efforts or conflicting tasks |
| | Collaboration and Support | Instances of team members offering help or collaborating to resolve issues |
| | | Improvement in team cohesion and support during the standups |
| **Progress Tracking** | Task Completion Rate | Percentage of tasks completed on time as discussed in standups |
| | | Progress toward sprint or project milestones as communicated during daily updates |
| | Visibility of Progress | Clear tracking of progress in relation to the sprint goals |
| | | Utilization of visual aids (e.g., Kanban boards, burndown charts) during standups |
| **Meeting Efficiency** | Duration of Standup | Adherence to the planned timebox for daily standups (usually fifteen minutes) |
| | | Efficiency in covering all necessary topics within the allotted time |
| | Meeting Structure and Discipline | Consistent adherence to the standup format (e.g., What did you do yesterday? What will you do today?) |
| | | Reduction in off-topic discussions or extended debates |

By regularly measuring these aspects of daily standups, marketing teams can ensure that these meetings remain efficient, effective, and tailored to the team's needs. Adjustments based on these evaluations can help maintain the relevance and effectiveness of the standup as part of the team's agile practices.

## THE AGILECORP MARKETING TEAMS' STANDUP EXPERIENCE

It's time to check in with the team at AgileCorp and see how these marketers have been using daily standups. They are now three months into their adoption of scrum and are currently working on a multichannel campaign for a new product feature launch. The standup takes place remotely every morning at 9:00 a.m., with team members joining from various locations.

During one of their standups, each member quickly shared updates according to the standard format. Emily, the product owner, began by summarizing the major achievements from the previous day, including final approval on several major ad designs. Next, Juan, a digital marketer, mentioned that he had successfully optimized the campaign's search engine ads but was facing delays due to slower than expected feedback from the analytics team on ad performance.

The social media manager, Liza, celebrated a significant increase in engagement from the latest social media blitz but noted she was encountering issues with scheduling tools that were causing posts to go live at incorrect times. The scrum master, Alex, noted down the issue and promised to coordinate with the IT department immediately after the standup.

In a retrospective dedicated to their daily standup activities, the AgileCorp marketing team noted several areas of success in their adoption of daily standups:

1. *Timeliness and efficiency*: The team was almost always well-prepared and kept their updates concise, regularly completing the standup in just under 15 minutes, which kept the meeting within the desired timeframe.

2. *Engagement*: Each team member was actively engaged on a consistent basis, listening to others' updates, and offering quick suggestions for any challenges mentioned.

3. *Progress tracking*: The use of a digital task board helped everyone visually track the progress of tasks and understand dependencies clearly. This was particularly important since the team members worked remotely and rarely met in person.

In that same retrospective, the team also identified some areas they still felt could be improved:

1. *Addressing blockers*: The team realized that while blockers were quickly identified, the resolution of these issues was not always prompt. They

agreed on a need for a more structured approach to address these blockers immediately following the standup.

2. *Scheduling tools*: The issues with the scheduling tools highlighted a broader problem with software reliability that affected several team members. The team decided to evaluate their current tools and look into alternative solutions if necessary.

3. *Increasing collaboration*: Juan's feedback delays underscored a need for better coordination with the analytics team. The team discussed establishing a mini daily check-in with key stakeholders from the analytics team during campaign peaks to streamline communication.

After the meeting, Alex, the scrum master, organized a quick follow-up session with the IT department to resolve the scheduling tool issue. Emily decided to arrange a biweekly sync with the heads of analytics to improve turnaround times for feedback, which was critical for John's work.

This experience underscored the value of the standup in identifying and addressing immediate issues but also highlighted areas where the team could improve their processes to make their daily meetings even more effective. The AgileCorp marketing team committed to continual adjustment of their standup practices, aiming for even greater efficiency and collaboration in their project workflows.

## CONCLUSION

Daily standups, when conducted effectively, are more than just routine meetings; they are a pivotal component of scrum that fosters transparency, collaboration, and swift responsiveness within marketing teams.

To maximize the benefits of daily standups, teams should regularly evaluate the efficiency and impact of these meetings and be willing to adapt their strategies based on team feedback and changing project needs. By doing so, marketing teams can ensure that their standups are not just a check-in, but a catalyst for dynamic growth and enhanced team performance.

### Note

1. Sutherland, Jeff, and J.J. Sutherland. (2014). *Scrum: The Art of Doing Twice the Work in Half the Time*. Crown Curr ency.

# 13

# *RUNNING A SUCCESSFUL SPRINT*

Thus far, the book has discussed the elements of planning and prioritization needed to work successfully as an Agile marketing team. Now it is time to talk about the day-to-day work of running a successful sprint.

This chapter discusses the individual components of a sprint and how to manage them well. This discussion will look at task management, how collaboration occurs within teams, how an agile marketing team adapts to changes, how to respond to blockers, as well as how clear communication is maintained throughout a sprint.

## TASK MANAGEMENT

Effective task management and workflow are critical components of a successful sprint. Properly managing tasks ensures that the team stays focused, progresses efficiently, and meets sprint goals. This section outlines the tools and techniques for managing tasks and maintaining a smooth workflow throughout the sprint.

### Tools for Task Management and Communication

As has been explored thus far, having a common visual frame of reference, as well as a centralized place to see the work in progress as well as what is in the queue is critical to the success of a marketing effort. While many tools will work in both Agile and non-Agile environments, the following sections explore some that work particularly well for Agile marketing teams.

## Kanban Boards

As seen in a previous chapter, a Kanban board is a visual tool that displays tasks in columns representing different stages of the workflow (e.g., To Do, In Progress, Done), and tools such as Jira (Figure 13.1) offer an easy drag-and-drop method to incorporating Kanban into a team's approach.

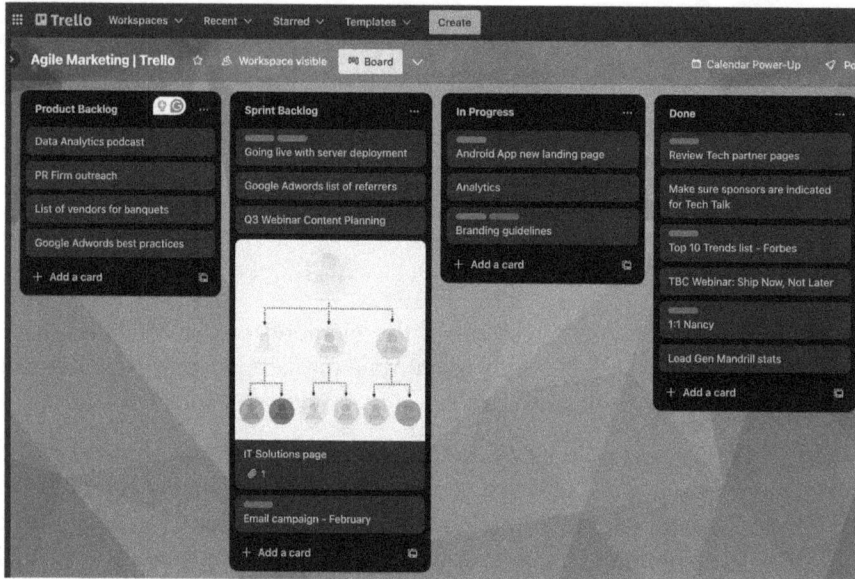

**FIGURE 13.1** Trello allows organizations to easily incorporate a Kanban board into their Agile marketing activities.

Each task is represented by a card that moves across the board as work progresses. This visualization helps the team see the status of tasks at a glance and identify bottlenecks.

Kanban boards are highly effective for managing workflows, maintaining transparency, and ensuring that work progresses smoothly through each stage of the sprint.

## Burndown Charts

An important component of a sprint is understanding how much work can be performed at optimal quality. This requires understanding the level of effort as well as the velocity, or how quickly the team can complete the work.

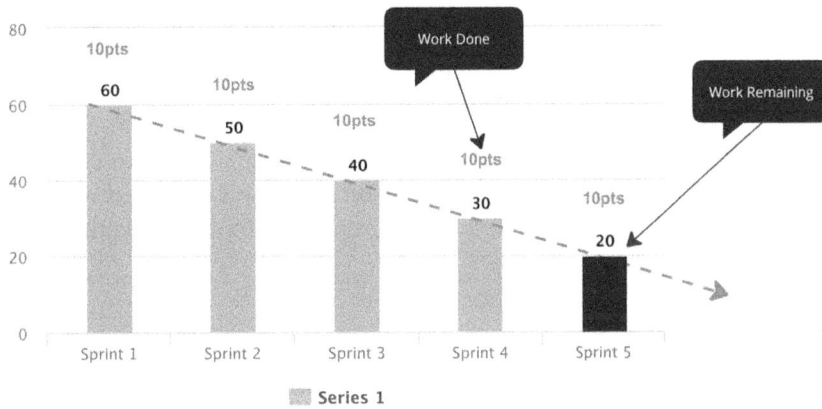

**FIGURE 13.2** A burndown chart tracks progress of a team against the sprint goals and tasks within a sprint.

A burndown chart (Figure 13.2) tracks the amount of work remaining in the sprint over time. It typically shows the ideal progress line versus the actual progress. Regularly updating the burndown chart helps the team monitor whether they are on track to complete the sprint goals. As can be seen in Figure 13.3, tracking actual progress against ideal progress allows a team to adjust. In the example, in sprints 1 and 2, the team was delivering less work than ideal, so they adjusted in sprint 3 and started to deliver more in order to make up for the shortage.

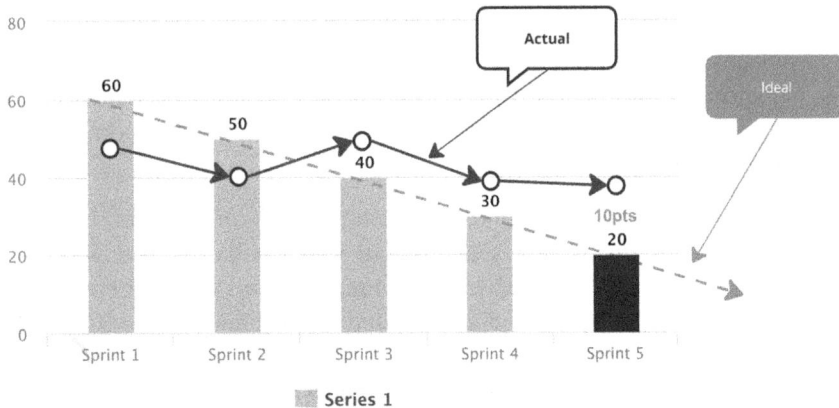

**FIGURE 13.3** Burndown chart with actual and ideal work amounts plotted.

Thus, effective use of a burndown chart will give teams advance notice of how they are tracking toward goals so they can adjust their efforts to make sure they achieve on-time delivery.

This tool provides a clear visual representation of progress, helping the team identify any deviations from the plan early and take corrective actions. Some of the project management software tools explored next have a burndown chart built into their standard reporting tools, although teams may need to create their own.

### Project Management Software

Project management tools like Jira, Trello, Asana, Adobe Workfront, and Monday.com are popular for managing tasks and projects in many types of environments, but Agile teams utilize them effectively when they are configured to be optimized for a scrum-based workflow. These tools offer features such as task assignments, progress tracking, and collaboration.

Vital to the success of an Agile marketing project, these project management platforms help visualize the workflow, track progress, and ensure everyone is aligned on what needs to be done and by when. The good news is that many team members may be familiar with them from their previous project work regardless of their familiarity with Agile methods like scrum, which makes the learning curve less steep.

### Other Helpful Tools

Of course, there are many other tools and software platforms that can be helpful, although they will not be reviewed in as much depth as many are not specific to Agile marketing. These include messaging platforms like Slack, Microsoft Teams, or Google Chat facilitate real-time communication and quick information sharing.

Particularly for remote teams, virtual whiteboarding tools like Miro can also help with brainstorming sessions and visual collaboration. Video conferencing tools such as Zoom, Microsoft Teams, or Google Meet enable face-to-face meetings, which are crucial for building rapport and discussing complex topics.

## Techniques for Efficient Task Management and Prioritization

It takes more than software to run a successful sprint. The following sections look at a few methods to make sure a sprint team's time is being managed effectively and that the teams are able to focus on the right things.

*Task Prioritization*

Prioritizing tasks ensures that the most critical items are addressed first, aligning the team's efforts with sprint goals.

Use techniques like MoSCoW (must have, should have, could have, won't have) prioritization or the Eisenhower Matrix to categorize tasks based on their importance and urgency. Each technique is explored briefly in the following sections, and if one of these seems optimal, readers are encouraged to explore them more before adopting them with their team.

*MoSCoW Method*

This prioritization technique is frequently used in many types of project management, and has four components:

1. *M: Must have.* These are deliverables that are critical to a projects success and thus nonnegotiable. The project will not be successful if they are not delivered.

2. *S: Should have.* These are important tasks, but not critical for the launch of a project or initiative. They should be included, if possible, but the M deliverables take precedence.

3. *C: Could have.* These are tasks or features that would have the ability to improve the project but can be postponed if needed so that the critical tasks can be completed on time.

4. *W: Won't have.* The last category is those tasks that are the lowest priority and are often left out of scope for an initial project or campaign delivery.

While there can be some subjectivity in this assessment, a clear definition of business value and objectives can help provide clarity to Agile marketing teams that may not immediately align on the previous definitions.

*Eisenhower Matrix*

Named after Dwight D. Eisenhower, thirty-fourth president of the United States, as well as a five-star general in World War II, he is generally attributed with having created this method for organizing his tasks.

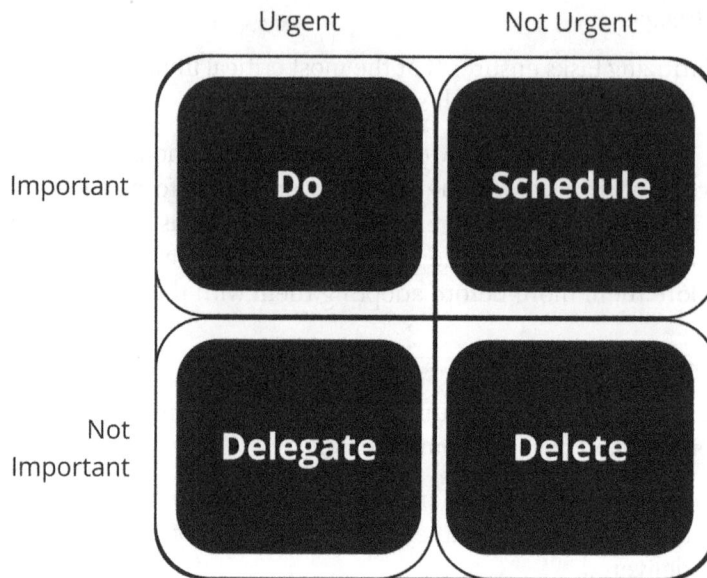

*FIGURE 13.4* The Eisenhower Matrix that is used to prioritize efforts.

The matrix (Figure 13.4) consists of four quadrants:

1. *Do first*. These are urgent and important tasks that require immediate attention while also contributing to long-term goals.

2. *Schedule*. These are important but not urgent and while they contribute to long-term missions, they don't require immediate attention.

3. *Delegate*. These are tasks that are urgent but not strategically important in the long term. They need to get done, thus must be delegated to someone, but they should be delegated to others that are not critical to completing the most important tasks.

4. *Don't Do*. These tasks are not urgent or important. While they may seem as if they need to be done, they should be removed from the schedule and postponed if not ignored indefinitely.

The Eisenhower Matrix offers many benefits, one of which is its simplicity. It can help a scrum master, for instance, easily help to prioritize items in a sprint backlog and offer a clear rationale when discussing with the sprint team.

There are many other methods that can be used to help prioritize a team's tasks. Regardless of the method used, effective prioritization helps focus the team on high-impact tasks, improving the chances of achieving the sprint objectives.

### Timeboxing

Timeboxing involves allocating a fixed amount of time for each task or activity. It helps in maintaining focus and preventing tasks from dragging on indefinitely.

The basic concept is that an individual or team gives themselves an immovable "box" of time in which to accomplish something. This includes the time to evaluate the task, perform the task, as well as to assess if it has been completed or not (and why not).

When implemented well, timeboxing enhances productivity, ensures timely completion of tasks, and helps manage the team's workload effectively. It encourages team members to more accurately and systematically measure the time that individual tasks take to accomplish and adjust work styles to be more accurate about how long the tasks will take.

### Task Breakdown and Estimation

Related to timeboxing is the need for breaking down larger tasks into smaller, manageable pieces makes it easier to estimate and complete them.

Use techniques like story points or T-shirt sizing (Figure 13.5) for task estimation. Ensure that tasks are small enough to be completed within a day or two. For instance, T-shirt sizing can be used to divide tasks into those that will take a certain amount of time to accomplish (e.g., two to three hours), or as a combination of time and resources (e.g., two team members spending four hours each).

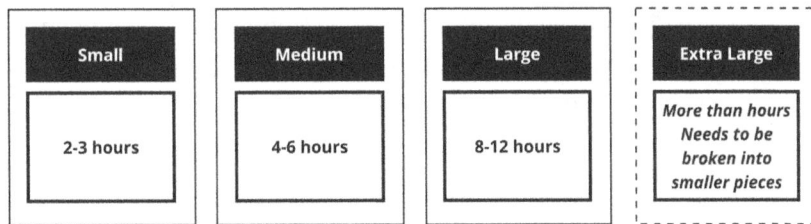

| Small | Medium | Large | Extra Large |
|-------|--------|-------|-------------|
| 2-3 hours | 4-6 hours | 8-12 hours | More than hours Needs to be broken into smaller pieces |

**FIGURE 13.5** T-shirt sizing approach, including a method to determine which tasks should be broken up into smaller ones.

This approach can also be a way to force teams to break larger tasks into more manageable ones. As shown in Figure 13.5, a task deemed "extra large" is suggested to be broken up into pieces rather than kept as a whole. This is because smaller tasks are easier to track and manage, reducing the risk of delays and improving the accuracy of progress tracking.

## Maintaining Velocity and Avoiding Scope Creep

So far, this chapter has looked at how to make sure a team is working on the right things and that they have a common view and visibility into what is being done. The following sections look at some ways to help maintain momentum within a sprint and make sure that challenges such as blockers and scope creep don't derail the success of a sprint.

### Clear Definition of Done

It is one thing to call a task complete, but it can be quite a different thing to agree as a group that the goals behind the task are accomplished. Thus, establishing a clear "definition of done" for each task ensures that everyone knows what constitutes task completion.

In the software world where scrum originated, the definition should include criteria like code reviews, testing, documentation, and any other specific requirements.

In a marketing context, however, this might be different. To use the example of when a marketing email is completed, one might want to look at the following:

- Does it meet the creative and branding requirements?
- Does it meet the content requirements of the marketing channel?
- Have the links on the call to action and elsewhere in the email been tested thoroughly?
- Have discount codes included in marketing messaging been tested?
- Has the email been tested thoroughly on different email clients as well as on desktop and mobile devices?

There might be plenty of other definitions of done as well, depending on the specifics of the email. Regardless, a clear definition of done helps maintain consistency in task completion and ensures that all aspects of the task are thoroughly addressed.

### Mitigating Against Scope Creep

Although it has its roots in the software engineering world, scope creep can apply to any type of work, including marketing. *Scope creep* occurs when new tasks or features are added to the sprint without proper evaluation, potentially derailing the team's progress.

Use a change control process to evaluate and approve any new tasks or changes. Ensure that any additions align with the sprint goals and are feasible within the sprint timeline. This could be as simple as a rule to not allow any new items to be added to a sprint backlog in the middle of a sprint.

Effective scope management prevents the team from getting overwhelmed by unplanned work and helps maintain focus on the agreed-upon objectives.

### Regular Check-Ins and Adjustments

Regularly checking in on task progress and making necessary adjustments ensures that the team stays on track.

While conducting daily standups is already a good way to discuss progress, blockers, and any adjustments needed, depending on how quickly a marketing initiative is moving, once a day might not be enough to get a general status update. Regular check-ins promote transparency, allow for timely identification of issues, and keep the team aligned and focused.

By leveraging these tools and techniques for task management and workflow, an Agile marketing team can ensure that their sprints are productive, focused, and aligned with their goals. Proper task management not only enhances efficiency but also fosters a collaborative and dynamic work environment, ultimately contributing to the success of the sprint.

## HANDLING BLOCKERS AND OTHER IMPEDIMENTS

Blockers and issues are inevitable in any marketing campaign or project, and effectively handling them is crucial for maintaining the momentum and success of a sprint when running a scrum team. Addressing, and resolving blockers quickly ensures that progress is not stalled and that the team can continue working toward their sprint goals. Following are some common types of blockers, strategies for identifying and addressing them, and the role of the scrum master in facilitating issue resolution.

### Common Types of Blockers

Many of these issues are likely recognizable whether teams are currently utilizing an Agile approach or not. After all, these are the items that most commonly get in the way of work being completed, regardless of whether scrum is being used or not.

- *Technical blockers*: As marketing becomes increasingly reliant on technology, technical blockers can pop up frequently. These can be things such as broken links in an email, or broken e-commerce functionality for a product promotion. These technical blockers often rely on external teams or third-party platforms to resolve.

- *Resource blockers*: These include unavailability of key personnel or insufficient budgeting to bring on external teams or full-time resources. For instance, if a team requires a designer to complete the work on the UX design for a landing page, but that individual is unavailable due to other commitments, this is a resource block.

- *Dependency blockers*: These consist of items that are necessary to have in place to accomplish the work at hand. For instance, if an email needs to be entered into a marketing automation platform, it requires an approved copy and design first. If the design is still waiting for compliance approval, this would be a dependency blocker.

- *Communication blockers*: These include miscommunications, lack of information provided in briefs or requirements documents, or unclear instructions. For instance, if a deadline for approvals is mistakenly set for three days later than it should be, that is a miscommunication that could have a major impact on the launch of a campaign, particularly if there is a short turnaround time involved.

### Identifying and Avoiding Blockers

Teams may find ways to identify some of those blockers listed in the previous section, but following are some tools that an Agile marketing team can utilize to identify and ideally avoid them.

- *Daily standups*: Use daily standup meetings to provide a forum for team members to raise any blockers they are facing. After all, those involved are already meeting as a team during this time, so it should be the perfect time to provide a transparent view of potential blockers.

- *One-on-one meetings*: There are times when daily standups cannot offer the ability for team members to talk in the depth they need to about potential blockers. Conduct regular one-on-one meetings to discuss individual challenges and blockers in more detail or make plans in the standup to follow up afterward if there is a potential issue that will take too long to discuss in that meeting.

- *Progress tracking tools*: Sometimes seeing where individual tasks are in relation to one another can highlight blockers and issues better than talking about them. Utilize tools like Kanban boards and project management software to visually track progress and identify stalled tasks.
- *Active listening*: Most team environments include a lot of activity, with many moving pieces. This makes it hard for any one person to keep track of everything and hear every detail that might indicate an issue.

Encourage all team members to actively listen and support each other in identifying and resolving blockers.

### Managing the Sprint Backlog

Part of running a successful sprint is to make sure that the backlog itself is maintained and up to date. While this has been discussed in terms of sprint planning, and the next chapter looks at how to use a retrospective to continuously learn, it is worth mentioning a few components of sprint backlog management here as well.

The scrum master is responsible for maintaining the status of the sprint backlog. Remember that this is different than the product backlog, which is maintained by the product manager based on the business goals that the marketing initiative is intended to accomplish. The sprint backlog, however, gives a visual representation of the work in progress within a sprint, thus the scrum master is keeping this up to date, based on information gleaned in standups and other communications.

One best practice that helps to keep the sprint backlog accurate and properly maintained is to wait until the daily standup to make updates to a visual representation of the backlog. This ensures visibility to all involved and allows for a discussion around completed items where the definition of done may be in question.

Note that this will also be covered in more detail when the roles and responsibilities of the scrum master are reviewed.

## AGILECORP'S SPRINT TO CAMPAIGN LAUNCH

The marketing team at AgileCorp, a technology firm specializing in business solutions, was preparing to launch a new project management tool aimed at small businesses. The marketing team was tasked with executing a launch campaign within a four-week sprint. The team decided to use the MoSCoW method for prioritization and had to overcome significant blockers to successfully launch the campaign on time.

During the sprint planning session, the marketing team, led by product owner Rupali and scrum master James, implemented the MoSCoW method to prioritize tasks. They used the framework to prioritize the team's work as follows:

- *Must have (M)*: Develop the main advertising creatives, set up the landing pages, and prepare the press release.
- *Should have (S)*: Create a series of instructional videos and blog posts about the product's unique features.
- *Could have (C)*: Develop a referral program to incentivize current customers to recommend the new tool.
- *Won't have (W)*: Launch a secondary social media campaign targeting a broader audience.

Being able to agree as a team that the secondary social media campaign was not necessary for launch helped the team focus on the higher priority items and not devote any effort to that task.

While their prioritization using MoSCoW was helpful, all was still not well. Although much of the work was proceeding according to plan, two major blockers emerged during the sprint.

The first was identified as a technical blocker. A critical issue was discovered with the landing page's lead form not capturing submissions correctly. James, the scrum master, facilitated a swift response by coordinating with the IT department to prioritize this fix. He arranged for extra testing sessions to ensure the issue was resolved quickly without pushing the launch date.

The second issue was a resource blocker. The team's lead graphic designer, Santiago, fell ill after a weekend trip, jeopardizing the timely completion of the advertising creatives.

Rupali, the product owner, reassessed the team's capacity and redistributed the graphic design tasks among other team members and a freelance designer. This redistribution ensured that the critical "must have" deliverables were not delayed.

Despite the challenges, the team managed to focus on the "must have" tasks, ensuring that the most critical elements of the campaign were ready.

The press release went out on schedule, the landing page was fully operational, and the initial batch of advertising creatives was well-received, generating significant interest and leads.

Following scrum best practices, the team had a retrospective at the end of the sprint and uncovered several valuable insights together. First, they were reminded of the importance of having flexible resource plans and backup options for roles that are critical to sprint goals. Second, they agreed that using prioritization methods like the MoSCow method can prove essential for focusing on what truly matters for the launch of a successful campaign. They agreed that both of these should be incorporated into future sprints.

The successful launch of AgileCorp's new product demonstrated the effectiveness of strategic task prioritization and swift problem resolution. The team's ability to adhere to the Agile principles of collaboration, adaptability, and continuous improvement under the guidance of their scrum master and product owner was crucial. This sprint not only resulted in a successful product launch but also strengthened the team's capability to manage future marketing projects under pressure.

## CONCLUSION

Running a successful sprint is critical to the success of Agile marketing efforts. As was seen with the AgileCorp marketing team, tough decisions around prioritization will need to be made, and there will often be blockers or other impediments that require team work to solve. While perfection is not the goal, keeping all of these areas in mind with an eye for continuous improvement will help keep the team's work moving and successful.

While this chapter briefly explored how the AgileCorp team was able to use a sprint retrospective to uncover some of their learnings, the next chapter will explore these important meetings in more depth.

# CHAPTER 14

# *RETROSPECTIVES*

An important component of a scrum approach is the retrospective, which is a meeting of the project team and stakeholders at the end of each sprint. Retrospectives promote the continued improvement of work and the processes by which work is accomplished, and the outcomes and next steps agreed upon within the retrospective are carried into the next sprint.

So, what makes a good retrospective? There are four components.

First, consistency in its approach from the leader of the meeting to the agenda. While no specific team member leads a retrospective as defined by scrum, the leader should remain consistent throughout the project. Similarly, the agenda should remain the same, although the group can set that agenda at the start of the project or in the very first retrospective.

Second, a good retrospective aligns the team on what worked well and what needs improvement. Remember, a retrospective exists to discuss both the work performed, as well as how the work was performed. While some team members may have strengths in different areas, it is important to discuss both aspects.

Next, a good retrospective allows the team to work together on the steps and actions needed to improve the work and the process of doing the work. This means that all team members should feel empowered to share ideas and weigh in on decisions made on how to do both.

Finally, a well-executed retrospective ensures common understanding while allowing for differing opinions and views to be expressed. Team members should walk away from the meeting with the same takeaways to launch into the next sprint as an aligned team.

## USING RETROSPECTIVES TO IMPROVE OUTCOMES

This section launches by exploring the principles that make up a good retrospective. These principles are also important to consider and remember throughout an Agile project.

First, a retrospective should embrace a culture of honest, open communication and feedback from all team members. While individuals on a team might have different communication styles, everyone should be made to feel comfortable expressing their true opinions and feelings so that the best possible decisions can be made.

Second, it is important that everyone walks away with a thorough and mutual understanding of what was discussed and what the potential outcomes should be. This requires ensuring the communication is clear, that no cliques or small groups have side conversations, and that everyone has their chance to voice their opinions.

Finally, while opinions may differ, it is essential that there are clear next steps and actions which are agreed upon by everyone. Having these next steps and actions defined ensures that the next sprint (which immediately follows the last sprint's retrospective) will benefit from the outcomes mutually agreed upon.

### Components of a Good Retrospective

Following is an exploration the components of a good retrospective in terms of what makes a good agenda. As mentioned earlier, the exact agenda for a retrospective may vary and can be created at the beginning of an Agile marketing project or during the team's first retrospective.

### Setting the Stage

The first component is to set the stage for the retrospective. The meeting facilitator bears much of the responsibility here, and they should have an agenda prepared that includes timelines.

Best practices also include ensuring that each team member has some form of verbal response at the beginning of the meeting, ranging from a fun icebreaker question to simply stating their name. While this act may seem like a small thing or an unnecessary one, it has the effect of getting everyone's mindset focused on the meeting at hand.

Setting the stage should also include reinforcing the principles of the retrospective, which were reviewed earlier, so that everyone feels comfortable openly sharing their thoughts and being decisive in the outcomes agreed upon.

### Sharing and Collecting Information

Second, the retrospective exists to share and collect information which can be used to improve the work on the project itself, as well as how the team performs the work.

Remember that everyone on the team should share during this portion of the meeting, and a few individuals should not dominate it. The facilitator should step in if there appears to be someone who is not as open to sharing or if someone is taking up all of the time with their views. Likewise, the full team should feel empowered to encourage participation.

This can be done by asking the following or similar questions:

1. *What worked well in the last sprint?* These are things teams should continue doing.

2. *What needs improvement?* These are things that went okay but could be made better.

3. *What went badly?* These are things that should either be avoided altogether or need greater effort to improve.

4. *What are one or two things to focus on for the next sprint?* These are useful items to gather when determining the next steps and actions, which will occur later.

A best practice is to make notes of these ideas and information in a way that everyone can see and refer to them. When in-person meetings are possible, this is often done on a whiteboard or with sticky notes on a wall. When meetings are done virtually, a collaborative tool can be used that allows everyone to see notes or contribute to them in real time.

### Analysis and Insights

After information is shared, it is time to analyze the data and generate insights that can be used to improve the work in the sprints that follow. The facilitator should lead this process and can refer to the notes taken to guide the team through using that information to come to conclusions about what worked well and what did not work well. Again, participation from the full group needs to be encouraged as everyone has valuable input here, not just those who might feel most comfortable speaking in front of the group.

By looking at the information and data collected, general groupings should be created around specific areas where the next steps and actions could be generated. For instance, if the communication between the marketing and design teams needs improvement, there might be several individual comments along those lines. Those could be grouped into a single insight that the team can brainstorm how to solve. For instance, perhaps the creative brief provided to the design team needs more information or different information to achieve better results.

### Next Steps and Actions

Once insights and idea groups have been generated, it is time to decide what to do with them. The facilitator should lead a discussion about this but still ensure that the full team contributes their thoughts and ideas, not just a handful of people.

For any insights and groupings created in the previous step, there should be at least one next step associated with it unless the group decides to deprioritize the item.

These next steps or actions should include who is responsible, as well as what the desired outcome will be.

### Closing the Meeting

Finally, the retrospective meeting should be closed. The facilitator will lead this, and one of the goals is to ensure that everyone leaves with a positive feeling that their contributions have helped to improve the work and that their ideas and contributions are valued and welcome.

In some cases, the facilitator will reiterate what was accomplished or have some type of ritual that everyone can participate in to close the meeting on a positive note.

### What to Avoid

Best practices for a retrospective have been covered, and this section will go over some things to avoid.

First, don't skip steps in the process because of a lack of timing or a feeling that some elements are unimportant. Retrospectives are most valuable when they are consistent and everyone is given time to contribute.

Second, don't allow a few people to dominate their discussion. As expert as these individuals may be, the team benefits from *everyone's* ideas and opinions, not just a handful.

Finally, don't avoid difficult decisions because they may hurt people's feelings or cause a disagreement. As long as everyone on the team understands that the purpose of the retrospective is to improve the work and that everyone has the team and project's best interests in mind, conflicts should be addressed directly and respectfully. When teams avoid making difficult decisions or having difficult discussions, resentment will build, and the work will suffer.

## AGILECORP'S RETROSPECTIVE REDO

The last look at the AgileCorp marketing team saw they had recently undertaken a new digital marketing campaign for the company's latest product launch. A few months later they were well into a new campaign, aimed to integrate cutting-edge AI tools with traditional marketing strategies to target a broad demographic. The Agile marketing team was set to evaluate their performance and strategies through a sprint retrospective.

While some of the team members were the same, there were several brand new team members hired specifically for this new product launch. During their first retrospective for the AI tools project, the team encountered several issues that hindered the effectiveness of the meeting.

First, the team did not have a consistent leader for the retrospective; as the meeting progressed, the role shifted between different senior team members. This lack of consistency led to confusion from the scrum team members, as each leader had a different style and wanted participants to focus on different aspects of the campaign when talking.

The second issue the team encountered was that the conversation within the retrospective was dominated by a couple of team members, which stifled broader team engagement. Some of the more junior team members who were more introverted felt overwhelmed and did not participate, leaving much of their feedback unexpressed.

Finally, everyone left the meeting without specific, actionable outcomes or assignments. This left the team with a sense of ambiguity about the next steps.

### Getting Back on Track

Fortunately, the AgileCorp senior leadership had brought on an Agile coach to help the scrum master, James, who had expressed some concerns about how the last retrospective went. With the help of the coach and cooperation among the team, they took several corrective measures for their next sprint.

First, James was appointed as the consistent leader for all future retrospectives. He prepared a standardized agenda that was to be used in every meeting, which included time for each segment and an opportunity for every team member to contribute. This was appropriate and complementary to his role as scrum master.

Second, James implemented a round-robin approach to participation in the next retrospective to ensure that each team member could share their insights and feedback without interruption. This structure prevented dominant personalities from overtaking the conversation and encouraged quieter members to speak up.

Finally, to make sure that everyone walked away with a clear set of next steps and what needed to be done in the next sprint, James facilitated a closing portion of the retrospective where the team collectively decided on specific actions to address the issues raised. Each action item was assigned a responsible team member and a deadline, ensuring accountability and follow-through.

The changes made a significant impact. The team left the retrospective with a clear understanding of what needed to be done and who was responsible for each task. The clear direction and increased participation levels led to a more focused and motivated team. In the subsequent sprint, there was noticeable improvement in the areas that had been highlighted during the retrospective, particularly in communication between the marketing and design teams.

By adjusting their approach to ensure consistent leadership, equitable participation, and actionable outcomes, the team was able to significantly enhance their collaboration and effectiveness, leading to more successful marketing campaigns.

## CONCLUSION

A retrospective is a great opportunity for a scrum team to reflect on their work and both successes as well as areas for improvement. When run well, the meeting provides everyone on the team an opportunity to share their thoughts and ideas. It also can be a motivational meeting to keep the team engaged and focused on the end goal of the project.

When next steps are clear, everyone walks away with a sense of purpose, urgency, and a common alignment toward achieving successful outcomes.

# IV

# THE MARKETING SCRUM TEAM

Thus far the text has discussed the components of scrum in terms of an Agile marketing team and will now look at each of the roles on a scrum team in more depth.

It will look in greater depth at the key areas and components of scrum in terms of the key roles of the team to give a better understanding of what the primary expectations of each role are as well as what success looks like for each role.

The following roles will be examined:

- product manager
- scrum master
- product team member, which can consist of a wide variety of marketing, creative, and related roles that will vary depending on the type and nature of marketing work being performed

Things will conclude by looking at some of the general characteristics of a good scrum team that all roles should strive to work toward.

# CHAPTER 15

# SUCCESS AS A PRODUCT OWNER

As briefly explored earlier, the role of the product owner is both critical to the success of an Agile project as well as a challenging position that requires a balance of skills and considerations in order to be successful. As a crucial bridge between the marketing team and its stakeholders, the product owner must balance creative demands with business objectives, ensuring that marketing efforts are both innovative and strategically aligned.

The product owner in an Agile marketing environment using scrum is responsible for defining the vision for marketing campaigns, prioritizing work items in the backlog, and ensuring that every sprint delivers value to the business and its customers. Unlike traditional project management roles that may focus solely on logistical or administrative aspects, the scrum product owner must have a deep understanding of market trends, customer behaviors, and the competitive landscape. This role requires a blend of strategic foresight, customer insight, and a keen sense of prioritization to steer the team toward achieving impactful marketing outcomes.

Furthermore, the success of the product owner hinges not just on their ability to manage the product backlog effectively but also on their skills in communicating with various stakeholders—from senior executives to team members and external partners. They must articulate and negotiate the needs of the business while championing the creative processes and ideas that emerge from within the team. The product owner must also be able to understand and interpret the needs of those stakeholders and at times explain them to others on their team.

This chapter will explore the essential functions and responsibilities of the product owner, including the skills and qualities that define a successful holder of this position, and the challenges they face.

## KEY RESPONSIBILITIES

Chapter 9 touched on the overall responsibilities of a product owner, but those things will be explored in more depth here. For this role to be successful, there are three key areas. It is also important to note that, of all the roles on the scrum team, the product owner is most likely to have many other responsibilities within the organization and may be involved in aspects of other products and initiatives. For instance, in a marketing context, a product owner might be the vice president of digital, with many projects and teams under her supervision. Or, in a much larger company, the product owner may be dedicated to anything from a portfolio of products to a single product.

This is important for both product owners as well as the rest of their teams to continually keep in mind—the needs of a single product may need to be balanced with several other initiatives. Three key responsibilities of this role will be explored next.

### Vision Setting for Initiatives

There are several considerations that a product owner should consider when setting the vision for their initiative. The following sections look at two of these.

#### Setting a Clear Strategic Direction

Setting a clear strategic direction involves defining what success looks like for each marketing campaign and how it aligns with broader organizational goals. This vision should be both inspiring and precise, serving as the north star that guides every decision and action within the team. For instance, a successful vision for a digital marketing campaign might be to increase market share among a younger demographic by 15% within six months using a targeted social media strategy. This vision not only sets a clear target but also aligns with broader business objectives like expanding into new market segments.

Effective strategic direction requires the product owner to have a deep understanding of the market landscape, customer behaviors, and competitive dynamics. This understanding enables the product owner to identify unique opportunities and potential challenges that the campaign might face. Communicating this vision clearly and passionately to the marketing team helps to ensure that everyone understands the campaign's objectives and is motivated to achieve them.

### Adaptability to a Changing Environment

The ability of a product owner to adapt is as critical as having a clear strategic direction. Adaptability involves the readiness and capability to modify the campaign's direction based on real-time performance data and changing market conditions. This might mean pivoting strategies when certain channels underperform or doubling down on tactics that are exceeding expectations.

A product owner excels in adaptability by staying closely connected with the analytics team to monitor campaign performance regularly. They must be comfortable making decisions that might deviate from the original plan but are necessary to capitalize on unforeseen opportunities or mitigate emerging risks. For example, if an initial content marketing strategy does not resonate with its intended audience as expected, the product owner might shift focus toward more engaging formats like video or interactive tools, based on user engagement data.

### What Success Looks Like

Successful vision setting in Agile marketing manifests as a series of well-defined milestones and outcomes that are understood and embraced across the team. It features regular checkpoints where the vision's relevance and progress are reassessed and refined. This practice keeps the team aligned while instilling a sense of ownership and accountability among team members.

The process of successful vision setting also includes engaging stakeholders from various departments to gather insights and feedback. This cross-functional collaboration enriches the vision with diverse perspectives, making it more robust and achievable. The product owner plays a pivotal role in facilitating these discussions, ensuring that the campaign vision supports and is supported by other business functions.

### What to Avoid

One significant roadblock in vision setting is the risk of becoming too rigid or attached to the initial plan. This rigidity can hinder responsiveness to market changes and can lead to missed opportunities or continued investment in underperforming tactics. Product owners should avoid the pitfall of *sunk cost fallacy*, where decisions are driven by previous investments rather than current realities and future potential.

Another area to avoid is the failure to communicate the vision effectively across the team and stakeholders. Misalignments in understanding can lead to discrepancies in execution, where team members may pursue conflicting priorities or strategies. It's crucial for product owners to ensure that the vision is not only communicated clearly but also reinforced regularly through team meetings, updates, and collaborative planning sessions.

Effective vision setting by the product owner involves a delicate balance between providing clear strategic direction and remaining adaptable to feedback and changing market conditions. By fostering a collaborative environment and maintaining open lines of communication, product owners can navigate potential roadblocks and lead their teams to successful campaign executions.

## Product Backlog Management

While the sprint backlog is managed by the scrum master, with strategic input from the product owner, the product backlog is the main focus of this role, as it provides the big picture of the initiative.

Thus, effective backlog *management* is a critical responsibility for a product owner, as priorities can shift rapidly due to market trends, consumer feedback, or any number of internal or external factors. This role must excel in prioritizing tasks within the product backlog to maximize business value, enhance customer impact, and ensure strategic alignment. This involves a continuous process of evaluating and reevaluating each task based on a variety of factors, including potential return on investment (ROI), customer needs, and alignment with long-term business goals.

Successful prioritization means both identifying the most important tasks while also being willing to defer or remove items that no longer serve the project's objectives. This is where methods such as The Eisenhower Matrix or MoSCoW method discussed earlier can be helpful in prioritization or removal of items in the backlog.

For instance, a product owner might prioritize a campaign adjustment over a planned content update if analytics indicate a shift in consumer behavior. Regular backlog grooming sessions ensure that every item is still relevant, properly prioritized, and ready to be pulled into upcoming sprints as needed.

*Providing Task Definition*

Part of effectively managing a product backlog involves ensuring that each item within that backlog is defined with clarity and sufficient detail so that the teams working on the tasks are able to focus on getting things done, not asking questions about scope.

This responsibility means that the product owner needs to provide comprehensive descriptions, clear acceptance criteria, and any necessary context so that when a task is moved into a sprint, the team can execute it without needing frequent clarifications. This clarity reduces the cognitive load on team members, allowing them to focus on execution rather than interpretation.

For example, instead of simply listing "update product video," a well-prepared backlog item would include specific details such as the target audience, key messages, desired call to action, and any brand guidelines that need to be adhered to. It would also specify what constitutes a "done" state, such as "Video is edited, approved by stakeholders, and uploaded to the specified platform."

This definition of done is the responsibility of everyone on a product team to hold each other accountable to define, but it starts with the product owner, and there is a huge opportunity for this role to set an example.

*Successful Product Backlog Management*

While there can be many considerations for a product owner to consider on any given product, the importance of backlog management is evident for any team who has worked in a scrum environment. Effective management results in a streamlined workflow that allows the marketing team to operate with high efficiency and responsiveness.

When done right, it ensures that the team always works on the most impactful tasks, aligns closely with the strategic goals of the organization, and adapts swiftly to changing market conditions. It also facilitates better forecasting and planning, as the product owner and the team have a clear view of upcoming work and can prepare accordingly.

*What to Avoid*

Several common pitfalls can undermine effective backlog management:

- *Overloading the backlog:* Adding too many items without regular grooming can lead to a cluttered and unmanageable backlog. This makes it difficult for the team to identify what's most important, potentially leading to priority dilution and team burnout.

- *Lack of stakeholder input*: Failing to involve key stakeholders in the backlog management process can result in misalignment with broader business objectives. Regular stakeholder engagement is crucial to ensure the backlog reflects both market needs and business priorities.

- *Inadequate descriptions*: Poorly defined backlog items can lead to misunderstandings and incomplete implementations. It's crucial that each item includes all necessary details to avoid back-and-forth during sprints, which can waste time and resources.

Effective backlog management is a cornerstone of a product owner's role in Agile marketing. It ensures that the marketing team remains focused on the most impactful tasks, adapts to changing market conditions, and aligns closely with strategic business objectives.

## Stakeholder Communication

While a keen eye for strategy is important, the product owner needs great communication skills to ultimately be most successful. This will range widely depending on the other roles that the product owner might play in the organization, as well as the organization itself.

### Alignment with Business Goals

The ability to align marketing initiatives with broader business goals hinges on the product owner's capacity to act as a bridge between the marketing team and key stakeholders. This includes senior management, sales and other departments, and external partners, each of whom might have different expectations and objectives.

A successful product owner must articulate how marketing activities can drive business outcomes, ensuring that all stakeholders understand and support the marketing strategies. This involves presenting marketing plans and campaign proposals in the context of business metrics such as revenue growth, market penetration, and customer engagement. For example, when launching a new product, the product owner should demonstrate how the marketing campaign will help achieve the company's sales targets and strategic business objectives. Regularly updating stakeholders on the progress and outcomes of marketing initiatives also reinforces this alignment and secures ongoing support.

*Integration of Stakeholder Feedback*

Another critical aspect of stakeholder communication that the product owner is responsible for is the collection and integration of feedback into the marketing strategy. Doing this effectively ensures that, for instance, marketing campaigns remain dynamic and responsive to the needs of the business and its customers. Effective feedback integration involves not only gathering insights from various stakeholders but also synthesizing this information to refine marketing tactics and strategic direction.

As an example, feedback from the sales team regarding customer inquiries and objections can provide valuable insights that shape content marketing and promotional strategies. The product owner must then take this feedback and work with the marketing team during sprint planning sessions to adjust the campaigns accordingly. This might include shifting the messaging to better address customer pain points or altering the media mix to better reach the target audience.

*Managing Stakeholder Expectations*

While it is not possible to make everyone happy all the time, being able to manage stakeholder expectations sets average or good product owners apart from great ones. There are a few things to keep in mind that can help here:

- *Transparent communication:* Establish regular communication channels to update stakeholders on progress, setbacks, and changes. Transparency helps in building trust and in setting realistic expectations.

- *Balancing competing priorities:* Often, stakeholders will have different and sometimes conflicting demands with varying levels of priority. It's important to prioritize these demands based on the strategic value they offer and the resources available. This might involve negotiating compromises or realigning expectations to what is feasible within the project scope.

- *Feedback integration:* Regularly collect and integrate stakeholder feedback into the project planning and execution process. This helps in making them feel heard and involved and can provide valuable insights that enhance the project's success.

- *Educating stakeholders:* A key part of managing expectations is effectively educating stakeholders on Agile principles and the scrum process itself, especially if they are accustomed to more traditional waterfall approaches to project management. A successful product owner explains to these stakeholders how iterative developments and feedback loops add value, allowing for flexibility and responsiveness that traditional methods lack.

*Successful Stakeholder Communication*

When done well, product owners that are able to more clearly communicate with stakeholders about key details of projects enable enhanced collaboration across departments and more coherent and unified marketing efforts. When stakeholders feel heard and see their input reflected in marketing activities, it not only improves the outcomes of these campaigns but also strengthens interdepartmental relationships.

The product owner should establish regular touchpoints and structured communication channels to facilitate this process. These could be formal meetings, digital collaboration platforms, or regular email updates. By maintaining transparent, consistent, and open lines of communication, the product owner helps ensure that the marketing team's work is not done in silos but is deeply integrated with the overall business strategy.

*What to Avoid*

Several challenges that regularly occur can impede effective stakeholder communication:

- *Overlooking nonmarketing stakeholders:* Failing to involve stakeholders from outside the marketing department, such as product development or customer service, can lead to campaigns that don't fully address all aspects of the customer experience.

- *Inconsistent communication*: Sporadic or inconsistent communication can lead to misunderstandings or misalignments with business objectives. It's crucial for the product owner to provide regular updates and actively seek stakeholder input to keep everyone on the same page.

- *Ignoring conflicting feedback*: As mentioned earlier, not all feedback will align perfectly, and some may even conflict. The product owner must navigate these waters carefully, balancing differing opinions and prioritizing feedback based on the strategic goals of the organization. Simply ignoring feedback is rarely the best option.

Successfully managing stakeholders requires a combination of good communication, strategic foresight, and diplomatic negotiation. By identifying stakeholders early and managing their expectations effectively, a product owner can ensure that the project remains focused on its goals while keeping those invested in its success informed and engaged.

## Collaboration with the Rest of the Scrum Team

Last but certainly not least in terms of key responsibilities of a product owner, effective collaboration with the rest of the scrum product team is essential. This positive collaboration not only enhances team cohesion but also drives creativity and innovation in marketing campaigns, which ultimately drives a better end result of all of these efforts. The next sections explore some techniques for building a cohesive team and establishing robust feedback loops that contribute to the continuous improvement of marketing efforts.

### Learning and Development

A good product owner engages the product team in regular activities that are not strictly work-related to strengthen relationships and improve communication. These could be weekly casual lunches, team outings, or creative workshops that encourage team members to think outside the box together.

Also, since marketing projects often require a range of skills from creative to analytical, organizing workshops where team members can share knowledge about their specific areas of expertise can enhance mutual understanding and respect. This cross-pollination of ideas not only broadens the team's skill set but also sparks innovation.

### Communicating Openly

Successful product owners establish and maintain open channels of communication where team members feel free to express their ideas, concerns, and suggestions without fear of criticism. This might include regular check-ins, open office hours with the product owner, or dedicated slots in meetings for open-floor discussions. While purely electronic, asynchronous communication channels like Slack and email are valuable, there are often benefits to real-time, one-on-one communication for building trust.

### Communicating the Vision

Along these lines, it is important to ensure every team member understands and is aligned with the project's goals and the broader marketing strategy. When team members see how their contributions fit into the larger picture, their sense of purpose and commitment to the project increases.

*Feedback and Reviews*

In addition to Implement iterative review sessions where marketing campaigns or projects are assessed at various stages, not just at the end. These reviews allow the team to adapt and refine strategies based on real-time feedback from stakeholders and market responses.

*Retrospectives on the Process Itself*

Looking at campaign and marketing initiative success is very important, but a successful product owner also makes sure to also conduct sprint retrospectives specifically focused on what went well, what didn't, and what could be improved. This is a critical component of the Agile methodology and helps in identifying lessons learned that can be applied to future sprints.

*Continuous Improvement*

Ensure that feedback—whether internal feedback or customer responses—leads to actionable steps. It's crucial that the insights gained from team discussions, customer feedback, and market analysis result in specific changes to tactics or strategies. This action-oriented approach helps to maintain the momentum of improvement and adaptation.

By fostering a collaborative environment and establishing effective feedback mechanisms, a product owner can ensure that the scrum team not only works harmoniously but also continuously innovates and improves. These practices not only enhance the team's productivity but also ensure that marketing strategies are responsive to the dynamic market conditions and aligned with customer expectations.

## SKILLS AND QUALITIES OF AN EFFECTIVE PRODUCT OWNER

An effective product owner running an Agile marketing scrum team embodies a set of crucial skills and qualities that enable them to navigate the complex interplay between strategic goals, team dynamics, and market demands. These skills are foundational to their role in steering projects toward success and delivering value to both the company and its customers.

When considering whether or not a role as a product owner is a good fit, it is important to have a good understanding of the types of skills and qualities needed. Following is an exploration of several categories of skills and qualities that will prove beneficial to this role.

### Communication Skills

Product owners are good communicators, whether that is in speaking, writing, and in some cases, illustrating the needs of the related stakeholders.

- *Clarity and precision*: As has been seen so far, the ability to clearly articulate the vision, goals, and requirements of marketing campaigns is essential. Product owners must communicate complex ideas in a way that is easily understandable for all stakeholders, including the marketing team, senior management, and external partners.

- *Active listening*: Effective communication is not just about speaking but also in the art of listening. Product owners need to actively listen to feedback from internal stakeholders and team members as well as external customers, all while integrating this input to refine strategies and product development. While active listening is beneficial for everyone on a scrum team, product owners can set the example here.

- *Negotiation and persuasion*: These two skills are crucial when dealing with stakeholders to balance different expectations and align them with the project's objectives, and to balance business priority, budget and resource constraints, and end customer needs. Product owners must be adept at negotiating priorities and resources and persuading stakeholders about the viability and strategic advantage of certain decisions.

### Strategic Thinking

Of course, a product owner is not simply all talk. They need to be able to think strategically and to be able to translate business strategy into actionable objectives. This takes several more skills.

- *Leading with vision*: Being able to set a long-term vision for marketing initiatives that aligns with the business objectives is a key quality and it is something that new product owners may take a little while to grow into. This involves anticipating market trends, understanding competitive dynamics, and positioning the company's marketing efforts to leverage its strengths and opportunities. It also involves being able to translate those items into something that is compelling to the team members that must ultimately do the work.

- *Problem solving and adaptability*: The marketing landscape can change rapidly. A successful product owner must be able to think on their feet and adapt strategies quickly. This requires strong problem-solving skills to navigate challenges and pivot plans effectively.

■ *Prioritization*: With often competing demands on resources and time, the ability to prioritize tasks based on their potential impact on business outcomes is crucial. Strategic thinking involves making tough choices that best align with the team's goals and available resources.

## Customer-Centric Focus

Product owners must also put their ego aside to make sure that their customers'—whether those are internal stakeholders, product team members, or external consumers—needs are met. This means that a product owner is continuously thinking about how to create the most value for these customers in how they prioritize tasks and measure success.

■ *Customer insight*: Understanding customer needs, preferences, and behaviors is central to crafting effective marketing strategies. Product owners must have a deep empathy for the customer experience to ensure that the products and campaigns developed meet and exceed customer expectations.

■ *Data-driven decision-making*: Utilizing data to understand customer behaviors and market patterns is crucial. Product owners should be adept at interpreting data analytics to guide marketing strategies and measure their effectiveness.

■ *Engagement optimization*: Continually looking for ways to enhance customer engagement through innovative marketing tactics. This includes testing new approaches, tailoring content to audience segments, and optimizing the marketing mix for maximum impact.

## ROI Focus

In addition to a focus on customers is a sharp focus on measurable results and ROI. Successful product owners run profitable projects and manage profitable product portfolios that make companies money while creating happy, loyal end customers.

■ *Aligning budgets with ROI*: Successful product owners ensure that marketing budgets are allocated based on the ROI of previous initiatives. This involves shifting resources away from low-performing areas to those that have historically provided the best returns.

■ *ROI-driven decision-making*: Product owners embed ROI considerations into the decision-making process. This means prioritizing marketing activities that are most likely to deliver measurable financial benefits, and being willing to cut or pivot away from those that do not meet ROI thresholds.

- *Continual optimization*: Product owners use the data collected from performance metrics to continually refine marketing strategies. For example, if analysis shows that video content yields a higher ROI than other content types, the product owner might allocate more resources to video production.

- *Stakeholder communication of results*: It is also important to regularly communicate the ROI of marketing activities to stakeholders to justify marketing expenditures and align expectations. This transparency builds trust and supports more informed strategic decisions across the business.

These skills and qualities are critical in fulfilling the role of a product owner effectively and in elevating the entire marketing team's capability to perform at its best, driving forward campaigns that resonate deeply with consumers and achieve substantial business impacts.

## CONTINUOUS LEARNING AND ADAPTATION

No matter the environment, continuous learning and adaptation are not just beneficial; they are necessary for staying competitive and effective. For a product owner, this means not only keeping up with shifts in marketing trends and consumer behavior but also actively pursuing personal and professional growth to enhance their strategic and operational capabilities.

This might include the following:

- Industry research such as industry news, read marketing blogs, and subscribe to relevant publications.

- Engaging with professional networks, online forums, and social media groups where marketing professionals gather. These platforms provide insights into challenges and solutions others are facing and new methods being tried in different markets.

- Regular attendance at marketing and industry-specific conferences which can provide a wealth of information on best practices and new tools.

- Using data analytics tools and customer feedback mechanisms to continually gather and analyze consumer behavior and preferences.

There are also plenty of opportunities for personal and professional growth, including:

- Pursuing formal qualifications such as a master's degree in marketing or certifications in specific areas like digital marketing, Agile management, or analytics.

- Enrolling in training courses to develop specific skills related to marketing technologies, leadership, strategic planning, or any other area that could enhance job performance.

- Engaging with mentors or coaches who can provide guidance, feedback, and insights from their own experiences.

- Regularly seeking feedback from peers, superiors, and team members. This feedback can be used for self-reflection and to identify areas for personal improvement.

- Encouraging and participating in innovation within the team. Trying new techniques and tools, experimenting with different campaign strategies, and learning from both successes and failures are essential practices that contribute to both personal growth and the evolution of marketing strategies.

By embracing continuous learning and adaptation, product owners can ensure they remain effective leaders in their field, capable of steering their teams through the complexities of modern marketing landscapes. This proactive approach to learning and growth not only enhances their capabilities but also sets a strong example for their teams, fostering a culture of continual improvement and innovation within the organization.

## AGILECORP'S PRODUCT OWNER EVOLUTION

Jasmine, the newly appointed product owner at AgileCorp, was tasked with spearheading a major digital marketing campaign to launch a new line of eco-friendly products. With a strong background in traditional marketing and a recent transition onto the Agile marketing team and their approach to scrum, Jasmine faced the challenge of blending her extensive experience with the dynamic requirements of Agile approaches.

The campaign kicked off with enthusiasm, but Jasmine quickly encountered difficulties. She realized that her traditional approach to campaign management—planning far in advance with little flexibility—was not well-suited to the fast-paced, feedback-driven nature of Agile marketing. Early campaign metrics indicated lower engagement rates than anticipated, and the marketing team was becoming frustrated with the lack of direction adjustment based on real-time data.

The low engagement rates were a wake-up call for Jasmine. In her next sprint review, feedback from the team highlighted the need for more responsiveness to customer interactions and market trends. Jasmine recognized that she needed to deepen her understanding of Agile practices and pivot her strategy to be more adaptive.

Jasmine took several steps to enhance her effectiveness as an Agile product owner:

- *Scrum training*: She enrolled in an intensive Agile certification course focused on Agile methodologies in marketing for product owners. This helped her understand the importance of iterative processes and continuous improvement cycles.
- *Engaging with industry peers*: Jasmine started participating in online forums and local meetups with other Agile marketing professionals. This networking helped her gain insights into how other companies were successfully managing their Agile marketing campaigns.
- *Experimentation*: She adopted a test-and-learn approach, initiating small-scale experiments within the campaign to test different messaging and channels. This allowed the team to quickly gauge what was resonating with the audience and adjust accordingly.
- *Regular feedback loops*: Jasmine increased the frequency of feedback sessions with her team and stakeholders to ensure all voices were heard and integrated into the campaign planning. This not only boosted team morale but also enhanced the campaign's alignment with customer expectations.

With these changes, the campaign saw a significant turnaround. Engagement rates improved as the team was able to quickly adapt to consumer feedback and refine their strategies. Jasmine's new approach also fostered a more collaborative and innovative team environment, where team members felt more valued and motivated.

Jasmine learned that being an effective product owner in an Agile environment requires flexibility, a willingness to learn continuously, and an openness to change. She realized that Agile is not just a methodology but a mindset that embraces adaptation and customer focus as routes to achieving better outcomes.

This experience transformed Jasmine's approach to her role. She became a champion of Agile methodologies within AgileCorp, advocating for their adoption across other departments. Jasmine's journey highlighted the importance of adaptability and continuous learning in the rapidly evolving field of marketing, proving that even experienced professionals could enhance their effectiveness by embracing new ways of working.

## CONCLUSION

This chapter has explored the multifaceted role of the product owner in Agile marketing teams. The product owner is not just a task manager but a visionary leader whose decisions and actions significantly influence the direction and success of marketing initiatives. Their ability to prioritize effectively, communicate strategically, and adapt quickly to changing market conditions positions them at the heart of the team's operations and success.

The product owner's role in bridging the gap between strategic business objectives and tactical team efforts is pivotal. They ensure that every sprint and every task within the product backlog is aligned with the broader strategic goals and definition of business value within the organization, thereby maximizing the impact and efficiency of marketing efforts. By maintaining a deep understanding of customer needs and market dynamics, Product owners guide their teams to not only meet but exceed market expectations.

However, the effectiveness of a product owner is not solely based on their current abilities but also on their capacity for ongoing learning and adaptation. The digital marketing landscape is continually evolving, with new technologies, platforms, and consumer behaviors emerging at a rapid pace. Therefore, a successful product owner must remain a perpetual student, always keen to learn about new trends, tools, and tactics that can enhance their team's performance.

Additionally, strong leadership development is critical to overall success. As leaders and owners of the strategic vision, product owners must inspire and motivate their teams, fostering an environment of creativity, accountability, and continuous improvement. They should strive to enhance their leadership skills through formal training, mentorship, and practical experience.

The role of the product owner is both demanding and rewarding. By embracing the principles of Agile, focusing on continuous personal and professional growth, and staying adaptable to the ever-changing marketing environment, product owners can lead their teams to remarkable successes. Their journey is one of constant evolution, where the rewards extend far beyond the immediate successes of their campaigns, contributing to the long-term resilience and competitiveness of their organizations.

# 16

# *SUCCESS AS A SCRUM MASTER*

The scrum master plays a crucial role in steering Agile teams to success, no matter how dynamic and chaotic the environment might grow at times. Unlike traditional marketing project managers, scrum masters do not simply oversee timelines and resources; they act as facilitators, coaches, and enablers of Agile principles and practices tailored to meet the unique demands of marketing projects and the teams that support them.

The scrum master's primary responsibility is to ensure that the marketing team fully embraces Agile principles and practices, adapting them to the fluid nature of goals and strategies. This role involves more than just managing tasks; it requires fostering an environment where continuous improvement, flexibility, and team collaboration are at the forefront. Additionally, the scrum master is pivotal in promoting an understanding of scrum methodology and Agile principles not just within the team but across the organization. By advocating for these Agile practices, the scrum master ensures that all parties involved in the marketing process—from digital creators and analysts to executives and clients—understand and support the Agile approach.

This chapter is going to discuss in more depth the specific responsibilities, challenges, and strategies that Agile marketing scrum masters can employ to lead their teams to greater success, and grow to be more proficient in their roles. This also includes how they can cultivate high-performing teams, implement effective scrum ceremonies, and drive the continuous evolution and improvement of marketing campaigns, initiatives, and other activities.

For those who are new to the role of scrum master or are considering whether or not this role would the right fit for your strengths and career goals, this chapter will be a great one to bookmark. Additionally, for those who are part of a scrum product team and want to better understand how a scrum master can help them in their role, this chapter will be a good review and reference.

## KEY RESPONSIBILITIES

Following is an outline of the tasks that a scrum master will perform that looks at a few high-level categories with several aspects that fall under each.

### Building and Maintaining a High-Performing Team

One of the key responsibilities of a scrum master is to build and maintain a high-performing team, which involves fostering positive team dynamics and a collaborative culture, as well as instilling a continuous improvement mindset that drives the team toward operational excellence and innovative outputs. The following are some of the ways that this is accomplished.

#### Project Management

While a scrum master is much more than a project manager, there are some more traditional elements of the role that might be familiar to those who have played a project management role on non-Agile or waterfall products.

Some of these elements include:

- *Effective planning*: This includes properly planning for all Agile ceremonies (sprint planning, daily standups, sprint reviews, and retrospectives). It also consists of having clear agendas, defined goals, and prepared participants to ensure that meetings are concise and productive.

- *Time management*: An effective scrum master strictly enforces time limits for each segment of the meetings to keep them focused and efficient. They use timers if necessary and are diligent about starting and ending on time to respect everyone's schedule.

- *Removal of impediments*: One of the primary duties of the role is to identify and remove any obstacles that may hinder the team's progress. This could range from technical issues, such as delays in data from analytics teams, to organizational barriers, like slow approval processes that stall campaign launches.

### Running Successful Meetings

One of the important aspects of a scrum master is their role in ensuring meetings are successful. At a fundamental level, they need to make sure that meetings start on time, have the right people attending, and follow the agendas that have been prepared. In addition, here are a few more important things they contribute to meetings:

- *Facilitation of meetings*: The scrum master organizes and leads key Agile ceremonies, including daily standups, sprint planning sessions, sprint reviews, and retrospectives. In a marketing context, this also involves ensuring that these meetings cater to creative brainstorming and strategic planning, crucial for marketing campaigns.

- *Engagement techniques*: Scrum masters use facilitation techniques to keep meetings engaging. This could include asking direct questions, using digital tools for live polling, or having different team members facilitate parts of the meeting to keep the energy levels high.

- *Ensure actionable outcomes from meetings*: This means ensuring that each meeting has clear, actionable outcomes. For sprint planning, this means tasks are clearly defined and assigned. For retrospectives, it means agreeing on specific improvements to implement in the next sprint.

### Ensuring Adherence to Agile Principles

As a scrum master in an Agile marketing team, one of the primary responsibilities is to ensure that the team adheres to Agile principles and that all Agile ceremonies are conducted effectively. This is essential in maintaining the agility and responsiveness required in the fast-paced marketing environment. This section outlines strategies to ensure adherence to Agile methodologies and tips for optimizing meetings and ceremonies.

- *Promoting agile principles*: Scrum masters regularly discuss Agile values and principles in meetings to remind the team of the Agile mindset. Encourage behaviors that reflect principles such as collaboration, flexibility, continuous improvement, and customer focus.

- *Providing visible artifacts*: A successful scrum master ensures that Agile artifacts such as the task board, burndown charts, and backlogs are visible and updated regularly. This not only helps in tracking progress but also keeps the team aligned with Agile practices.

- *Continuous education*: They regularly schedule training sessions and workshops not just for new team members but also as refreshers for the existing team. This helps everyone stay current on Agile and scrum practices and principles.

- *Agile coaching*: Teams of all experience levels need coaching from time to time, and this role can play that in limited measures. Sometimes, a scrum master doesn't have all the tools and experience needed to help a team in areas they need to focus. So they may bring in an external Agile coach can provide new perspectives and insights that reinforce the importance of Agile methodologies. This can be particularly beneficial during the initial phases of Agile implementation or when the team is going through significant changes.

### Optimizing Team Dynamics

A scrum master serves several types of roles. This also includes being a strong center to a team that provides both technical and project support, as well as the role of a facilitator and one that works to increase the morale and relationships within the team members. In this capacity, here are a few more areas that they play a role:

- *Support for the product owner and team*: The scrum master acts as a coach and advocate for the product owner and the marketing team. This support includes helping the product owner manage and prioritize the backlog effectively and ensuring the team remains focused on and motivated by the sprint goals.

- *Establishing clear roles and responsibilities*: They ensure that each team member clearly understands their roles and the expectations associated with these roles. Clarity provided by the scrum master prevents overlaps and gaps in responsibilities, which can lead to confusion and inefficiency.

- *Promoting open communication*: A successful scrum master encourages open and honest communication among team members. They facilitate an environment where feedback is given constructively and received openly. They also use tools and techniques such as regular one-on-ones, team meetings, and open feedback sessions to promote dialogue.

- *Cultivating trust and respect*: Building trust within the team is crucial for effective collaboration, and an effective scrum master does things like organizing team-building activities that are not just fun but also include problem-solving exercises that require team members to work together.

These activities help in forging strong relationships based on mutual respect and understanding.

### Continuous Improvement of Projects and Team Dynamics

A core component of the Agile principles readers have gotten to know over the course of this book is to embrace continuous improvement. A scrum master should live up to this ideal in everything they do. Here are a few ways they can lead by example:

- *Effective retrospectives*: While holding regular sprint retrospectives is a given, a successful scrum master takes extra care to ensure that these retrospectives result in actionable insights that are implemented in subsequent sprints. This could involve adjusting processes, refining communication strategies, or introducing new tools. Rather than simply going through the motions, someone who is successful in this role makes retrospectives a valuable and integral part of the process.

- *Encouraging a growth mindset*: They also promote a culture where learning from failures is valued as much as celebrating successes and encourage team members to take calculated risks and explore new ideas. This mindset fosters innovation and continuous growth.

- *Providing training and development opportunities*: A good scrum master facilitates ongoing learning and professional development, and they identify training needs based on team performance and individual aspirations. Additionally, they support team members in acquiring new skills and knowledge that are beneficial to their roles and sometimes find creative methods to fill in those gaps.

- *Measuring and sharing progress*: Implement metrics to measure improvements in team performance and process efficiency. Share these metrics with the team regularly to demonstrate the tangible benefits of their efforts toward continuous improvement.

The role of a scrum master demands both a deep understanding of Agile principles as well as the ability and willingness to apply them to even the most challenging marketing projects and campaigns. They must foster an environment where strategic goals are met without compromising the success metrics of the teams and their stakeholders.

By focusing on these areas and balancing all of the areas discussed, a scrum master can cultivate a team environment that supports the current project needs while adapting and evolving to meet future challenges. This proactive approach to team dynamics and continuous improvement ensures that the Agile marketing team remains resilient, motivated, and consistently capable of delivering exceptional results.

## SKILLS AND QUALITIES OF AN EFFECTIVE SCRUM MASTER

To be an effective scrum master, one needs to go beyond a mere understanding of Agile principles and scrum rituals. In addition to these foundational elements that any member of a team must have, effective scrum masters are skilled facilitators and communicators who are adept at fostering a supportive and productive team environment. Next are some of the essential skills and qualities that define a successful scrum master in an Agile marketing team.

### Facilitation Skills

While the term *leader* was mentioned earlier, that is less accurate than *facilitator*. After all, Agile principles support the idea of self-organizing teams that require less direct management—or micro-management—and more guidance and enablement. To clarify, here are a few ways that a scrum master can play the role of facilitator:

- *Guiding agile ceremonies*: An effective scrum master must excel in facilitating key Agile meetings such as daily standups, sprint planning sessions, sprint reviews, and retrospectives. These meetings are crucial for maintaining the momentum of marketing campaigns and ensuring alignment with project goals.

- *Efficient meeting management*: It's important for scrum masters to keep meetings focused and on track. This involves setting clear agendas, keeping discussions relevant and brief, and ensuring that every team member has the opportunity to contribute.

- *Conflict resolution*: Agile environments can be fast-paced and stressful, which may lead to conflicts. A skilled scrum master can navigate interpersonal conflicts and facilitate resolutions in a way that strengthens team cohesion rather than detracting from it.

### Optimize Processes and Flexibility

There are some similarities between a scrum master and a more traditional project manager. One area where this is the case is in the need for them to make sure that the processes that the teams are using are optimal, as well as that the right things are being worked on in the right order. The following list looks at a few areas related to optimization of the work being performed:

- *Prioritization and flexibility*: An effective scrum master will implement a robust system for prioritizing tasks that can quickly adapt to changing priorities. Working with their teams, they use techniques like the MoSCoW method to adjust priorities without disrupting the ongoing workflow. Flexibility in task management ensures that the team can respond swiftly to urgent tasks without losing sight of the broader campaign goals.

- *Streamlined processes*: They optimize internal processes to reduce bottlenecks and enhance efficiency, which could involve automating routine tasks, simplifying approval processes, or setting up quick daily check-ins to address urgent issues. Streamlining these processes helps the team to keep pace with the demands of a fast-moving marketing environment.

- *Time boxing*: Scrum masters who are effective members of their teams often use time boxing to manage tasks effectively within tight deadlines because allocating fixed time periods for certain tasks helps prevent overrun and keeps the team focused on meeting deadlines. This method also helps in managing team workload and preventing burnout, because there are times when simply prioritizing one thing over another is not possible.

## Adaptive Communication

Marketing moves at as fast a pace as just about any area within a business, and thus Agile marketing teams need to adapt and adjust on a near continual basis. The scrum master thus has to master the art of communication amidst this constant flux. Here are some ways that they can do this:

- *Diverse team dynamics*: Marketing teams often comprise individuals from various professional backgrounds, including creative, analytical, and strategic roles. A scrum master must be able to adapt their communication style to effectively connect with different types of team members.

- *Stakeholder engagement*: Communicating with stakeholders is a critical part of a s master's role. They must be able to articulate project progress, negotiate resources, and manage expectations, all while advocating for the needs and priorities of their team.

- *Transparency and clarity*: Keeping communication clear and transparent helps in building trust within the team and with external stakeholders. A scrum master should ensure that information is shared openly and that team members are kept informed about changes and decisions.

### Supporting the Rest of the Product Team

Beyond empowering teams with the information, tools, and communication they need, a good scrum master is there to support the needs of team members when it comes to understanding their challenges, defending decisions and timeline or scope changes to stakeholders, and other sometimes complex areas that involve emotional support as much as they involve technical support. Here are a few ways that a scrum master can be effective by providing empathy and supporting their team:

- *Understanding team needs*: Empathy is crucial for a scrum master to truly understand and support the needs of their team. This involves being attentive to the well-being of team members, recognizing their efforts, and providing support during challenging phases of a project.

- *Encouraging a supportive culture: Scrum masters* should foster a team culture that values mutual support, collaboration, and respect. This creates an environment where team members feel valued and motivated to contribute their best. This also reflects how a scrum master supports the teams' decisions to stakeholders and even to the product owner.

- *Motivation and positive reinforcement*: Recognizing and celebrating successes, big or small, can significantly boost team morale. A scrum master should consistently acknowledge individual contributions and team achievements to maintain high spirits and motivation.

By adopting these strategies, a scrum master can equip their Agile marketing team to effectively handle the challenges of a fast-paced and uncertain marketing landscape. These approaches help in managing the immediate challenges of a product team and contribute to building a strong, adaptive, and cohesive team capable of sustaining high performance over time.

### Stakeholder Management as a Scrum Master

Effectively managing relationships with stakeholders is crucial, and while it may not require a concentrated amount of effort every day, it can make the difference between success and failure of a project and a scrum team in the bigger picture. Stakeholder management involves several things, including ensuring that stakeholder needs are met while also protecting the team from any undue interference that could disrupt the Agile process. Some of the ways that this role manages stakeholders to ensure successful project delivery are explored in the following list:

- *Clear communication channels*: This includes the establishment and maintenance of open and clear lines of communication with stakeholders that might consist of providing regular updates about project progress, upcoming sprints, and any changes in strategy. This type of transparency helps in managing expectations and builds trust between stakeholders and the marketing team.

- *Involvement in planning*: It is important to involve stakeholders in the planning phases of campaigns where appropriate because it is during these initial stages that big decisions need to be made, and that the trajectory for a project or campaign is set. This could mean including stakeholders in certain sprint planning sessions or strategic meetings where their input could be valuable. This involvement helps stakeholders feel connected to the process and gives them a firsthand understanding of the team's approach and challenges.

- *Setting realistic goals:* It is important for the scrum master to help set realistic goals with stakeholders. This might involve discussing what can be realistically achieved in each sprint and over the course of the project. Setting feasible goals helps prevent disappointment and ensures that marketing efforts are aligned with business objectives.

- *Boundary setting*: While stakeholder input is invaluable, the scrum master must also protect the team from interference that could disrupt workflows. This includes managing how and when stakeholders interact with the team, ensuring that these interactions do not detract from the team's productivity and focus.

While much is often written about the more technical and project management-related roles of a scrum master, it is important not to underestimate this component of their role. Those marketers that are interested in becoming a scrum master on an Agile marketing team would do well to take this into account.

## PERSONAL DEVELOPMENT FOR SCRUM MASTERS

Those who are already a scrum master for a marketing team already know the importance of staying up to date with the latest best practices. For readers of this book who are considering it as a potential role, there are several things to think about, and they will be covered in this section.

As with any role, scrum masters should spend time focusing on personal professional development to stay effective in their role and be the best possible support to their teams as well as to the stakeholders supporting their work. Continuously enhancing their marketing knowledge, expertise in exercising Agile principles and scrum methods, alongside developing strong leadership skills, is essential. This is a win–win, benefiting their individual career path as well as their teammates.

Next is a look at two big areas that scrum masters can focus on when looking at personal development.

### Skills Development

The first area is skills development, which, outside of Agile best practices can depend a lot on the types of marketing work that the scrum master works within.

- *Continuous agile learning*: Best practices involving interpretation of Agile principles evolve, and new frameworks and tools to best utilize scrum approaches emerge regularly. Scrum masters should stay updated by attending training sessions, workshops, and seminars.

- *Agile certification education*: Pursuing advanced certifications in Agile methodologies or marketing can also be beneficial. Certifications such as Certified ScrumMaster (CSM), Advanced Certified ScrumMaster (A-CSM), or even specific marketing certifications can deepen understanding and validate skills.

- *Community participation*: Engaging with associations, communities, and networking opportunities and insights into how various challenges are tackled across different industries. This can range from organizations such as the Agile Marketing Alliance, to a more general organization like the American Marketing Association.

- *General marketing education*: The marketing landscape changes rapidly, and while a scrum master may focus a lot of their energy on learning Agile and scrum best practices, having a solid understanding of the evolving best practices within the marketing profession will help them play a stronger role on their teams.

- *Mentorship opportunities*: Different people learn in different ways, and some benefit from less formal education and training than others. Mentorship is another opportunity to grow professionally, and either as a mentor or a mentee, participating in mentorship can significantly enhance leadership skills. Mentors can provide guidance and feedback based on their experiences, while acting as a mentor can refine one's leadership style and problem-solving approaches.

By investing in their personal development, scrum masters not only enhance their capability to effectively guide and support their teams but also position themselves as invaluable leaders within their organizations. This ongoing development is crucial in maintaining the agility and effectiveness of the marketing team, ensuring they can adapt to new challenges and continue to deliver outstanding results.

## AGILECORP'S SCRUM MASTER BREAKTHROUGH

It's time to return to the team at AgileCorp, where the company recently expanded its marketing efforts to launch several new products aimed at different consumer segments, some of which none of the team members had relevant experience reaching in past work experience. Sarah, the scrum master, was tasked with leading the Agile marketing team through this complex and multifaceted campaign.

### The Challenge

The team struggled with coordinating across different product launches, resulting in a few missed deadlines, poor planning, and ineffective use of resources. The rapid pace and overlapping schedules overwhelmed the team, and the Agile marketing practices they were using seemed insufficient to handle the complexities of the marketing demands.

Sarah realized that the way she was managing the product team as a scrum master wasn't working. By her estimation, the way she was approaching things needed a significant overhaul to meet the unique challenges of their marketing campaigns, and account for some of the unknowns that they continually experienced.

### The Solution

She decided to focus on two main areas for improvement: enhancing her leadership skills and implementing advanced Agile practices tailored to marketing.

First, to give herself the necessary tools to grow, Sarah enrolled in an advanced leadership development program focused on scrum and Agile marketing environments. Here, she learned about strategic decision-making and effective communication, which are crucial for managing complex projects and diverse teams.

Next, Sarah organized workshops specifically designed for her marketing team, facilitated by an external Agile coach who specialized in marketing. These workshops addressed unique challenges such as managing simultaneous campaigns and integrating rapid market feedback into the ongoing projects. This fresh external perspective also provided some new ideas, and the team also had a safe environment to ask questions to an expert with more extensive experience.

Then, knowing that some of the missed deadlines and crossed wires in communication were due to the project management and communication platforms the team was using, Sarah introduced new digital tools for better project tracking and communication, allowing the team to update their progress in real-time and making it easier to adapt quickly to changes.

Finally, Sarah established regular feedback sessions that not only focused on the progress of marketing campaigns but also on the team's well-being and workload management. This helped in identifying burnout early and adjusting workloads accordingly.

Taking this a step further and recognizing the need for better coordination with other departments in addition to her own, Sarah facilitated monthly cross-functional meetings where representatives from sales, product development, and customer service could align with the marketing team's efforts and timelines.

## The Results

The renewed focus on specialized Agile training and enhanced leadership skills paid off. The marketing team became more cohesive and responsive. Campaigns were better coordinated, and resource allocation was optimized, leading to a 30% increase in campaign output without increasing the team's workload.

Campaigns that initially struggled with engagement saw improvements in both reach and customer interactions, thanks to the rapid integration of market feedback and the efficient pivoting of campaign strategies.

Sarah's commitment to personal development and her strategic overhaul of the team's Agile practices led to significant improvements in team performance and campaign success. As shown with the success of the team at AgileCorp, a scrum master can have a big impact in transforming challenges of a marketing team into opportunities for growth and success. Her experience underscores the importance of continuous learning, adaptability, and proactive leadership in maintaining the effectiveness of Agile marketing teams.

## CONCLUSION

This chapter has explored the multifaceted role of scrum masters within Agile marketing teams, highlighting their importance as facilitators, mentors, and strategic leaders. As the Agile landscape continues to evolve, particularly within the fast-paced and often unpredictable realm of marketing, the scrum master's role becomes increasingly vital in steering teams toward efficiency, innovation, and success.

Scrum masters are the linchpins that hold Agile marketing teams together. They ensure that Agile practices are not only implemented but optimized to suit the specific challenges of marketing. By effectively managing team dynamics, facilitating Agile processes, coordinating with stakeholders, and fostering an environment of continuous improvement, scrum masters enable their teams to remain adaptable and responsive to market demands.

However, the effectiveness of a scrum master is not solely defined by their ability to manage current projects but also by their commitment to personal and professional growth. In an industry where change is the only constant, scrum masters must continuously seek to enhance their skills and adapt their strategies. This includes staying informed about the latest Agile methodologies and marketing trends, developing leadership skills, and fostering a culture of learning and adaptation within their teams.

The role of a scrum master is crucial to the success of a product team, and they are a key link between the product owner and the marketing team members that perform the daily work of taking a marketing initiative from concept to execution. By embracing the principles discussed in this chapter and committing to ongoing development, scrum masters can lead their teams to achieve remarkable successes, delivering projects that resonate with consumers and achieve significant business impacts.

# CHAPTER 17

# SUCCESS AS A PRODUCT TEAM

Each member of the product team plays a key role in the successful execution of projects, which can vary greatly within an Agile marketing approach—from initiatives and projects like a Web site launch, to an ongoing product marketing campaign. For instance, one may be part of a team at a large organization that is focused on supporting a company's Web site, or its email marketing, social media marketing, digital advertising, or any of the other multitude of marketing channels available. Or, the team might oversee all marketing channels at once for a smaller organization, or for one product at a larger company.

Additionally, when comparing the two, a marketing team often has a more diverse set of roles than a software engineering team using scrum might be composed of. Whether their expertise lies in marketing, creative design, analytics, or technical development, every individual contributes to the overall agility and effectiveness of the team.

Within the scrum framework, each team member has both a specific set of tasks as well as sharing a common goal of enhancing product value through iterative development. The diversity of roles—from creative professionals who craft compelling content to analysts who decipher data landscapes and technical experts who implement complex backend systems—is able to create engaging experiences and campaigns for their intended audiences. However, harnessing this diversity requires a deep understanding of how Agile principles can be applied across various disciplines within marketing.

This chapter will examine the key responsibilities of a product team as well as the skills and qualities that make up a good team member. Without getting into too many details about the specifics of different types of marketing tactics, it will also explore how to overcome some common challenges and take a look at how other members of the product team at AgileCorp are doing in their Agile marketing implementation.

## KEY RESPONSIBILITIES

In Agile marketing product teams, every member plays a critical role that extends beyond mere task execution to include strategic collaboration and active participation in scrum ceremonies. These roles, although varied, are united by a common goal to swiftly respond to market dynamics while producing high-quality creative output. It's time to explore the key responsibilities and unique challenges that members of a team face.

### Individual Task Execution

Each member is responsible for completing tasks that directly contribute to the team's marketing goals. For instance, a marketing team responsible for Web content may be responsible for writing the Web content, creating graphics, publishing the content through the content management system, and measuring the effectiveness of the content. This includes several disciplines from marketing strategy, copywriting, graphic design, content management, and marketing measurement.

Similarly, other marketing tactics and strategies will include a diverse mix of team members. In still other cases, a marketing team may work in coordination with a separate creative team that consists of copywriters and designers, or with a separate technology team that publishes content to the Web.

Because of this, these tasks vary widely in marketing, perhaps to a greater extent than in most other applications of Agile or scrum. That said, the fundamentals of what it takes to be a good product team member still applies.

### Participation in Scrum Ceremonies

Active participation in scrum ceremonies is crucial for every member of a product team. These meetings and processes—including those previously discussed such as daily standups, sprint planning, sprint reviews, and retrospectives—are not just formalities; they are structured opportunities to align, adjust, and learn as a team. The next sections look at how a product team relates to these important components of scrum.

*Daily Standups*

- *Provide clear, concise updates*: During daily standups, each team member should provide brief and focused updates on what they accomplished the previous day, what they plan to work on today, and any obstacles they are facing. Keep updates relevant to the team's goals to maintain the efficiency of these meetings, but don't skip details that might help fellow teammates understand potential implications to their work.

- *Engage in active listening*: It's important to listen actively to peers during standups because they may share information that is relevant in ways that the person sharing doesn't fully understand as they are laser-focused on their own role and work. This active listening helps in understanding team dynamics and project progress, and it can identify opportunities where one might assist a teammate or collaborate on challenges.

- *Be prepared for meetings and activities*: Product team members should come prepared with updates and any notes on obstacles or requests for help. This preparation makes the standup more effective and respects the team's time and makes sure that important elements or implications are not glossed over.

*Sprint Planning*

The process of mapping out the work to be performed is, as discussed in previous chapters, a critical part of scrum and it sets the stage for the success of each sprint. Product team members can actively contribute by incorporating a few key behaviors:

- *Engage in goal setting*: Sprint planning is a collaborative effort to set goals and define tasks for the upcoming sprint, as previously explored. Team members can ensure greater success by engaging actively by suggesting tasks, questioning assumptions, and understanding the scope and purpose of the work ahead.

1. *Commit to tasks*: When tasks are being assigned, one should ensure that they fully understand their responsibilities and commit to realistic delivery timelines, because the rest of the team—as well as other teams they are coordinating with—may be depending on their work. If there's uncertainty, it's the right moment to ask for clarifications or additional resources needed to meet expectations.

- *Promptly raise and voice concerns:* Part of effective collaboration as a team is making sure that each member is proactive in all things, even if they don't necessarily think there are dependencies. If one foresees potential issues with the planned workload or deadlines, the sprint planning meeting is the right place to voice these concerns. This proactive approach can help adjust plans before the sprint starts, avoiding stress and rushed work later.

### Sprint Reviews and Retrospectives

As important as planning and regular updates in standups are to the success of a task in progress, one of the most important things a product team member can do is assist in making sure that the marketing work as well as the processes that the Agile marketing team engage in are continuously improving. There are several things a good team member can keep in mind to do so:

- *Open sharing of accomplishments and learnings*: During sprint reviews, showcase what has been completed, focusing on how the work contributes to the campaign's goals. Be open about what worked well and what didn't, as this will guide future strategies.

- *Offer constructive feedback*: In retrospectives, there can be a tendency to focus on the positive, or to avoid what might be deemed as criticism. Great team members provide constructive feedback aimed at improving processes, discussing what should be started, stopped, or continued in a constructive way that offers both an assessment of what was not optimally done but with some ideas of how it could be improved. This is not about airing grievances but rather about proposing actionable changes that could benefit future sprints and the team's progress as a whole.

- *Take a solution-oriented approach*: Reviews and retrospectives are a great opportunity to bring the best ideas for how to make things better. Bring suggestions for improvement to retrospectives, not just problems. Being solution-oriented helps the team move forward and shows one's commitment to the team's continuous improvement.

By actively engaging in these scrum ceremonies, team members ensure that they are not just passive participants but active contributors to the project's success, as well as the long-term success of bigger initiatives and the company as a whole. This engagement fosters a collaborative and transparent team environment where each member feels valued and accountable, driving the overall effectiveness and efficiency of the Agile marketing team.

## Collaborating Effectively with Peers

Success with Agile marketing incorporates effective collaboration, as it is one of the cornerstones of the Agile principles that scrum is based on. It involves not just working alongside one another but actively engaging in ways that enhance team dynamics, support a healthy work environment, and constructively resolve conflicts.

### Team Dynamics

While fostering a strong team was discussed in Chapter 16 in the discussion of being successful as a scrum master, it is important that each individual product team member takes responsibility for fostering a strong dynamic within their team as well. Here are some areas individual team members can actively contribute to a stronger and more cohesive team:

- *Open communication*: It is incumbent on each individual to create an environment where open communication is encouraged and practiced. This means regular sharing of ideas, concerns, and feedback in a respectful and constructive manner. While this can take many forms and may be experienced differently for fully in-person versus hybrid or fully remote teams, successful members will utilize tools and practices that enhance communication, such as regular team meetings, shared digital workspaces, and informal catch-up sessions.

- *Multidisciplinary curiosity*: Because marketing teams often comprise individuals with diverse skill sets, members of a successful product team are curious about the work of other team members, and they take an opportunity to educate each other about the unique needs and considerations of individual roles. This takes the form of cross-training teams to have a better understanding of more of the marketing process which in turn can yield more thoroughly thought-out approaches.

- *Openness to new technology*: With the increasing reliance on digital platforms including AI-based tools and approaches, team members often need to integrate new technologies into their strategies and workflows. Keeping up with technological advances and understanding how to leverage them effectively in marketing campaigns is a critical challenge.

- *Embrace diversity and inclusion*: The unique professional and cultural backgrounds, skills, and perspectives within the team are an asset, and should be embraced as such. Ensure that all team members feel valued and included, and that their ideas are considered and respected. Diversity in thoughts and approaches can lead to more innovative solutions and a more enjoyable workplace.

- *Address conflicts early*: Successful teams address disagreements or misunderstandings early before they escalate into bigger issues. This involves recognizing signs of conflict and having the courage to initiate conversations to resolve issues.

- *Learn from conflicts*: It is important to view conflicts as opportunities for learning and growth. After a conflict is resolved, take the time to reflect on what caused the disagreement and how it was resolved.

Collaborating effectively with peers in an Agile marketing environment requires a combination of good communication, empathy, respect for diversity, and effective conflict resolution skills. By cultivating these aspects, team members can enhance their working relationships, contributing to a more cohesive, productive, and innovative team.

### Interfacing with the Scrum Master and Product Owner

Effective interaction between product team members and other key roles like the scrum master and product owner is crucial for maximizing team performance and achieving successful project outcomes. These relationships are critical to success, make the work performed easier to do, and can make it more productive and enjoyable.

- *Understanding roles and responsibilities*: It is vital for team members to fully understand the distinct roles and responsibilities of the scrum master and product owner, because in fast-moving environments there is not always time to run between different roles to get answers to timely questions or to make decisions quickly. Remember that the scrum master facilitates the scrum process, ensuring the team works efficiently and effectively on a day-to-day and sprint-to-sprint basis, while the product owner defines the vision and priorities of the project at a higher level and also has closer connections to other executives and stakeholders in the organization. Knowing these roles and understanding their implications helps team members know whom to approach with specific issues and requests.

- *Facilitate their efforts*: The scrum master is a key ally to the product team and can unblock efforts, get clarity from key stakeholders like the product owner, and generally make sure the team's work is running smoothly. Thus, product team members can support the scrum master by adhering to the scrum practices, participating actively in all scrum ceremonies, and being open to changes and adjustments in processes. Supporting the product owner involves understanding the project's goals and requirements, providing insights that might affect project priorities, and being proactive in delivering tasks that align with the project's strategic vision.

- *Engage in proactive communication*: Given the importance of speed and clarity, a successful product team maintains open and proactive communication with both the scrum master and product owner. The team informs them of any impediments or concerns as soon as they arise, and provide suggestions for improvement that might benefit the project or the team's workflow.

By effectively supporting and interacting with the scrum master and product owner, and by utilizing established channels for ongoing feedback, team members can significantly contribute to the smooth running of Agile processes. This collaboration not only enhances the team's overall performance, but it also drives the successful delivery of marketing projects, ensuring that strategic objectives are met efficiently and effectively.

## SKILLS AND QUALITIES OF AN EFFECTIVE TEAM MEMBER

Success in Agile marketing requires more than just proficiency in one's specific role; it demands a set of core skills and qualities that facilitate effective collaboration, rapid adaptation to change, and continuous innovation. These following sections will look at some essential skills and qualities that every member of a product team should cultivate to excel in their roles and significantly contribute to their team's success.

### Adaptability

As the word *agile* would suggest, a key aspect of a working team is the ability to be nimble and adjust approaches to best suit the project, campaign, or initiative they are contributing toward. A few ways to look at adaptability are the following:

- *Adjusting strategy when needed*: Agile approaches to marketing thrive on flexibility. Team members must be capable of quickly adjusting strategies based on consumer feedback and market trends. This involves being open to changing course and reevaluating the team's approach, often at a moment's notice, although never without data and consensus to support the change.

- *Responsiveness to feedback*: Effective team members actively seek and respond constructively to feedback from both their team and the target audience. This responsiveness is crucial for refining marketing tactics and ensuring that campaigns perform optimally when faced with dynamic factors both internally and externally.

- *Continuous learning*: Possessing the ability to learn from experiences and apply that knowledge to new situations is a key aspect of adaptability. Team members should continually seek to expand their knowledge and skills to stay relevant and effective in their roles.

## Communication Skills

While Agile marketing teams may be great at communicating the value of a product or service to an external audience, they can often suffer from internal communication issues that hinder their ability to do their best work. While some of the scrum rituals and the Agile principles help to foster better communication and understanding, there are some key things to keep in mind to be more successful as a team:

- *Clarity and conciseness*: There was an earlier discussion about how clarity can impact specific points in the scrum process, but this is something that should be carried out through all opportunities that a team has to communicate with each other and with other teams they may be working alongside. Clear and concise communication is vital in Agile environments where quick decisions are common, and so is the active listening approach mentioned earlier. Team members must articulate their ideas and concerns effectively, ensuring that misunderstandings are minimized and that every team member is aligned with the current objectives.

- *Cross-functional communication*: Given the multidisciplinary nature of Agile marketing teams, members must be adept at communicating across different areas of expertise which may include different channels (e.g., email, social media, advertising, Web), tactics (e.g., SEO, growth marketing, branding), or product-specific (e.g., Adobe Photoshop, Salesforce, HootSuite). Taking the time to understand what other team members are working on, and some of the key elements of their work ensures that creative ideas, technical requirements, and strategic objectives are understood and integrated effectively by all team members.

### Creativity and Innovation

- *Contributing new ideas*: Creativity is at the heart of marketing. Team members should regularly contribute fresh and innovative ideas for campaigns, messaging, and problem-solving. This creative input is vital for developing campaigns that capture attention and engage consumers.

- *Problem-solving skills*: The ability to creatively solve problems when campaigns don't go as planned or when unexpected challenges arise is crucial to success. Product team members should use their creativity to find effective solutions quickly and efficiently and embrace these difficulties as a learning experience to help themselves, their teams, as well as other teams in the company to do better in the future.

- *Willingness to experiment*: Embracing a trial-and-error approach is part of the innovative process in Agile marketing. Team members should be willing to experiment with new concepts, tools, and processes, learning from both successes and failures to continuously improve the team's outputs.

By developing these skills and qualities, members of an Agile marketing team can enhance their effectiveness and adaptability, ensuring that they are not only meeting the demands of their roles but are also driving the team toward achieving its strategic goals. These competencies foster a proactive and productive environment that is essential for the success of Agile marketing initiatives.

## AGILECORP'S PRODUCT TEAM LEARNS SOME LESSONS

The marketing team at AgileCorp recently embarked on a rather ambitious project to launch a new product focused on small businesses. In addition to Rosa the scrum master, the product team consisted of Emily, a digital marketing strategist, and Tom, a creative content designer, as well as a couple other members.

The launch of the new small business-focused software was slated to coincide with a major industry conference, giving the team a tight timeline to work within, and the launch campaign required innovative marketing strategies and creative content that could stand out in a highly competitive market. Emily struggled with utilizing analytics to optimize the campaign effectively, while Tom faced difficulties in aligning his creative designs with the strategic goals of the marketing campaign.

The initial phase of the campaign did not perform as expected and fell flat as the industry conference passed by without a resounding success for the new product. Engagement rates were low, and the feedback from the target audience indicated that the messaging was not resonating well. Additionally, a competitor stole much of the attention and focus at the conference, and this setback served as a catalyst for Emily and Tom to seek new learning opportunities and refine their approaches.

### Emily's Improvements

Looking to the Agile principles that involve continuous improvement, Emily reflected on the initial results of the software launch campaign and realized she needed a deeper understanding of data analytics to better gauge campaign performance and user engagement. She enrolled in an advanced analytics course that helped her learn how to interpret data more effectively and adjust strategies in real-time.

Armed with new analytical skills, Emily was able to identify which aspects of the campaign were underperforming and why. She adjusted the digital marketing strategies accordingly, which significantly improved the campaign's subsequent phases, as we will soon see.

### Tom's Improvements

Like Emily, Tom realized that he was lacking in a few key areas that negatively affected the small business campaign that AgileCorp just launched. To help shore up some of these gaps, he participated in a workshop on integrating strategic marketing goals with creative design. This training helped him understand how to align his designs more closely with marketing objectives and user expectations.

Utilizing feedback from the team and target audience, Tom revised his designs to better reflect the campaign's core messages and appeal more directly to the target demographic. While he would need to wait and see, he felt confident that this revised approach would help to improve the results of the initiative.

### Campaign Turnaround

The improvements made by Emily and Tom had a profound impact on the campaign. Even though the industry event had passed, there was still plenty of room for success. Engagement rates with the target audience of small businesses increased by over 50%, and the feedback from the target audience turned overwhelmingly positive. The successful turnaround of the campaign was largely attributed to the targeted skill enhancements and the application of new learnings.

As important as its initial successes, the learnings from this project were documented and shared with the entire marketing team, becoming part of AgileCorp's knowledge base to support future efforts. Emily's analytical techniques and Tom's approach to creative alignment were incorporated into the standard operating procedures for future marketing projects. Both team members also became mentors within their teams, helping to elevate the overall capabilities of the Agile marketing department.

By addressing their initial shortcomings, Emily and Tom not only improved their own skills but also contributed to the long-term success and innovation of their team's marketing strategies.

## CONCLUSION

This chapter looked at the important roles that each member plays within an Agile marketing product team. From embracing their core responsibilities to overcoming common challenges, the effectiveness and success of an initiative heavily rely on the active and engaged participation of every team member. The chapter explored whether in roles related to marketing, creative, analytics, or technical aspects, each member's contributions are crucial to navigating the Agile landscape effectively.

Growth of product team members requires continuous learning and adaptation. The fast-paced nature of the marketing environment, coupled with the iterative process of Agile, demands that team members not only adapt to changes quickly but also proactively seek ways to improve both their skills and their work processes. This ongoing personal and professional growth is essential not just for the success of individual campaigns but for the long-term development of the team and the organization.

Furthermore, the collaborative spirit of scrum emphasizes the importance of each member's engagement in all aspects of the team's activities—from daily standups and sprint planning to reviews and retrospectives. It is through this proactive involvement that teams can truly embody the Agile principles of continuous improvement and responsiveness to change.

Members of an Agile marketing team are encouraged to pursue opportunities for enhancing their skills, to learn from both successes and failures, and to remain committed to the collective goals of the team. By doing so, they not only enhance their own career, they also contribute significantly to the team's ongoing success and innovation.

Remember that a team's journey into Agile marketing will require continual evolution, and investments in these approaches will pay off with better work, sustained results, and continuous improvement.

# V

# ADOPTING AGILE PRACTICES AS A MARKETING ORGANIZATION

Readers are now prepared to begin practicing Agile marketing using scrum processes and methods, having reviewed the principles, practices, and roles involved. While there may be a learning curve for all team members that should not keep anyone from beginning their journey.

In fact, this part of the book will discuss several ways to get started that have a relatively low impact, and also some of the ways of thinking and culture changes that will help a team's adoption of Agile and scrum.

This will also prepare individuals to work collaboratively with other teams, departments, and areas of an organization that may or may not already be using scrum or other similar methods.

The next chapter will begin our exploration of adopting these practices as a marketing organization by taking a look at what it means to have an Agile mindset.

# 18

# *Adopting an Agile Mindset*

As readers have likely seen in their own experience, or surmised from reading the preceding pages, while there are some aspects of Agile and scrum that may be familiar, there are also approaches that may be brand new to many approaching it for the first time.

Even marketing teams that are excited about a move to more Agile approaches can still have some big changes to make, behaviors to learn (or unlearn), and other potential roadblocks ahead. Adoption of Agile principles and scrum methods work more smoothly with the right mindset, which often requires a shift from more traditional and waterfall methods. To help with this, keep a few things in mind when moving from more traditional marketing approaches to a scrum approach. These will be explored in this chapter.

## FOCUS

In marketing, *focus* traditionally refers to the priorities a team sets to achieve its goals. Traditionally, this focus has revolved around the four ‟P"s: price, place, promotion, and product—elements that are controlled internally by the company. However, as marketing teams adopt Agile and scrum methodologies, a significant mindset shift is necessary, moving from an internal, producer-centric focus to a customer-centric approach. This shift is crucial for teams transitioning to Agile marketing because it aligns more closely with the dynamic nature of consumer behaviors and market conditions.

Traditionally, marketing strategies have been producer-centric, designed around the four "P"s. This approach dictates that marketing efforts be centered on what the company wants to push to the market—whether that be launching new products, pushing for higher sales, or controlling the market perception of their brand. Decisions are typically made based on historical data and projections that favor the company's planned trajectory, often at a scheduled, campaign-oriented pace.

Agile marketing upends the traditional approach by prioritizing the customer's perspective and needs, and unlike the linear and somewhat rigid focus of traditional marketing, it is iterative and responsive, emphasizing flexibility and continual adaptation to customer feedback and behavior.

This customer-centric approach allows marketers to respond quickly to changes in the market or in consumer preferences, which is more effective in today's fast-paced, digital marketplace. Rather than pushing products through predetermined campaigns, Agile marketers pull insights from actual customer interactions and data, adjusting their strategies in real time to better meet customer needs.

To adopt a customer-centric focus, teams can look at the following:

1. *Listen actively to the customer*: To successfully adopt a customer-centric focus, marketers must first become adept at listening to their customers. This involves not only collecting data from customer interactions across various touchpoints but also actively seeking customer feedback through surveys, social media listening, and direct engagements. The insights gathered are then used to inform marketing decisions, ensuring that strategies are genuinely reflective of customer needs and not just company objectives.

2. *Iterate based on feedback*: Agile marketing thrives on *iteration*—making continuous, incremental adjustments to marketing strategies based on real-time feedback. Marketers need to embrace the idea that strategies are perpetually in a state of flux, rather than set in stone. This requires a cultural shift within the marketing team, moving away from the "set it and forget it" campaign mentality to a more dynamic, ongoing optimization process.

3. *Empower teams to make decisions*: In traditional setups, decisions often come top-down, but Agile marketing promotes a more decentralized approach where the teams closest to the customer feedback have the authority to make decisions. This empowerment not only speeds up the

response times but also enhances the team's engagement and accountability. Encouraging cross-functional collaboration and open communication channels are essential to facilitate this empowerment effectively.

By prioritizing the customer's voice, responding agilely to feedback, and empowering teams, organizations can ensure that their marketing efforts are more aligned with the market realities and customer needs, thereby enhancing both customer satisfaction and business outcomes.

## GOAL-SETTING

*Goal-setting* is an essential activity that outlines the expected achievements of a team, the campaign or initiative being run, as well as company-wide goals. Traditionally, these goals are set well in advance, often on an annual or quarterly basis, and usually follow a rigid structure with little room for adjustment once they are agreed upon. However, when adopting Agile and scrum methodologies, marketing teams are encouraged to rethink how they set goals to allow for greater flexibility and responsiveness. This shift is crucial for keeping pace with market changes and enhancing customer engagement.

In a conventional setting, marketing goals are typically defined at the start of a fiscal year or quarter and are designed to align with the strategic objectives of the business. These goals might include specific revenue targets, market share increases, or other performance metrics. Once set, the strategies and tactics to achieve these goals are planned out, often with little scope for change as market conditions evolve. This approach assumes a predictable environment where variables change minimally over time.

Contrary to the traditional approach, Agile goal-setting embraces flexibility and iterative adjustments. While Agile marketing teams also set long-term goals and business key performance indicators (KPIs) which may not be as flexible, how these are achieved can often be considered adjustable based on ongoing feedback and market dynamics. This adaptability allows teams to pivot or alter their strategies to maximize opportunities or mitigate risks as they arise. For instance, rather than having a fixed goal to increase Web site traffic by 20% over the quarter, an Agile team might adjust this target based on new customer insights or changes in digital consumption behaviors.

Furthermore, Agile marketing places a strong emphasis on customer-centric goals alongside typical sales-related objectives. This means incorporating KPIs that reflect customer satisfaction, engagement levels, and brand loyalty—metrics that are continually refined through customer interactions and feedback loops.

A few ways that teams can adapt to a more Agile approach with their goal-setting are outlined in the following list:

1. *Set flexible goals*: Start with clear, but flexible goals that allow for adjustments. Establish mechanisms for regularly reviewing these goals (e.g., during sprint reviews) and make adjustments as necessary based on performance data and market feedback.

2. *Balance long-term and short-term objectives*: While maintaining focus on long-term strategic goals, Agile marketing teams should also set short-term objectives that can be quickly achieved and iterated upon. This dual focus helps maintain strategic direction while leveraging immediate opportunities and feedback.

3. *Incorporate customer-centric metrics:* Expand the traditional sales-focused KPIs to include customer-centric metrics. For example, consider customer retention rates, net promoter scores (NPS), or customer engagement levels as part of goal-setting. These metrics offer a more holistic view of marketing effectiveness and can guide more nuanced strategic adjustments.

By adopting an Agile approach to goal-setting, marketing teams can ensure they remain relevant and responsive in a rapidly changing market. This flexibility not only enhances the team's ability to meet and exceed customer expectations but also aligns more closely with the dynamic nature of today's digital marketplace. Agile goal-setting empowers teams to navigate uncertainty with confidence and make strategic decisions that drive sustained business growth and customer satisfaction.

## PLANNING

Planning also varies between traditional and scrum approaches. Traditional marketing planning often involves creating detailed plans well in advance, based on assumptions that the market conditions and consumer behaviors will remain relatively stable. However, for teams adopting an Agile approach, there's a significant shift toward more flexible, responsive planning practices.

In more traditional, waterfall environments, marketing plans are laid out with a long-term view, where activities for the next quarter or year are mapped out in advance. These plans are often detailed and prescriptive, with specific campaigns, budgets, and expected outcomes delineated early in the planning process, and the assumption is that external factors will remain constant, or changes can be predicted. However, this approach leaves little room for adapting to unforeseen changes, making it risky in environments where market dynamics can shift rapidly.

In contrast, Agile planning recognizes the fluid nature of marketing dynamics and customer behaviors. It incorporates a sprint-based approach where planning is iterative and evolves over time. This means that while there is an overarching strategy or goal, the specific tactics and activities are planned in shorter cycles or sprints, typically lasting a few weeks. After each sprint, the team reviews the results, learns from the data, and adjusts the plan accordingly. This iterative process allows for incorporating new insights, responding to changes in the market, and refining strategies based on what is working.

Here are some things to keep in mind when changing a planning mindset to a more Agile one:

1. *Iterative planning*: Embrace the concept of iterative planning where the strategy is outlined but the specific tactics are flexible and reviewed regularly. This approach requires setting short-term goals at the beginning of each sprint, assessing the outcomes at the end, and using the insights gained to influence the next cycle of planning.

2. *Flexibility and responsiveness*: Maintain flexibility in the planning process to accommodate new information and changes in the market. This may mean adjusting campaign tactics, reallocating budgets, or shifting focus based on real-time data and feedback from customers.

3. *Regular reviews and adaptations*: Schedule regular review sessions to evaluate the effectiveness of marketing activities. These reviews should not only assess performance against goals but also consider external changes that could impact future plans. The ability to adapt quickly is a competitive advantage in agile marketing.

Planning in a scrum environment empowers marketing teams to be more adaptive, responsive, and effective in their strategies, and by moving away from rigid, long-term plans to more flexible, iterative planning cycles, teams can better align their activities with current market conditions and consumer needs. This shift enhances the agility of the marketing team while driving better outcomes by ensuring that marketing efforts are always aligned with the most relevant and current opportunities.

## TIMING

Timing is crucial for the success of any campaign or initiative. Traditional marketing methods often employ long phases or cycles for project completion, typically planned well in advance around fixed stages. These phases are designed to align with broader marketing and product launch schedules but can lack the flexibility to adapt to changes or seize emergent opportunities. Agile and scrum methodologies introduce a different perspective on timing, emphasizing shorter cycles and responsiveness, which is vital for adapting to the fast-paced nature of modern markets.

Traditionally, marketing projects are segmented into extended phases akin to the software development lifecycle (SDLC) explored at the beginning of the book, with each phase lasting several weeks to several months. This method involves comprehensive planning and execution stages that lay out tasks sequentially. The major drawback of this approach is its rigidity; once a timeline is set and tasks are defined, deviating from the plan due to changing market conditions or new customer insights can be challenging and often requires extensive reviews and adjustments.

Scrum methodologies drastically alter the approach to timing by segmenting work into sprints—short, consistent cycles that allow for continual reassessment and adjustment. These sprints, typically ranging from two to four weeks, enable marketing teams to remain agile, allowing them to adjust their strategies based on real-time data and feedback without waiting for the completion of long phases. This method ensures that marketing efforts are continuously aligned with current market demands and can adapt to new opportunities or challenges as they arise.

Keep the following in mind as ways to make the transition to a more Agile method of thinking about timing:

1. *Short cycles for quick adaptation*: Adopting shorter cycles or sprints allows for rapid testing and iteration of marketing strategies. This approach enables teams to quickly learn what works and refine or pivot strategies accordingly. It reduces the risk associated with longer project phases by allowing incremental adjustments before significant resources are committed.

2. *Regular reviews and feedback integration*: To make the most of agile timing, regular sprint reviews and retrospectives are essential. These meetings should assess the effectiveness of current strategies and integrate new insights from market feedback. This process helps ensure that marketing efforts are not only timely but also highly responsive to customer needs.

3. *Balancing speed and quality*: While agile emphasizes speed and flexibility, it is crucial to balance these with the quality of output. Ensure that the desire to push out marketing deliverables quickly does not compromise the quality of the content or the strategic coherence of marketing campaigns.

Embracing scrum transforms how marketing teams plan and execute their strategies, offering a competitive edge in today's dynamic market environment. By adopting shorter, more responsive cycles, marketing teams can ensure their initiatives are more aligned with current trends and customer expectations, leading to higher effectiveness and better overall business outcomes.

## WORKLOAD

While the overall *amount* of work would likely not vary greatly between a Scrum-based and approach versus a traditional one, the difference is in how and when the work is performed.

Traditional marketing methods often distribute workload without a clear prioritization, which can lead to inefficient resource utilization and project delays. Agile and scrum methodologies introduce a structured approach to managing workload, focusing on prioritizing tasks that deliver the most business value and ensuring a sustainable pace for team members.

In more traditional marketing settings, workload is usually assigned based on the project phases. Tasks are often laid out at the beginning of these phases without a clear prioritization, leading to scenarios where work is performed based on availability or perceived urgency rather than strategic importance. This approach can result in key deliverables being rushed or overlooked as deadlines approach, impacting the overall quality and effectiveness of marketing campaigns.

Adoption of Agile marketing, and in particular scrum, radically changes the approach to workload management by utilizing tools like the sprint backlog. This tool helps prioritize tasks based on their contribution to business goals and the overall campaign strategy. Each task is evaluated and prioritized by the product owner with input from the entire team, fostering a collaborative environment where every team member agrees on the workload and understands its relevance to the project's success.

Additionally, a scrum approach necessitates delivering a working product at the end of each sprint, which can range from two to four weeks. This continual delivery ensures that the project progressively builds toward a complete product with each sprint, allowing for regular feedback and adjustments. This approach not only enhances productivity but also ensures that the team is not overloaded, as work is broken down into manageable chunks that deliver tangible results.

Making a shift to an Agile mindset is not always easy for some teams, but here are a few things to keep in mind when thinking about workload:

1. *Prioritize based on value*: Shift the focus of workload management from simply completing tasks to delivering value. Prioritize work items that offer the most significant impact on the campaign's goals, ensuring that resources are allocated efficiently.

2. *Encourage team collaboration in planning*: Workload management should be a collaborative effort involving all team members. This inclusion helps ensure that everyone has a say in the prioritization process, understands the workload, and commits to the sprint goals, which enhances overall team productivity and morale.

3. *Maintain regular reviews*: Regular sprint reviews and retrospectives are essential in Agile workload management. These reviews allow the team to reflect on what has been accomplished, what needs to improve, and how to adjust the workload to meet changing requirements or to address any issues that might have arisen.

Adopting Agile methodologies for managing workload in marketing not only helps in aligning tasks with strategic business outcomes but also ensures that the team can adapt to changes effectively.

## COLLABORATION

Finally, collaboration, while a fundamental of any type of marketing approach, differs between traditional and Agile or scrum methods.

Teams using more traditional approaches to marketing often work in silos on specific tasks, which can lead to challenges in integration and alignment. Agile marketing, leveraging the principles of scrum, emphasizes a more integrated and dynamic approach to collaboration, ensuring that all team members work together closely throughout the project lifecycle.

In traditional marketing frameworks, teams are often organized by function, with each group working independently on their components of a project. For example, creative teams, digital teams, and analytics teams might work separately, only coming together to integrate their work at predetermined milestones. This siloed approach can lead to issues such as misaligned objectives, inconsistencies in the final product, and the need for significant revisions once all elements are combined.

Agile marketing transforms collaboration by fostering a team environment where multidisciplinary groups work together in short cycles or sprints. This structure allows for continuous communication and adjustment, with team members from different disciplines (such as creative, analytics, and technology) collaborating from the start of a project to its completion. Agile teams prioritize work collectively and make decisions in a way that aligns closely with real-time feedback and project goals, enhancing both the efficiency and the effectiveness of marketing campaigns.

New and better means of collaboration can be one of the biggest immediate benefits of an Agile approach to marketing. Here are some things to keep in mind:

1. *Foster a team-oriented culture*: Cultivate a culture that values open communication, mutual respect, and shared goals. Encourage team members to view the project from a holistic perspective rather than just through the lens of their specific roles.

2. *Implement regular cross-functional meetings*: Hold regular meetings such as daily stand-ups, sprint planning sessions, and sprint reviews that involve all team members. These meetings ensure everyone is aligned on the project's objectives, progress, and challenges, facilitating more integrated and effective solutions.

3. *Encourage active participation and shared decision-making*: Empower all team members to contribute ideas and make decisions collectively. This shared decision-making process improves project outcomes by incorporating diverse perspectives while enhancing team members' commitment and satisfaction.

Adopting an Agile approach to collaboration involves a significant shift in how teams communicate and work together. By breaking down silos and encouraging continuous, cross-functional collaboration, Agile marketing teams can react more swiftly and effectively to changes in the market or project requirements.

## SOME ADDITIONAL BEHAVIORS TO ADOPT

In addition, there some more things that teams can keep in mind to enhance the adoption of scrum:

- Avoid perfectionism, which can often cause teams to spend an inordinate amount of time and resources on a task or initiative before getting feedback on it.

- Partake in more frequent reviews, which can avoid the trap of perfectionism, as well as allow teams to take the very latest and best insights and findings and incorporate them into their work.

- Undertake greater collaboration, which follows some of the core principles of Agile, increases the diversity of ideas and solutions, and ultimately leads to stronger results.

- Talk about successes and failures in a judgment-free environment so everyone can learn from both. The success of a team depends on this type of dynamic.

- Talk about working on the work. This is important to remember: Taking an Agile approach means that teams are not only focused on creating great work but are also focused on improving the *ways* that they work. Talking about these processes and methods will help the team develop more language around them and ultimately find better ways to complete the work.

## BEHAVIORS TO AVOID

Just as there are behaviors teams want to adopt, there are several behaviors that teams should set aside or avoid when embracing an Agile mindset. These include:

- micromanaging team members—this prevents experimentation and exploration of new ideas and ways of working that can achieve better results

- assuming there is a single approach to success

- solely focusing on results instead of the growth of knowledge and the team

- forming cliques of a few individuals or working in silos instead of being more collaborative

- holding back information instead of being more transparent and trusting the team to do great things with full information

## CONCLUSION

Being successful with Agile marketing using scrum depends on the adoption of the practices and roles, yet long-term growth requires a mindset shift from all those involved. This mindset shift is as much about changing old behaviors as it is about adopting new ones.

# CHAPTER 19

# LEADERSHIP'S ROLE

Chapter 18 showed how an Agile mindset helps teams do their best work, and as will be explored more in this chapter, when there is adoption of this mindset by leaders and role models within a company, it can ease the pain of adoption of this sometimes completely new approach to doing business.

The next section takes a look at leadership's role in the successful adoption, implementation, and improvement of Agile marketing in an organization.

## FOSTERING COLLABORATION

Going back to the Agile principles that were explored at the beginning of this book, one of the key ideas expressed in those is that of the self-organizing team that, based on the guidance of the product owner and their definition of business value, determines the best way to achieve the goals of the initiative.

Given this foundation, a key component of being a leader among Agile teams is the ability to create the type of collaborative environment in which teams can work well together. Thus, the first component that will be explored is how a leader should foster greater collaboration, which needs to include the elements.

### Creating a Culture of Openness and Trust

Trust and openness lead to better teamwork, increased innovation, and a stronger sense of belonging among team members, and because of this, a collaborative environment thrives on openness and trust. Thus, team members should feel comfortable sharing ideas, feedback, and concerns without fear of criticism or retribution.

A leader can support this by encouraging open dialogue, celebrating diverse perspectives, and building a culture where everyone's input is valued.

### Encouraging Cross-Functional Collaboration

Cross-functional collaboration leads to more comprehensive and creative solutions, as team members bring different perspectives to the table. Because marketing teams often include members with diverse skill sets, such as content creators, designers, analysts, and strategists, cross-functional collaboration leverages these varied skills to achieve common goals.

A leader can support this by organizing regular cross-functional meetings, promoting knowledge sharing, and using collaborative tools to facilitate teamwork.

## ENSURING CLEAR COMMUNICATION

Building on the importance of collaboration is the need to make sure that teams are all on the same page. Thus, clear communication and transparency are fundamental to the success of any team, Agile or not. But when adopting a new approach, such as scrum, these elements ensure that everyone is aligned, informed, and able to collaborate effectively. The following sections discuss some things that leaders can do.

### Establishing Communication Protocols

Leaders should use and set standardized communication channels for different types of interactions, such as email for formal communication, instant messaging for quick questions, and video conferencing for meetings. There is no one right way to do this across different companies, but within a team and an organization, a leader can set standards here that will help everyone have clearer communication.

A leader can also implement regular updates, similar to how scrum utilizes daily standups and weekly check-ins, to keep everyone informed about progress and any changes. This can be especially important when big changes are taking place, such as the initial adoption of scrum.

### Encouraging Open and Honest Communication

Leaders can encourage an open-door policy where team members feel comfortable sharing their thoughts, concerns, and ideas without fear of judgment. This includes the leader, but it should also include other team members and peers and the way they communicate with each other.

Promoting active listening practices where team members pay full attention, ask clarifying questions, and provide constructive feedback can often begin with the way a leader behaves and other team members learn by observing.

### Promoting a Culture of Transparency

Leaders should make it a habit to share information openly, including project updates, successes, challenges, and lessons learned, as this will provide a good example of how scrum teams should do it in their work. If team members have worked previously within different types of environments, some of those prior experiences may have been extremely siloed or closed off and not encouraging transparency. A leader has an opportunity to be a good influence here.

It is important to acknowledge and celebrate individual and team contributions to build a positive and transparent team culture. Scrum rituals like retrospectives provide a great opportunity to do this, although a leader may not want to wait until the end of a sprint to do so.

Transparency in communication builds trust and ensures that everyone is aware of each other's contributions and challenges, and it fosters a sense of shared responsibility, helps identify and address issues promptly, and promotes a collaborative approach to problem-solving.

## ENHANCING TEAM ENGAGEMENT

A leader has a responsibility to promote a culture where each member is contributing to their fullest. While everyone on a team has a role to play in team engagement, there are some things that leaders can do that help set the stage. The following sections explore these.

### Ensure Everyone Has a Voice

In any team, as with just about any group of people, there will be some that naturally speak up more and voice their thoughts and opinions. While these people can have incredibly important things to say, a leader needs to set an example by ensuring that *everyone* has the ability to share their ideas and feedback.

As a leader, this might mean using different approaches to acquire feedback from different individuals. While some might be more willing to speak up in a group setting, others, may find it more comfortable to share things offline or asynchronously. A leader needs to strike the right balance between encouraging some of the more introverted team members to feel more comfortable to speak up, while not causing more discomfort and disengagement by not providing different means of gathering ideas.

### Building Cohesion Through Social Interaction

Good leaders know that strong social bonds can improve team cohesion and morale, leading to better collaboration. Whether a team regularly works together in the same office, or has a hybrid or fully remote work environment, social interaction is a key component to building cohesion.

To build better cohesion, one can organize team-building activities, virtual coffee breaks, and informal social gatherings to build relationships and foster a sense of community.

Ensuring that everyone is aligned, informed, and engaged will contribute significantly to the success of the sprint, leading to better outcomes and a more dynamic, motivated team.

## ADAPTING TO CHANGES

The ability to adapt to changes quickly and effectively is crucial for the success of any marketing team. It's essential to look at the importance of flexibility, techniques for handling unexpected changes, and strategies for maintaining momentum despite disruptions.

### Embracing Change as a Constant

Great leaders know that when teams have truly embraced Agile principles in their work, change is not seen as a disruption but as an opportunity to improve and refine strategies. Flexibility is embedded in the Agile mindset, allowing teams to pivot and adjust their approaches based on new information or shifting priorities.

Embracing change leads to more resilient and responsive marketing strategies, enabling teams to capitalize on emerging trends and avoid potential pitfalls.

### Staying Open to New Ideas and Information

As a leader, it can be tempting to not want to appear weak and change one's mind on key decisions that have already been made. That, however, is not what an Agile mindset is all about. When new information is available, any member of a team—including its leadership—should be willing to reexamine the thought processes that led to a decision being made.

Doing so sets an example to others on the team to not give in to stubbornness and to let objective data and information drive actions and key factors in campaigns and initiatives.

The ability to exhibit the humility to rethink one's decisions also sets a great example to team members that are often tasked with making quick assessments in a fast-paced environment.

## HELPING TEAMS OVERCOME OBSTACLES

While the ultimate goal of a leader whose team adopts Agile principles and an approach such as scrum is to build a self-sufficient and self-organizing group, there are inevitably times when there are obstacles to overcome.

At first, even small hurdles may seem insurmountable, but a good leader is able to build a team's resilience over time so that they are increasingly self-reliant, and only the largest of obstacles are cause for bringing the leader back to help them solve it.

Following are a few ways that a leader can help their teams in overcoming obstacles.

### Prioritizing and Reprioritizing Tasks

Agile teams must be adept at reprioritizing tasks to accommodate new information or shifting priorities, and leaders can play a key role in helping to teach tools that will help their teams make better decisions in the future.

As discussed in previous chapters, there are many potential frameworks that can make prioritization easier. Consider using one of the two explored earlier: the MoSCoW (must have, should have, could have, won't have) or the Eisenhower Matrix to reevaluate task importance and urgency.

Leaders who are successful in this have more efficient teams, who are able to increase their sprint velocity. Thus, reprioritizing tasks ensures that the team focuses on the most critical and impactful activities, optimizing resource allocation and effort.

## Determining the Root Causes of Challenges

There can be some issues that crop up that are unlikely to return often, if ever. Yet many obstacles are the result of recurring issues that will continue to appear unless the root cause is dealt with.

These issues can be particularly vexing, as their immediate cause may be easily identified, yet solving a single step may not completely resolve the challenge.

A helpful tool that leaders can show their teams, and ultimately have the teams run themselves is called the 5 Whys, and it has its origins in lean approaches, as discussed in the beginning of this book, have similar roots as scrum.

### The 5 Whys

The 5 Whys is a tool that can help get teams "unstuck" when there are challenges that they are unable to diagnose solutions for. Originally developed as a root cause analysis tool as part of the Toyota Production System by Sakichi Toyoda,[1] this technique became a key component of the lean approach, which shares many ideas and principles with Agile.

The 5 Whys is a simple yet effective tool that helps diagnose a problem's root cause. It is deceptively simple yet very effective in producing important insights.

To use it when faced with a challenge, one simply asks "why" the challenge occurred five times, and they will inevitably get to the root of the issue. In some cases, it may not even take five times to get there! Following is an example of this, using the late delivery of an email marketing campaign as the problem.

- *The challenge is defined as this*: The email campaign launched two days late.
- Then, ask "why?" the first time:
  - The initial answer is: Because the final approved version wasn't ready to send until yesterday.

- Ask "why?" a second time:
  - Because the copywriting team sent it to the designers late.

- Then ask "why?" a third time:
  - Because they only got finalized requirements two days ago.

- Then ask "why?" a fourth time:
  - Because the creative brief wasn't clear in its direction for messaging.

- In this case, the fifth "why?" reveals the underlying issue:
  - Because the process of writing creative briefs is inconsistent and needs improvement.

Suppose the questioning had stopped earlier in this process. In that case, the team might have simply pointed fingers at a specific person or role instead of getting to the bottom of a systemic problem that can be solved, and that will hopefully help to avoid this challenge in the future.

As effective as this can be, there has been plenty of scepticism expressed about the 5 Whys technique. For instance, why is five the magic number and not three, six, or thirteen? As previously mentioned, sometimes it doesn't even take five times asking to get to a root cause, but in other cases, five questions may not get to the reason. In the case that using the 5 Whys doesn't get the team the answer they need, they may need a more thorough root cause analysis tool, such as the Ishikawa diagram, sometimes known as the Fishbone diagram.[2]

It is highly recommended to use the 5 Whys technique the next time a team is faced with a dilemma for which a simple, single answer doesn't help.

## MAINTAINING MOMENTUM

Finally, a leader is responsible to make sure that even a high-performing team *stays* high-performing and doesn't experience dips in productivity for just about any reasons.

A few ways that a leader can support a team and ensure that it maintains momentum during its campaigns and initiatives are examined in the following sections.

### Regularly Reviews and Adjustments

While scrum provides opportunities for Agile teams to review their work and make adjustments, a leader may find it necessary to separately conduct regular reviews of progress and adapt plans as necessary to stay on track despite changes.

A leader (when they are able to attend) can use daily standups, midsprint reviews, and continuous feedback loops to monitor progress and identify areas needing adjustment, but there are also times when taking a step back and looking at the work across a longer time period is needed. As a leader, regular review of how the team is working overall allows for meaningful course corrections and maintaining momentum.

### Promoting a Culture of Resilience

A resilient team is better equipped to handle setbacks and maintain a positive attitude, driving sustained effort and progress, and cultivating a resilient team culture helps members remain motivated and productive in the face of challenges.

Leaders can often lead by example here by showing that, despite setbacks and hurdles faced, there is always a path forward. Team members can see how leaders respond to these impediments and learn tools and methods to apply to their own work.

### Encouraging Continuous Learning and Improvement

A commitment to continuous learning and improvement helps teams adapt to changes and evolve their practices. To encourage greater continuous learning and improvement, conduct sprint retrospectives to identify lessons learned, invest in training and development, and stay updated with industry trends and best practices.

The benefits can be numerous. Continuous learning fosters a growth mindset, equipping the team with the skills and knowledge to navigate changes successfully.

By prioritizing flexibility, implementing structured processes for handling changes, and maintaining a resilient and adaptive team culture, a team can effectively manage unexpected changes and continue to drive successful sprints. Adaptability is a key strength in agile marketing, enabling teams to thrive in a dynamic and ever-changing environment.

## GAINING SUPPORT FROM THE TOP

It's time to look at this from the point of view of a team member and discuss a few ways that marketing team members can ensure they are gaining the leadership support they need.

A marketing team needs leadership support for its efforts. This change will be new for existing marketing team members and other teams that are interfaced with, including legal and IT.

As with any change initiative, it can only go so far without support from the top. As motivated as individual team members and contributors may be to make change happen, there will inevitably be roadblocks on the way, and often, this will take a leader or executive to help clear them so the team can focus on the work at hand.

### Keeping Leadership Informed

Make sure to keep leadership informed of what is being done and of any foreseeable potential challenges so team members can work collaboratively and try to get ahead of any possible setbacks before they happen. When an inevitable challenge rears its head, leadership will already be aware of what the desired accomplishment is and will be supportive in helping see things through to a successful conclusion.

### Collaboration and Communication

Effective collaboration and communication are the cornerstones of a successful sprint. In an agile marketing team, these elements ensure that all team members are aligned, informed, and able to work together seamlessly. Following is a look at the best practices for fostering collaboration and maintaining clear communication throughout the s print.

## AGILECORP'S LEADERSHIP CONUNDRUM

The marketing team at AgileCorp recently transitioned its marketing team to a scrum framework. While the transition promised enhanced adaptability and faster turnaround times on many of its campaigns and initiatives, it also surfaced new challenges that required astute leadership to resolve.

The chief marketing officer (CMO), Sarah, identified two critical issues that were impeding team performance and took proactive steps to address them.

## Lack of Team Engagement and Collaboration

The first issue related to the team's collaboration and communication. During the regular sprint reviews and daily stand-ups, Sarah noticed that the discussions were dominated by a few outspoken team members. This imbalance in participation led to several other team members remaining silent, contributing to a lack of diverse ideas and engagement in the team.

Recognizing the importance of every team member's voice in fostering a truly collaborative environment, Sarah decided to lead by example to rectify this issue. She implemented a structured approach to communication in meetings:

- *Round-robin contribution*: Sarah introduced a round-robin system in meetings, ensuring that each team member had the opportunity to speak and share their insights or updates without interruption.
- *Encouraging quiet members*: Sarah personally coached quieter team members, encouraging them to prepare points in advance of meetings and publicly praised contributions that added value, regardless of the team member's usual level of participation.
- *Setting ground rules*: Clear ground rules were set about the duration and focus of contributions during meetings to prevent any individual from monopolizing the conversation.

These changes fostered a more inclusive atmosphere where all team members felt valued and responsible for the team's success. Over time, the team experienced a significant increase in engagement and collaboration, with more balanced participation across all members.

## Campaign Creative Delays

The second issue that the marketing team faced was persistent delays in design approvals for their email campaigns. The approval process had become a bottleneck, causing frustration and delays in the campaign launches.

*Action*: To tackle this issue, Sarah employed the "5 Whys" technique in a problem-solving session with the team:

1. *Why are design approvals delayed?* The initial designs often required significant revisions.

2. *Why do the initial designs require significant revisions?* The design team's initial outputs often did not meet the expectations set by the marketing strategy team.

3. *Why were expectations not met?* There was a lack of clear communication and understanding between the design and strategy teams regarding the campaign objectives.

4. *Why was there a lack of clear communication?* The briefs provided to the design team lacked sufficient detail and context.

5. *Why were the briefs inadequate?* The strategy team assumed certain industry knowledge that the designers did not possess.

Based on this analysis, Sarah initiated a series of workshops between the design and strategy teams to align their understanding and expectations. She also updated the briefing process to include detailed explanations and examples to ensure clarity. Furthermore, Sarah established a preliminary review step where designs could be discussed in a less formal setting before formal submission for approval.

These measures streamlined the approval process, significantly reducing delays. The design team was able to produce more accurate initial drafts, and the strategy team was more effective in communicating their needs.

Under Sarah's leadership, AgileCorp's marketing team not only overcame initial hurdles in their Agile adoption but also enhanced their operational efficiency and team morale. Her proactive and inclusive approach to leadership helped in cultivating an environment where continuous improvement was encouraged, and challenges were met with collaborative solutions. This case study underscores the critical role leaders play in ensuring the successful adoption and implementation of Agile methodologies in marketing.

## CONCLUSION

Despite the strong role of individual team members on a scrum team, leaders still have a decisive part to play in their success. By fostering collaboration and communication, and ensuring adaptivity and problem-solving are streamlined and supported, leaders have a critical place in the success of any organization adopting Agile marketing and scrum.

### Notes

1. Ohno, Taiichi (1988). Toyota production system: beyond large-scale production. Portland, OR: Productivity Press. ISBN 0-915299-14-3.

2. Ishikawa, Kaoru. (1968). *Guide to Quality Control.* JUSE.

# CHAPTER 20

# WHERE TO START

Although a team may be ready and excited to adopt scrum for their marketing needs, it makes sense to be careful about how they initiate their first forays into Agile approaches.

The next chapter looks at some specific examples of how scrum and adoption of Agile principles changes some of the ways that a team may currently be approaching their marketing work.

This chapter talks about how to get started with the first few projects by examining a few different approaches.

## PILOT PROJECTS

When considering pilot projects, it's best to implement select elements that don't disrupt the rest of the organization, such as performing the work in two-week sprints, adopting the Agile team approach, or considering performing a pilot project that utilizes Agile methods and a scrum team. See where there are elements that work well, and where there may be others that need to adapt more fully to the organization.

Pick a project or initiative that is not too complex or time-consuming because it's desirable to get learnings from project initiation, execution, as well as wrap-up. Picking too long a project won't yield that critical step of being able to take an objective step back and review it.

It's not uncommon to run several concurrent campaigns to different audience segments. Instead of switching all of the campaign planning and execution to use scrum processes at once, pick one small team and one campaign to start using the process. This might be a paid social media campaign that requires creative assets and integration with a Web site landing page but is limited in scope and timing. That last part is particularly important in order to make sure there are visible results from the effort and to allow the team to give feedback on what worked and what didn't.

### When to Use the Approach

A pilot project is best used when an organization wishes to test Agile methodologies on a small scale before rolling them out more broadly. It's particularly effective in environments where there is skepticism about Agile or where the risk of broader organizational disruption needs to be minimized. This approach allows the team to demonstrate the benefits of Agile in a controlled setting.

### When Not to Use the Approach

Avoid using a pilot project if the organization requires immediate and broad transformation across multiple teams or disciplines. This approach might also be less effective in highly interconnected environments where changes in one team could significantly impact others, making isolated changes less informative.

### Advice on Getting Started

Choose a project that is manageable yet significant enough to showcase tangible benefits. Ensure it involves cross-functional team members to incorporate diverse insights and skills. Set clear objectives and success metrics from the start, and make sure to communicate these goals to all stakeholders to align expectations and support.

## ADVANCE TEAMS

As mentioned in the previous section, initial adoption of scrum can be as affected by the work an individual chooses to perform first as much as it is by the teams chosen to perform the work.

Pick an "advance team" to run the first scrum project and choose the individuals on that team carefully. Make sure they are open to new things, and excited about the possibilities of a more Agile approach.

Don't just pick people that will say "yes," however—make sure that the team members on this advanced team will be honest and share the good things as well as the areas for improvement. After all, continuous improvement is a big part of scrum, and one needs team members that can help improvement happen as quickly as possible.

### When to Use the Approach

Advance teams are suitable when an organization has some experience with Agile practices and wants to deepen their Agile capabilities. This method works well when scaling Agile practices across new areas or larger groups, serving as champions of the change.

### When Not to Use the Approach

Do not use advance teams if the organization is completely new to Agile, as these teams require members who are already somewhat familiar with Agile practices. It's also less suitable in smaller organizations where there aren't enough resources to dedicate a team exclusively to advancing Agile practices.

### Advice on Getting Started

Select team members who are enthusiastic about Agile and possess a mix of skills and influence within the organization. Provide them with advanced training and the authority to make decisions about Agile processes. Their role will be to mentor others, so choose individuals who are respected and possess good communication skills.

## STARTING WITH SPECIFIC DISCIPLINES

Another way to approach initial forays into scrum is to apply it to specific areas of marketing work. In some cases, a digital marketing team that has had past experience working closely with software engineering or Web development teams, might at least have some passing familiarity with Agile approaches, or they might have been part of a scrum team already.

In this case, starting your Agile marketing efforts with a digital marketing team with some prior experience makes it a little simpler to get up to speed and quickly understand some of the unique hurdles that other teams newer to scrum may face when applying these approaches in an organization.

### When to Use the Approach

This approach is ideal when certain departments or disciplines within the organization show a natural affinity or readiness for Agile, such as marketing or product development. It can be particularly effective when these areas are more adaptable or innovative by nature.

### When Not to Use the Approach

Avoid this method if there is a need for a uniform change across the entire organization or if the selected discipline is too isolated, which could prevent the Agile practices from spreading effectively to other areas.

### Advice on Getting Started

Begin by conducting training sessions focused on Agile principles tailored to the specific discipline. Integrate Agile tools and techniques that directly address the unique challenges and workflows of the discipline. Establish clear communication channels between this discipline and others to facilitate knowledge transfer and encourage wider adoption.

## FOCUSED COLLABORATIONS WITH MORE EXPERIENCED TEAMS

Another option is to intentionally partner with another area of the business that is already using a scrum approach. As mentioned earlier, software engineering or Web development teams are often a good partner to pick, both because they are more likely than other teams to have experience with scrum or other Agile-based approaches, and these teams also tend to work on marketing-related projects on a regular basis.

One way to do this is to simply adopt the Web development team's sprint cycle and build schedules and Scrum rituals by using the other team's schedule. The marketing team would still have individual sprint planning, standups, and retrospectives, but the timing of the two respective team's sprints would line up.

Syncing sprints with another team presents the opportunity to share in some of the ritual meetings, which can prove beneficial at times. For instance, a daily standup might be too much to share between a marketing and engineering team, but a retrospective might give everyone the opportunity to share what is working and what isn't with the collaboration.

There will be further exploration of collaborating with other teams in the next part of the book.

### When to Use the Approach

Use this approach when there is an existing successful scrum team within the organization and other teams are looking to adopt Agile practices. This method leverages the existing knowledge and successes of the experienced team to boost the confidence and capabilities of new teams.

### When Not to Use the Approach

This may not be suitable if the experienced scrum team is stretched thin or if their expertise does not easily translate to the needs or functions of the new team. It also requires careful consideration if the organizational culture varies significantly across teams.

### Advice on Getting Started

Facilitate structured collaboration sessions during which members of the new team can observe and participate in scrum events with the experienced team. Consider temporary cross-team assignments to deepen understanding. Ensure that the experienced team has the capacity and support to mentor effectively without impacting their own productivity.

## CONCLUSION

How teams start their adoption of Agile marketing and scrum is important, so it is worth spending time thinking about the best projects and team configurations to start with.

There are likely other scenarios or combinations of the preceding items that might work best in an organization. The best thing to do is to figure out what will work best with teams, organizations, and the tools at one's disposal.

# CHAPTER 21

# AGILE MARKETING IN ACTION

Many teams start a journey toward Agile marketing because of its potential benefits of their output and, thus, the effect it will have on their external customers. While Agile approaches can have a meaningful and measurable impact on end customers, they can also directly and positively impact teams and the internal processes used to get work done. This section explores several ways that Agile approaches, such as using scrum, can help deliver better results more effectively and efficiently.

What's more, Agile principles support systems of continuous improvement, which allow organizations to focus on maximizing results from their efforts.

## MARKETING AND ADVERTISING CAMPAIGNS

When discussing the use of Agile with marketing and advertising campaigns, there are three categories to consider: efficiency, effectiveness, and improvement.

Looking at efficiency and how it corresponds with a marketing and advertising campaigns, here are some ways that Agile approaches help:

- A scrum-based approach to team coordination and campaign asset creation means that one can maximize work on high-priority tasks and items with a self-organizing team.

- The sprint-based model allows teams to set realistic time frames of when assets and deliverables can be delivered, even across different teams like creative, analytics, and others.

When looking at effectiveness and as it pertains to marketing and advertising campaigns, here are some ways that Agile approaches help:

- An Agile mindset includes building in learning and testing from the beginning. Instead of trying to launch a full-featured campaign that tries to anticipate every scenario, an Agile approach allows one to start with a minimum viable product (MVP) and gain quick learnings that will help the rest of the campaign be more effective in the long run.

- This mindset is also beneficial in terms of gaining inputs from a team, rather than a single individual. Because of Agile's focus on democratizing approaches, the full team has the opportunity to weigh in and contribute ideas that can benefit a marketing campaign's effectiveness.

Finally, when looking at continuous improvement in marketing and advertising campaigns, here are some ways that Agile can help:

- An iterative approach to testing and learning means that the results that obtained from marketing and advertising campaigns will build and improve over time due to a consistent approach to determining what works best and where there is room for improvement.

- Continuous improvement methods also mean that the processes used to create campaigns will be improved over time.

### An Example

Here's an example of how Agile improves marketing and advertising campaigns:

- Using a traditional approach, a lot of planning and work goes into building and launching a marketing campaign without the guaranteed success of the initiative, creating risk.

- While research can be done, and past performance of similar campaigns can be compared, there is a lot of effort and time spent across marketing, creative, analytics, engineering, and others to get all of the assets and elements ready for a campaign.

- Because of the amount of planning that goes into the campaign, it can often be difficult to change direction or modify the initiative substantially enough to have the biggest impact.

    ▪   Using an Agile approach, however, builds a minimum viable product (MVP) campaign and iterates and optimizes as things progress. This allows the team to incorporate the latest learnings into their campaign.

This means that the marketing campaign is Agile and adaptive *by design*, and changes and improvements aren't an afterthought.

## CONTENT CREATION

Content is a fundamental part of any marketing initiative, and beyond the content needed for campaigns as were just explored, effectiveness within the process of content creation can make a big difference in how successful a marketing team can be. It's time to delve deeper into content creation using the same three categories of efficiency gains, effectiveness, and the ability for marketing teams to improve their efforts over time.

Looking at efficiency and content creation, here are some ways that Agile approaches help content creation:

    ▪   Agile practices, and scrum in particular, emphasize focusing on the outputs—in this case, content—that will achieve the highest business value for the organization. Therefore, a large content creation task can be split into sprints where teams can focus their energy on the tasks that will have the greatest impact.

    ▪   This approach allows focus which can drive greater efficiency.

Here are some ways that effectiveness in Agile approaches help content creation:

    ▪   Focusing on content that will have the greatest business impact first also means that this content will reach customers first.

    ▪   When high-impact content is prioritized and rolled out to customers, it stands to reason that there will be greater marketing impacts, delivering measurable outcomes.

Finally, when looking at continuous improvement in content creation, here are some ways that Agile approaches help:

    ▪   There are always ways to improve content, whether adding more detail, rewriting to be more succinct, offering supporting links, or helpful videos, images, and other graphics. Agile practices allow for iteration of content over time to become more effective and to base decisions on data from real customers.

- Likewise, with the personalization of marketing content increasing, one can start with an MVP that has a single version of copy and images and then add complexity and variations over time.

### An Example

Here is an example of how Agile improves content creation.

Using a traditional approach, a large set of content of all kinds is sent to a team to create. The team works until all of the work is completed without getting any feedback on if their work is impactful to customers.

However, if an Agile approach is used, batches of content are prioritized with the sets estimated to make the most impact first. Using an iterative, sprint-based approach, content can be rolled out to customers in batches while feedback is collected on its effectiveness. In this case, customers can also include internal audiences, which may be waiting on key components of a campaign or project to continue their work.

The Agile approach allows teams to be most efficient and effective and ultimately deliver the best content to customers.

## ANALYTICS AND REPORTING

Looking at efficiency and analytics and reporting, here are some ways that Agile approaches help:

- There is an abundance of data, whether Web, social, email, advertising analytics, or any other channels and measurements that can be used to gauge the success of one's efforts.
- Using Agile principles to minimize waste and prioritize items that contribute to the greatest business value, teams can focus on their efforts by analyzing and measuring only the metrics that matter.
- Minimizing waste and prioritizing items with the highest business impact also helps reduce being individuals on a team being flooded by dashboards with endless charts that don't directly relate to marketing performance.

When looking at effectiveness and analytics and reporting of marketing efforts, here are some ways that Agile approaches help:

- Using Agile approaches and the focus just discussed that allows one to narrow in on the most meaningful metrics to one's goals means that one can more easily see where their marketing efforts are effective and where they are lagging.
- Agile's focused approach that prioritizes creating business value allows marketing efforts to be laser-focused on achieving meaningful outcomes and keeps the whole team aligned on what success looks like.

Finally, when looking at continuous improvement in analytics and reporting on marketing efforts, here are some ways that Agile approaches help:

- Building on initial successes, it is important that one doesn't simply "set it and forget it" when it comes to achieving their marketing goals.
- Agile's continuous improvement mindset keeps the marketing team continually looking at not only how to achieve better results for their customers but also how to make the work easier and more efficient and to be able to do more with fewer resources.

That's a win–win!

## An Example

Next an example of how Agile improves analytics and reporting.

- Using a traditional approach, there is not a shared understanding of business value, so different teams and team members may prioritize using their own metrics for success.
- Additionally, with a lack of focus and prioritization, it is often difficult to achieve optimal success.
- Finally, once success is achieved, without Agile methods of continuous improvement, there is a danger that results may stagnate, and unnecessarily complex or burdensome processes to measure and produce work may cause long-term inefficiencies and increased time to deliver and even increased costs.

When using an Agile approach, however, there are many benefits:

- Creating business value is central to the team's work, and Agile principles of teamwork, collaboration, and mutual understanding mean that everyone is aligned on what ideal outcomes look like. This includes the analytics and metrics used to measure success.

- This alignment creates greater focus, which allows the team to collaborate more effectively to deliver better results and articulate where improvements are needed.

- Finally, achieving success is only the beginning. Through a process of continuous improvement, the team keeps finding ways to improve the measurement process, as well as the results from customers.

## DIGITAL TRANSFORMATION

Many organizations are undergoing large-scale digital transformations that involve marketing efforts and often include several business areas. Adopting Agile approaches can make the marketing component of a transformation more successful, regardless of whether the entire enterprise utilizes Agile approaches.

Looking at efficiency and digital transformation initiatives, here are some ways that Agile approaches help:

- Digital transformation is generally centered around creating greater business value, improving the customer experience, and improving operational efficiency. Agile principles embrace all of these ideas and align team members around them.

- The Agile mindset can create a more efficient way of rallying a team behind a large-scale initiative such as a digital transformation.

- A sprint-based approach can also be incredibly helpful in digital transformation initiatives because it allows a marketing team to sync with other teams in other areas of the organization to deliver pieces of a larger project.

When looking at effectiveness and digital transformation initiatives, here are some ways that Agile approaches help:

- Prioritization not only helps with efficiency but helps a large project with many moving parts to be more effective more quickly.

▨ Agile's focus on prioritizing high-impact work based on creating business value means that the most important pieces get worked on first, showing quick wins that benefit the business, the customer, and the team's morale.

Finally, when looking at continuous improvement as the team undergoes digital transformation, here are some ways that Agile approaches help:

▨ The most successful digital transformation initiatives are those that are done using an iterative Agile approach.

▨ This means proofs of concept (POCs) and minimum viable products (MVPs) are created to test a hypothesis, a set of integrations, processes, or a customer experience.

▨ Using a continuous improvement approach means that a daunting task that is part of a multiyear cross-departmental initiative can be broken down into more manageable pieces, and each can be tested and improved over time.

### An Example

Here is an example of how Agile improves digital transformation.

Using a traditional approach:

▨ A multiyear plan with many requirements is planned and designed using the "waterfall" method discussed in an earlier course.

▨ This means that while there is a detailed plan with dependencies, roles, and responsibilities, there is also a lack of flexibility if external or internal factors change during the course of the transformation.

▨ Because of this, a digital transformation initiative can be derailed in multiple ways if there is a major shift in the market, platforms change, or a customer shift or need becomes apparent midway through the initiative.

When using an Agile approach, however, there are several advantages:

▨ While there is a goal for transformation, planning is broken into more manageable sprints, where adjustments can be made based on internal or external factors, which may require rethinking part of the initiative.

▨ This sprint-based approach focused on delivering the most business value as soon as possible allows a multiyear project to start showing results much more quickly.

■ Through a series of proofs of concepts (POCs) and minimum viable products (MVPs), this means that a digital transformation that might take eighteen to twenty-four months to complete may start showing results and providing teams with initial learning on how to improve in a matter of months. This helps justify the investment much more quickly.

## CONCLUSION

Of course, there are many other potential applications of scrum in marketing efforts, but hopefully these examples show a sense of how one can apply Agile principles and practices to their specific needs.

The next chapter explores how to measure the success of one's efforts to incorporate scrum into marketing practices.

# CHAPTER 22

# MEASURING SUCCESS

In addition to the success of the marketing initiatives and campaigns that are the end result of the work, such as product sales, customer engagement, or return on ad spend (ROAS), an Agile team should continually strive to improve the way that work is delivered. This requires its own set of metrics and measurements. This chapter will focus on one metric in particular: velocity, and then briefly explore several others.

## VELOCITY

Velocity is a metric that quantifies the amount of work a team can complete in a single sprint or iteration, typically measured in story points or any other consistent unit of measurement the team agrees upon. This key performance indicator helps teams predict how quickly they can work through the items in the product backlog, providing a clear picture of the team's capacity and helping in future sprint planning.

Velocity is calculated by summing up the points for all fully completed user stories at the end of each sprint. It's important that the stories are fully completed; partial work does not count because unfinished tasks do not deliver value until they are complete. By tracking velocity over several sprints, marketing teams can establish an average velocity, which can then be used to forecast the completion of future projects and sprints. This measurement not only aids in setting realistic expectations but also in adjusting workloads for optimal team performance.

Several factors can impede a marketing team's velocity. Common obstacles include:

- overcommitment to too many tasks
- underestimation of the effort required for tasks
- lack of clear priorities
- insufficient team skills or resources
- external dependencies that cause delays

Interruptions and scope changes during the sprint can also reduce velocity, as can team dynamics and communication issues.

## Improving Velocity

Improving velocity begins with refining the estimation process to ensure it accurately reflects the complexity and effort of tasks. Regular and effective backlog grooming sessions can help in clearly defining and prioritizing tasks based on their value and urgency. Streamlining processes and removing impediments promptly during the sprint also contributes significantly to maintaining or increasing velocity. Additionally, continuous team training and development ensure that all members are well-equipped to handle their responsibilities efficiently.

Increasing velocity should not compromise the quality of the work delivered. To maintain this balance, it's crucial to establish robust definition of done (DoD) criteria that encompass not only task completion but also quality benchmarks. Regular code reviews, pair work, or, in the context of marketing, content and campaign reviews can help maintain high standards. Automating repetitive tasks and testing can also save time and reduce errors, thereby supporting both velocity and quality.

Thus, velocity is a critical metric that represents the amount of work a team can complete in a given sprint. It is measured by adding up the points for completed tasks and helps in planning and forecasting. Challenges to velocity can arise from various internal and external factors, but with careful planning, clear communication, and continuous improvement practices, these can be overcome. Balancing the drive for increased velocity with the need to maintain high quality is essential for sustaining long-term success in marketing environments.

## OTHER METRICS TO MEASURE SUCCESS

In addition to increasing a team's velocity, there are many other ways to measure success that are specific to scrum.

1.  *Sprint burndown chart*: Mentioned earlier in the book, this chart tracks the amount of work completed from the sprint backlog over the duration of the sprint against the total work that was originally planned. It helps teams visualize daily progress and identify whether they are on track to complete the work by the end of the sprint.

2.  *Release burndown chart*: Similar to the sprint burndown, the release burndown chart tracks the remaining work across multiple sprints toward a larger release. This is useful for teams working on bigger projects that span multiple sprints, providing a macro view of progress toward long-term goals.

3.  *Lead time*: Lead time measures the time taken from when work begins on an item until it is fully completed. This metric is crucial for assessing the team's efficiency in processing tasks through the workflow.

4.  *Cycle time*: Cycle time tracks the amount of time it takes for a team to complete a task from the moment it starts working on it. This metric is key to understanding process efficiency and can help identify bottlenecks in the workflow.

5.  *Cumulative flow diagram*: This diagram provides a visual representation of the different stages of work for a project over time. It helps teams visualize work in progress, completed work, and work that hasn't been started yet, thus identifying any potential bottlenecks.

6.  *Employee satisfaction*: Agile and scrum also focus on the team's dynamics and morale. Regularly surveying team satisfaction and using this data as a feedback mechanism can help measure the cultural impact of scrum adoption.

7.  *Retrospective action item completion*: The success rate of implementing action items identified in retrospectives can indicate how effectively a team is adapting and improving its processes.

These metrics, when monitored regularly, can provide a comprehensive view of the team's performance and the overall success of scrum adoption in an Agile marketing setting. It's not necessary to measure all of them to be able to gauge improvements or areas of weakness, but collecting data on several may provide insights into the bigger picture.

## OVERALL MARKETING IMPROVEMENT

Of course, in addition to these, another way to measure the adoption of scrum is to look at improvements in marketing-specific metrics. These do not require adopting new measurements, but instead require one to look at the success of their marketing efforts before and after their teams adopted Agile approaches.

Thus, using existing marketing metrics product sales, customer engagement, customer satisfaction, or other KPIs, it will become apparent how building a nimbler and more responsive team can provide customers with better and more relevant marketing content and initiatives. This, in turn will result in a compelling before and after story.

Doing this, however, requires being able to have consistent "apples to apples" metrics that allow team members and stakeholders to realistically compare the results of their efforts before and after adopting scrum.

## AGILECORP'S AGILE MARKETING GROWING PAINS

AgileCorp's marketing team faced some significant hurdles during the initial stages of their scrum adoption. Despite enthusiasm for the new Agile approach, the team struggled with meeting sprint commitments and delivering projects on schedule. Key issues included inaccurate estimation of task complexities and a lack of understanding of team capacity, which led to frequent spillovers of work and delayed campaign launches. The unpredictability of their delivery schedule caused frustration within the team and skepticism among stakeholders about the effectiveness of scrum practices.

To address these challenges, the team decided to focus on two critical metrics: velocity and lead time. They began by tracking the number of story points completed in each sprint to measure their velocity. This metric provided clear insight into the actual capacity of the team and helped in future sprint planning by setting more realistic expectations based on historical performance data. Additionally, they measured the Lead Time for each task to identify where delays were occurring in their process. This measurement highlighted significant bottlenecks in the creative development and approval stages that were previously unnoticed.

With a better understanding of their true velocity and the specific areas causing delays, AgileCorp's marketing team implemented targeted improvements.

They adjusted their sprint planning to better match the team's realistic capacity, ensuring that commitments were achievable. They also introduced more frequent check-ins during the sprints, specifically around the creative development phases, to ensure that any blockers were addressed promptly. To improve lead time, they streamlined the approval process by setting predefined criteria and involving decision-makers early in the creative process.

These adjustments led to a significant improvement in the team's performance. The more accurate setting of expectations and the focused resolution of bottlenecks increased the team's velocity by 30% within a few months. Moreover, the reduction in lead time enhanced the overall agility of the team, allowing them to adapt quickly to new market opportunities and feedback. The successful adjustment of their scrum practices restored confidence in the Agile transformation among stakeholders and contributed to a more motivated and cohesive team. This case study illustrates the power of key performance metrics to diagnose and resolve issues in Agile marketing practices, ultimately leading to enhanced productivity and better alignment with business goals.

## CONCLUSION

Adoption alone is not enough to be successful with scrum in marketing. As it is with marketing work, one needs to measure their success in order to know the areas where improvement is needed, and the areas where the team can celebrate success.

While there are many methods that can be used to measure improvement, it's best to pick only a few to avoid being overwhelmed, but more than a single method in order to gain perspective to spot areas to be improved.

This chapter discussed some specific behaviors and approaches to keep in mind, and the next chapter will talk about some mindset shifts and some of the philosophical differences between traditional marketing methods and Agile approaches.

# CHAPTER 23

# BUSINESS VALUE

While the Agile principles make sense to many and might be a compelling enough reason to consider this approach, adopting scrum for marketing ultimately needs to bring a return to the business. Fortunately, for businesses using Agile, some compelling numbers support this. According to a report by Simform, companies that adopt Agile practices achieved 60% higher revenue growth, and 49% saw increased customer satisfaction, which can lead to sustained growth.[1]

This book previously discussed that the product owner's role is to prioritize and deliver business value by ensuring that the appropriate items from the product backlog make it into the current sprint backlog and the current iteration of the product.

This means that, in marketing terms, the product owner needs to ensure that the most value to both customers and business is delivered first and foremost when approaching an Agile marketing initiative or campaign. Of course, the term "business value" may seem more straightforward than it actually is to define.

Additionally, despite a wealth of writing and documentation on Agile principles, scrum practices, and other topics, the concept of business value is one that is the least well-defined.

## DEFINING "BUSINESS VALUE"

Simply put, the business value is the return on investment achieved by an initiative. But determining that value is more difficult than it might seem. While it may be easy to define, it is often much harder to quantify.

## LEADERS AND STAKEHOLDERS

In addition to the question of what business value is, and just as important, who is chiefly concerned with realizing business value?

While everyone on a scrum team has a responsibility to create a great work product, a product owner's role is directly and specifically related to creating and delivering what executives need to ensure the business is strategically and financially successful, which is also a definition of business value. In a discussion of business value and Agile marketing, a key stakeholder would be the chief marketing officer, although there may be several roles in an organization that a marketing team

One of the big implications of business value is how leadership and stakeholders perceive the results and outcomes of work performed by the team that the product owner prioritizes work for. In other words, the business value is how the output of teams is measured in relation to their importance to the business.

For instance, a marketing team whose primarily accomplishment was gaining more Instagram followers for the company's profile might not be deemed as a key contributor to business value the way that a team that drove a 25% increase in sales from marketing efforts. In the former's case, there would need to be a strong relationship between an increase in social media followers and revenue to convince an executive that they were outperforming the team that drove the sales increase.

Of course, business value does not always need to directly translate to revenue, although that is often the case, as will be explored now.

## TANGIBLE AND INTANGIBLE BUSINESS VALUE

An often helpful approach to understanding business value splits everything into two categories: tangible and intangible.

The tangible business value consists of all the things that can quantify, and is often related to revenue and costs, although not exclusively. However, tangible business value does always directly impact the bottom line. It includes things like:

- revenue growth
- lost revenue
- increased/decreased expenses

- return on investment (ROI)
- cycle time reduction
- conversion rates
- customer retention
- percentage of market share
- decreased work effort
- sprint velocity

While some of these might be easier to calculate than others, they all are quantifiable, and once a measurement is agreed upon, it can be relatively easy to set benchmarks for future reference, as well as to compare one requirement to another. After all, comparison is a key action related to business value as product owners are likely to need to compare several potential activities to prioritize, and their relative business value is a key way they will know what do recommend to add to a sprint backlog.

While *tangible* business value is quantifiable, *intangible* business value includes things that, while able to be measured, may not have as direct an impact on the bottom line or may be more difficult to measure their direct impact on the bottom line. Intangible business value includes things like:

- brand reputation
- positive/negative customer sentiment
- net promoter score (NPS)
- employee satisfaction
- analytics reliability
- campaign bugs/issues
- legal and contractual compliance
- regulatory compliance
- risk avoidance or mitigation
- reduced resources

As can be seen, it can be more difficult to calculate the financial value of some of these items. As an example, what is the impact of an increase in brand reputation to the bottom line, and furthermore what metrics are used to measure brand reputation? There are several ways to do this, but many companies have not defined a correlation between the two.

Likewise, net promoter score (NPS) is quantifiable by using surveys of customers, but many companies have not tied that score to a direct increase or decrease in revenue.

Even more complicated are things like risk mitigation or avoidance of a potentially negative outcome in general. These can be difficult to calculate in terms of financial metrics, yet can have a severe impact if they are not avoided.

## CUSTOMER VALUE PYRAMID

A different way to look at business value is by using the business value pyramid. This approach starts at the bottom with the more basic or functional benefits and builds toward the more transformative values. Note that this example is looking at benefits in terms of the customer only, not in terms of the business. For this reason, if this is used, it is most likely used in addition to other more financial and risk-oriented methods of measuring business value.

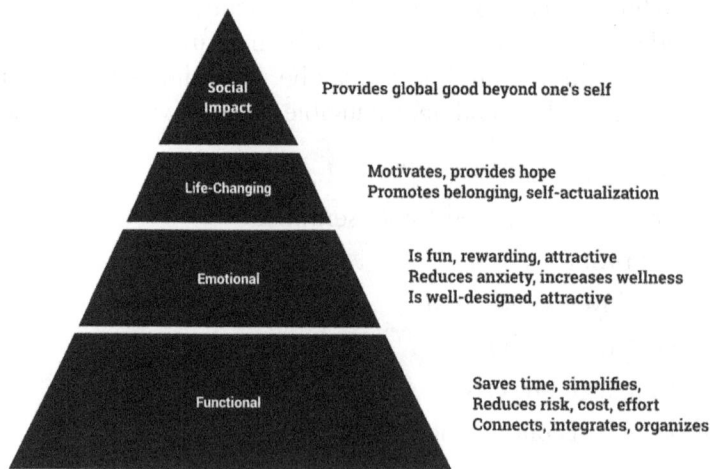

**FIGURE 23.1** Business value pyramid.

The following list describes each element of the pyramid (Figure 23.1) from the bottom up:

- The bottom of the pyramid begins with the functional elements. These are things that, for instance, save time or simplify, reduce risk, cost, or effort, or connect, integrate, and organize things more effectively.

- The next step in the pyramid includes the emotional elements. These include things that are fun, rewarding, or attractive, or things that reduce anxiety or increase wellness, as well as those things that are well-designed and attractive.

- The next step is life-changing elements. These motivate and provide hope or promote belonging or self-actualization.

- At the top of the customer benefits pyramid are those items that transcend an individual customer and provide global or societal impact or good. While not every product or decision can do this, it is a good exercise for businesses to undertake as they calculate the business value of their work.

## CALCULATING BUSINESS VALUE

There is no single way to calculate business value, and methods can range from the very simple to much more complex. But as seen from both the categorization of tangible and intangible values, as well as the business value pyramid, there are many factors that can contribute, yet quantifying each individual value and being able to understand relative value between them can be a challenge.

To get a better understanding of some ways to calculate business value, two different methods for evaluating will be looked at. They are:

- simple business value calculation
- business value realization formula

### Simple Business Value Calculation

While the previous examples provide some robust methods to calculate business value, there can be a much simpler method, which is to use a straightforward return on investment (ROI) calculation, which takes the benefits minus costs into account. Figure 23.2 exemplifies a simple version of the formula.

$$\text{ROI} = \frac{(\text{Benefits - Costs})}{\text{Costs}}$$

*FIGURE 23.2* Simple calculation of business value.

ROI is calculated by subtracting the costs from the benefits and then dividing that difference by the costs. This is very straightforward when "benefits" is calculated in terms of something like revenue which can easily quantified. When the benefits are intangibles, then an arbitrary number must be assigned to them to properly complete this.

For many, this can be an easy way to make a quick decision when required, but it may not be robust enough to handle complex business needs and instances where there are multiple aspects that need to be prioritized and accounted for.

### Business Value Realization Formula

For more complex calculations that follow a similar approach to the ROI model, this section explores the business value realization formula introduced by Andrew Kaminski and modified slightly.[2]

It is a relatively simple formula that looks like the following:

$$\textit{The formula: } BV = a(BV1) + b(BV2) - c(BV3)$$
$$\textit{Business Value} = BV$$

BV1, BV2, and BV3 are each different elements of business value. For instance, the potential to generate revenue, increase customer retention, delivery efficiency, and so on.

The variables a, b, and c equal different weights of relative importance for each item. For instance, BV1 may be more important to the business than BV2. Therefore, "a" would have a higher value.

Subtract the last item (dBV3) if this is a negative value. For instance, if there is a risk to the organization, one might weigh that highly (i.e., "c" would be a high value) and subtract it since it is a negative value.

### A Real-World Scenario

This section makes this a little more real by plugging in some real-world scenarios.

Values are assigned based such as the following:

- BV1, the first variable, which is of potential benefit to the organization = potential to generate revenue = 4 (out of 5)

- BV2 = the second variable, which is another benefit to the organization. This is defined as the potential to increase customer retention = 3 (out of 5)

- BV3 = the third variable is actually a risk or detriment, or the cost to implement = 5 (out of 5). Because it is a risk, subtract this variable's value instead of adding it.

- A, or the first weighted variable = priority of BV1 (potential to generate revenue) = 3 (out of 5). This means we value the potential to generate revenue as a 3 out of 5.

- b = priority of BV2 (potential to increase retention) = 4 (out of 5). This means we value the potential to increase retention as a 4 out of 5.

- c = priority of BV3 (cost to implement) = 4 (out of 5). This means we value the cost of implementing this initiative as a 4 out of 5.

To replace the values with numbers, the formula is:

$$BV = 3(4) + 4(3) - 4(5) = 4$$

What should be done with this formula?

### Which Initiative Should One Invest In?

The best way to use this method of business value realization is to prioritize initiatives, whether marketing campaigns, new projects like a Web site or mobile app redesign, or any initiative that requires large investments of time and resources.

When one is able to calculate the business value for multiple current or potential projects, it can help to understand where further investments should be made.

For instance, if one has three initiatives, one with a business value of 12, another with a value of 18, and a third with a business value of 5.5, which would they invest in? With that context alone, it's a no-brainer to invest in initiative 2 since its value of 18 is 33% more than the next most valuable initiative.

## DEFINING BUSINESS VALUE WITHIN AN ORGANIZATION

While there can be commonly used methods of calculating business value, two organizations might value the same item differently. This is why methods such as the business value realization formula include relative weights as part of their calculation. It lets one adjust the priority for their company, even allowing for changes over time.

For this reason, it is important to clearly understand how an organization prioritizes and values items and to pay careful attention to trends and shifts over time. What might be valuable at one point in time might change based on internal factors, such as cost-cutting measures, or external ones, such as competitive pressures.

## CONCLUSION

In a scrum team, the product owner is chiefly responsible for understanding and articulating business value, but it is important that they communicate this to the rest of their team.

The main reason this is so important is that because scrum masters and product teams work collaboratively and democratically, they can ensure their work is delivering the maximum value when they have a solid understanding of business priorities.

Additionally, the nature of Agile allows teams to respond to changes and fluctuations over time. Understanding shifting priorities allows the full Agile marketing team to anticipate and respond to necessary changes based on internal and external factors.

### Notes

1.  Akiwatkar, Rohit. (November 10, 2022). "Agile adoption statistics: How is software development changing?" Simform blog. *https://www.simform. com/blog/state-of-agile-adoption/*. Retrieved January 21, 2023.

2.  Kaminski, Andre. Measuring Business Value in DevOps and Agile Projects. April 14, 2019. *https://www.linkedin.com/pulse/measuring-business-value-devops-agile-projects-andre-kaminski/* Retrieved January 21, 2023.

# CHAPTER 24

# CONTINUOUS IMPROVEMENT

Central to Agile principles is a focus on the regular and systematic improvement of the work output, the way teams communicate and work together, and the improvement of the work process. This all adds up to what is termed *continuous improvement*, or CI. While CI is not "officially" a part of scrum or Kanban, it is certainly something that an Agile marketing team will want to embrace and adopt.

This chapter starts on continuous improvement in action by defining what continuous improvement is by looking at it in three ways.

1. First, in general, *continuous improvement* is analyzing both outcomes and the processes that create them and finding ways to adjust and optimize them incrementally over time.

2. Second, in terms of Agile or scrum, *continuous improvement* is a core part of these practices that are implemented in areas like the sprint retrospective and sprint planning to ensure that the product iteration, as well as the processes used to do the work, is always running at peak efficiency and effectiveness.

3. Finally, in terms of Agile marketing, *continuous improvement* is the practice and mindset of ensuring that marketing campaigns and programs are analyzed, adjusted, and revised to produce maximum results while being produced with maximum efficiency by internal teams.

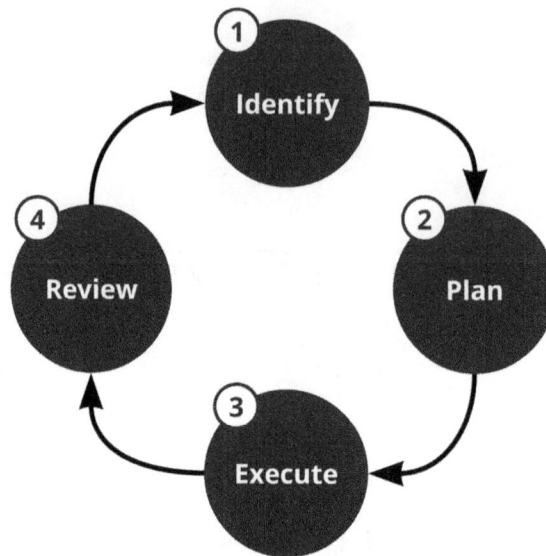

**FIGURE 24.1** Continuous improvement diagram.

Continuous improvement can be explained in 4 steps, as featured in the diagram (Figure 24.1):

1. *Identify*: Here are steps in the process workflow or methods used in projects and campaigns that might pose an opportunity for improvement.

2. *Plan*: In this step, there is collaboration on the team, including discussions and other work around improving the processes and methods. The sprint planning process is a great time to do this.

3. *Execute*: In this third step, changes identified and planned earlier are implemented into the workflow. The execute phase can be integrated into a sprint backlog, and the work can be performed as part of a sprint, for instance.

4. *Review*: In this final step, the team will review how effective the changes were and if there is still room for improvement. If there can be further improvements, identifying and planning can then be performed in a new continuous improvement cycle. A good time for the review phase is at a sprint retrospective.

Once this process has been completed, it starts again, similar to how a new sprint begins in the scrum process once another one has ended. Keep in mind it's possible to utilize this continuous improvement model while engaging in scrum practices within sprint planning, sprints, and retrospectives.

## WHY IS CONTINUOUS IMPROVEMENT SO IMPORTANT?

Why is continuous improvement so important when implementing Agile marketing practices? The following list explores two big reasons why.

- The first way to look at this is in the potential gains marketing campaigns and initiatives stand to benefit from. Unlike traditional methods of marketing that plan months in advance and offer less room for modifications and adjustments, Agile and scrum practices encourage making tangible changes to improve outcomes. These practices also encourage changes in how the work is performed. The overall culture of improvement fostered by this means that teams are likely to see quicker gains in improvement.

- Another way to explain the benefits of continuous improvement is to understand and embrace the fact that teams will not always make the best decisions and choices the first time, but that is okay. In fact, it is better to learn what *doesn't* work as quickly as possible, in order to move on to the next ideas that will work better until the most optimal way of marketing and reaching audiences is found. The culture of continuous improvement also openly shares successes and failures, knowing that both are critical to achieving end goals.

## THE COSTS OF AVOIDING CONTINUOUS IMPROVEMENT

Another reason why continuous improvement is so important when engaging in Agile practices is that *not* implementing feedback and learning has two types of cost.

1. The first type is a loss in efficiency or an opportunity cost. Remember, teams are engaging in Agile practices for a reason. The incremental approach that sprints allow means teams can learn quickly and apply those learnings to the next sprint and iteration. If they fail to utilize the benefits of sprint retrospectives and other agile practices emphasizing continuous improvement, they will lose efficiency and effectiveness. There will still be some benefits from a sprint-based approach, but one of the major ones will not be utilized.

2. The second cost is a loss of morale in the team performing the work. Think about it: If one is on a team and provides helpful feedback that can help improve both the outcomes of their work as well as the efficiency of how they *achieve* those outcomes and their ideas are never listened to or

implemented, it's going to cause a lessening of morale. This will further reduce efficiency and possible outcomes and may worsen if this morale loss spreads among the entire team.

## TWO TYPES OF CONTINUOUS IMPROVEMENT

There are two ways to look at continuous improvement, and the following sections will look at each in more detail.

1.  The first type of continuous improvement is *internal improvement*, which often includes process enhancements and other ways of enhancing the way that work is performed.

2.  The second type is called *customer-facing improvement*, which, in the case of Agile marketing, most often includes the sales and marketing results gotten from campaigns and projects.

### Continuous Improvement Type 1: Internal Improvement

The first category of internal improvement, or how well processes and teams work to achieve goals, can include several things. For instance, how much time does it take to create a new advertising campaign from start to finish? What hurdles need to be overcome to get from concept to launch, including the marketing strategy and goals, the creative direction, the technical execution, vendor and partner alignment, and more? What are the areas that seem to take too long or go too much back and forth?

Additionally, how many defects are there in items created, such as new Web site landing pages for the campaigns? Or, how many rounds of revision does marketing collateral require before it is ready to launch? Measurements of these types of internal improvement include measuring the time to launch a campaign, the overall hours spent per project or campaign, or the vendor costs per campaign.

Teams might be capturing some of these in their internal project management or workflow applications already, or they might need to find ways to start measuring and tracking these things to implement them into a system of continuous improvement. Either way, doing this and combining it with a sprint-based approach will allow a team to identify and improve areas that are current or potential problems that either delay the launch of projects or campaigns or inhibit their effectiveness due to defects and bugs more quickly.

## CONTINUOUS IMPROVEMENT TYPE 2: CUSTOMER-FACING IMPROVEMENT

The second continuous improvement category is customer-facing improvement, which includes the results from customers interacting and engaging with marketing campaigns and projects.

This category includes things like the effectiveness of a campaign promoting a new product or service. Or, it could include individual marketing tactics and approaches, such as advertising, social media, or email. It could also include overall customer sentiment about a brand, a product or service being offered, or an individual experience.

Customer-facing improvement is measured through many of the measurements probably already being used to measure the effectiveness of marketing efforts. For instance, product sales or signups for a new subscription service can measure the effectiveness of a campaign. Advertising clicks or email opens could measure the tactic of advertising or email marketing.

Finally, customer satisfaction (CSAT) or net promoter score (NPS) can measure customer sentiment and their opinion of a brand, product, service, or even individual experience.

## INTEGRATING CI INTO SCRUM SPRINTS

With a good understanding of continuous improvement (CI) to match previous work on understanding sprints, it is possible to more closely tie the two concepts together (See Figure 24.2).

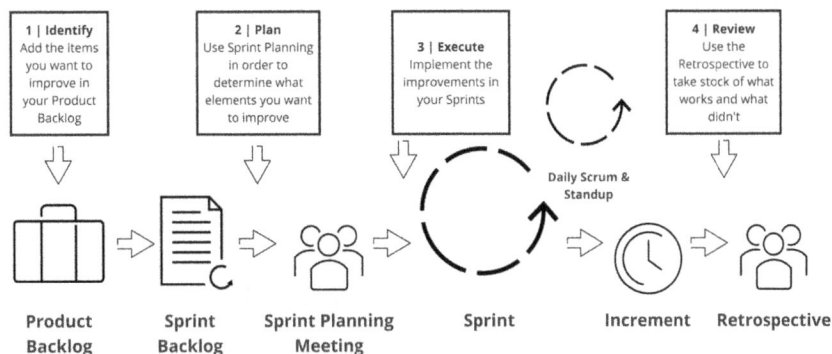

**FIGURE 24.2** Continuous improvement and the scrum workflow.

At the beginning of a product or campaign, teams will have several items they want to create and processes that will need to be implemented. Whether this is a marketing campaign that spans several mediums, or a project such as the launch of a new Web site, there will be a product backlog of items that need to be accomplished. This will incorporate the "identify" portion of continuous improvement. Note that this list will need to be revisited at several points throughout the campaign or project because the retrospectives will encourage this.

Next, begin sprint planning and create the sprint backlog. This aligns perfectly with the "plan" phase of continuous improvement. In this phase, use the sprint planning process to plan how to implement the improvements identified and prioritized to move to the current sprint.

Following this, move to the work performed within a sprint and, with it, accomplish the "execute" phase of continuous improvement. While performing the work, the team should pay close attention to what works well and what does not.

Finally, the sprint retrospective aligns perfectly with the "review" phase of continuous improvement. In the retrospective, teams will take stock of what worked, what could be improved, and how this might be implemented in a future sprint. As noted before, these improvements should include both the results of the work, such as the open and click-through rates of an email campaign, and the process by which that email campaign was created. The team will then take those ideas of how to improve and start the process all over again as they plan the next sprint.

## ENCOURAGING HOLISTIC FEEDBACK

Many components are necessary to ensure an organization, marketing team, and marketing campaigns and efforts can benefit from continuous improvement. This chapter has talked about several of them already, but there is one important one not yet discussed in as much detail.

This is the importance of getting good ideas and information from the entire team working on marketing efforts. While some team members may be outspoken and provide feedback willingly, encouraging holistic feedback from the entire group is vital to ensure that the best ideas are heard, which can solve the most diverse set of issues.

Retrospective leaders must find ways to draw out those that may be quieter or less eager to share feedback in front of a group. Instead of waiting for people to speak up, create a format for collecting feedback that allows everyone to have a voice and a chance to share. Collect this feedback visually so everyone can see it side by side.

Additionally, the team's culture should encourage positive and negative feedback without fear of anyone taking it personally. This can take practice, even for seasoned teams, particularly when working with a new group of people. But with practice, it will enable better results and a closer team dynamic.

## CONCLUSION

Despite a formalized system of continuous improvement not being outlined in scrum, the concept of continually making work output as well as processes better and better performing over time is inherent in the original Agile principles. Additionally, as this chapter has shown, continuous improvement can be incorporated into the sprint process effectively.

# WORKING COLLABORATIVELY WITH SCRUM

Now that we have explored the fundamental principles of Agile, as well as the components and individual roles of scrum as applied to marketing, it is time to look at how Agile marketing fits within the larger context of an organization.

After all, marketing teams, whether they embrace Agile principles or not, are part of a system of teams, processes, and technology that need to work together to perform the work necessary to grow and maintain a business.

This part of the book will be looking at how Agile marketing teams can be effective in their work where collaboration is a necessary component of success. This collaboration may take many forms, and may involve working with other teams using scrum, or teams using other Agile approaches. It may also involve working with teams that use waterfall methods and thus require innovative approaches to incorporating a team's sprint-based approaches with a more linear method of delivering work.

CHAPTER 25

# WORKING WITH OTHER AGILE TEAMS

A marketing team may either be new to scrum or have been using it for some time, while other teams may have varying levels of experience with Agile principles as well as with scrum specifically.

After all, marketing teams regularly collaborate with others in an organization, such as software engineering or data teams, customer service teams, sales teams, and many others. While all of these groups may not be using scrum, if your team does, chances are at least one other team is also doing so.

This chapter will discuss what to keep in mind when working with other nonmarketing teams utilizing Agile practices, particularly scrum. These include the following:

- the team's adherence to scrum practices and finding ways to standardize that adherence
- syncing sprints across teams to deliver work most effectively and efficiently
- platform considerations in terms of Agile project management and requirements gathering

## ADHERENCE TO SCRUM PRACTICES AND AGILE PRINCIPLES

An important consideration when working with other teams who have adopted Agile practices is how strictly they adhere to scrum practices and Agile principles. There are a few questions to be asked as other teams' adherence to scrum is evaluated.

### Sprint Backlog Behaviors

How strict are the other teams about maintaining their sprint backlog? In other words, do they "work in" additional items without a formal review process? This might affect the ability to ensure they can complete items you are depending on getting done in their sprint cycle.

### Shared Definition of Business Value

What is the other team's definition of business value? The concept of business value will be reviewed in more detail later in this chapter. It was reviewed in an earlier chapter as one of the key drivers of prioritization of items within a sprint backlog. If another Agile team doesn't share the same definition of business value, it's entirely possible that their prioritization of specific items may not match yours. This can cause a mismatch of deliverables over time and unnecessarily delay items you and your team deem high value.

### How Feedback Is Shared and the Role of the Retrospective

Finally, will the other team take external inputs in their sprint retrospectives? If you and your Agile team have areas for improvement or areas of strength to share, it can be incredibly valuable to other Agile teams within the organization. They have to be open to this feedback, however. When done well, this can be incredibly beneficial.

Likewise, the previously mentioned suggestions should be considered for your own Agile marketing team. The goal should be to make it as easy and beneficial as possible to work with the team!

## SYNCING SPRINTS ACROSS TEAMS FOR CAMPAIGN-BASED WORK

The following sections talk about syncing scrum sprints across multiple Agile teams to ensure the most continuous and efficient results for Agile marketing efforts.

### Sprint Length

First, consider the length and start time of the different teams' sprints. Generally speaking, the duration will be either two or four weeks, and the implications are obvious. If one team is on a two-week sprint cycle, and another team is on a four-week cycle, there may be two weeks of "downtime" to wait on an item that is part of a critical path.

For instance, if a team needs to launch a new advertising campaign in two weeks, but their technology team is on a four-week sprint cycle, the advertising campaign may be at risk of not launching on time if it takes the full four-week sprint to finish a related task.

### Sprint Synchronization

Sprint start time is another key consideration. For instance, if two teams have the same sprint start date, there may not be enough time to prioritize items from one product backlog to get them into another Agile team's backlog for prioritization.

For this reason, one team may want to end their sprints one day earlier to ensure they have enough time to perform a retrospective, then have the sprint prioritization begin in time to work with another Agile team to ensure it can be added to their queue.

### Sprint Backlog Coordination

Finally, teams should ensure they thoroughly understand the inputs and requirements needed to provide another Agile team to ensure they have enough information to add an item to their sprint backlog and understand its priority.

Teams that work together often will generally understand these things already, but if there are new team members, particularly product owners or scrum masters, they will want to ensure that all involved have the latest information.

## THE SCRUM OF SCRUMS

The *scrum of scrums* is a coordination technique used in organizations with multiple teams working on the same project or interconnected projects. This method is particularly useful in large-scale scrum implementations, where individual teams' activities may impact one another.

The main goal of a scrum of scrums is to ensure that teams are aligned with the project's overall direction and dependencies and roadblocks are managed effectively across teams. In practice, it functions as a higher-level stand-up meeting where representatives—often the scrum masters—from each team meet to discuss their progress, challenges, and plans.

### Areas to Avoid

While the scrum of scrums can significantly enhance interteam coordination, several pitfalls can hinder its effectiveness:

1. *Lack of clarity in communication*: If team representatives are not clear in conveying their teams' updates or issues, it can lead to misunderstandings and misalignments that compound delays across teams.

2. *Inconsistency in meetings*: Irregular scheduling of these meetings or failure to hold them can lead to lapses in synchronization, causing teams to drift from the project's main objectives or duplicate efforts.

3. *Domination by certain teams*: Sometimes, more vocal teams might dominate the discussion, overshadowing quieter teams which may also have critical input or pressing issues.

### Running a Successful Scrum of Scrums

To maximize the benefits of a scrum of scrums and mitigate potential drawbacks, consider the following approaches used to be successful in a smaller setting, though be ready to deal with them at a more complex level because of the sizes of the teams involved:

1. *Regular and structured meetings*: Ensure that the scrum of scrums is held at a regular frequency, ideally at the same time and place to maintain routine and to help multiple participants from the different teams to be able to plan with regularity. The meeting should be time-boxed to remain focused and efficient, similar to daily stand-ups in individual teams.

2. *Clear agenda and documentation*: Each session should have a clear agenda, and minutes should be documented and shared with all participants, often with a representative from each team taking the lead on sharing and disseminating information. This practice helps keep meetings on track and ensures that all points of discussion are recorded for future reference.

3. *Focused representation*: Each team should send a representative who is knowledgeable and empowered to make decisions or commitments on behalf of their team. This often means the scrum master, but in some cases, it could be a technical lead or another role depending on the discussion's focus.

4. *Resolve dependencies and blockers*: Use the scrum of scrums primarily to address and plan around dependencies between teams and to bring up and resolve blockers that affect multiple teams' progress.

By understanding and implementing these practices, organizations can ensure that their scrum of scrums meetings enhance collaboration and efficiency across teams, driving larger project successes in an integrated Agile environment.

## MULTICOMPANY PROJECT WORK

Most of what has and will be discussed in this book looks at Agile approaches within a single company, but in-house marketers frequently work with external agencies and consultancies to plan, execute, and measure their work.

For this reason, it is important to consider how a multicompany project would be managed, and how this impacts the areas discussed earlier, such as the following:

- sprint length and synchronization
- sprint backlog planning
- feedback loops that utilize retrospectives
- A scrum of scrums to coordinate all the teams working on a project

Strong project management is required, but these initiatives can be successful when the preceding items are accounted for, and when an agreement that continuous improvement of processes is a shared goal.

## AGILECORP'S MULTITEAM SPRINT ALIGNMENT

The marketing team at AgileCorp was gearing up for a major product launch that involved close collaboration between the marketing and software engineering teams.

Both teams adopted scrum methodologies, but with a crucial difference in their sprint schedules: The marketing team operated on three-week sprints, while the software engineering team utilized two-week sprints. This discrepancy in sprint length led to coordination challenges, impacting the timely rollout of interdependent tasks crucial for the product launch of their new app marketplace, which had high expectations for driving revenue in the organization.

There were several challenges that this misalignment of sprint schedules cause, including the following:

1. *Misalignment of deliverables*: The marketing team's longer sprint cycles often meant that they were out of sync with the faster-paced software team, leading to delays in receiving the latest product updates and features. This misalignment affected the marketing team's ability to plan and execute campaigns that were dependent on software releases, such as feature announcements and user education content.

2. *Inefficient communication and planning*: The differing sprint schedules made it difficult for the teams to hold effective joint planning meetings. Key decision points often missed alignment, resulting in the marketing team either waiting for software updates or the software team not receiving timely feedback on necessary adjustments from marketing insights.

## Adoption of a Unified Sprint Schedule

Recognizing these challenges, the leaders of both teams convened to discuss potential solutions. After several strategy sessions, they decided that aligning their sprint schedules could enhance synchronicity and efficiency.

Although members of the marketing team had grown comfortable with the three-week cadence that seemed to be working well, they agreed to standardize on a two-week sprint cycle for both teams, facilitating more frequent check-ins and smoother collaboration.

## Better Alignment, Better Results

Despite some initial hesitation related to changing the sprint schedule, it quickly became apparent that the modification paid off. Several benefits started to emerge, including the following:

1. *Synchronized planning and execution*: With both teams on a two-week sprint cycle, planning and execution became more synchronized. This allowed for agile responses to market feedback that the software team could quickly iterate upon, which in turn enabled the marketing team to adjust their strategies in a more dynamic manner.

2. *Enhanced communication*: The new sprint schedule facilitated more frequent scrum of scrums meetings, improving communication between teams. These meetings helped to quickly identify and resolve dependencies and blockers, leading to smoother workflow and project progress.

3. *Improved product launch efficiency*: The aligned sprints led to a more coordinated launch effort. Marketing was able to plan and execute

campaigns that were closely tied to the software's readiness, ensuring that all marketing materials accurately reflected the product's capabilities at launch.

The decision to synchronize sprint schedules marked a significant turning point for AgileCorp. The alignment of operational rhythms between the software engineering and marketing teams led to a highly successful product launch, characterized by timely releases and highly effective marketing campaigns.

This exemplifies the importance of flexibility and adaptability in Agile practices, especially when cross-functional collaboration is crucial to a project's success. The teams' ability to evaluate their processes critically and make necessary adjustments paved the way for improved efficiencies and set a precedent for future projects at AgileCorp.

## CONCLUSION

Working with small teams that work together regularly can pose its own challenges, but working across multiple teams in an organization can drive greater complexity. By accounting for the larger demands that this can bring and introducing new elements such as the scrum of scrums, organizations can be more successful in their scrum implementation on larger initiatives.

Now that readers have explored how to work most effectively with other teams that use scrum or other methods based on Agile principles, the next chapter will explore ways to work with non-Agile teams.

# CHAPTER 26

# WORKING WITH NON-AGILE TEAMS

Working with other teams that are also using scrum can present its own host of challenges (and opportunities) for a marketing team, however there are many companies which have not been consistent in their adoption of such practices, and even within a large marketing team, adoption can vary. Thus, there is a very likely situation that individuals find themselves in a company where some teams have adopted Agile approaches and others have not.

Therefore, it's beneficial to talk about the scenario of working with other teams that do not yet utilize Agile principles including scrum, or other practices. While there are some challenges with this, there are many organizations in this situation, as many companies do not uniformly adopt Agile across all teams and departments at once. There are some benefits to being early adopters and some areas to be aware of.

This chapter is going to focus on the challenges when Agile scrum frameworks in marketing must interface with traditional, nonscrum teams within the same organization. Additionally, this chapter will underscore the importance of creating a harmonious working relationship between different methodologies to achieve organizational goals.

For a more in-depth review of the differences between more traditional, waterfall approaches and scrum approaches, please refer back to Chapter 1 where both approaches were explained and contrasted. For the purposes of this chapter, readers should have at least a general understanding of the key differentiations between more waterfall and scrum approaches to project management and ways of working.

## ACKNOWLEDGING THE DIFFERENCES

Beyond a fundamental understanding of the differences between scrum and waterfall methods is to ensure that teams and departments that collaborate frequently are aware of the different ways of working, regardless of the methods they subscribe to. When teams work differently, it is important to acknowledge these differences, and where possible embrace the areas where the dissimilarities can complement efforts, as well as work together to identify further areas for improvement in the way that teams collaborate.

## KEY DIFFERENCES AND CHALLENGES

As explored already, scrum is iterative and incremental, where work is divided into two-, three-, or four-week sprints and the scope of work can adapt based on ongoing feedback and changing requirements as well as organizational priorities. This flexibility allows marketing teams to pivot quickly in response to market changes or new insights.

Conversely, waterfall methodologies follow a linear and sequential approach, where each phase (such as planning, execution, and evaluation) must be completed fully before moving on to the next. This method is often more rigid but provides a structured and predictable project timeline.

While a host of challenges may occur when teams reconcile these two methods, there are three challenges that are most common:

### Misaligned Timelines

One of the most prominent challenges when integrating scrum with waterfall methods in marketing projects is aligning timelines between a scrum, sprint-based approach and a waterfall approach that has a series of cascading dependencies that generally offer little room for deviation.

This difference can lead to issues when scrum teams are ready to adapt or pivot, while waterfall teams are not yet prepared to move on or adjust their plans.

### What to do about it

While either method of working can yield an on-time project, syncing workstreams between a sprint-based approach and a waterfall project management approach with cascading dependencies takes some preplanning to be most effective.

Synchronizing sprints with traditional project milestones requires thoughtful planning strategies that accommodate the agility of scrum without undermining the structured nature of traditional methodologies. One approach is to align sprint reviews and planning meetings with the phase reviews of waterfall projects. This ensures that at the end of each sprint, both Agile and traditional teams are on the same page regarding progress, upcoming goals, and resource allocation.

Furthermore, hybrid planning methods that incorporate both Agile's flexibility and waterfall's phased structure can be developed. For example, while the broader scope and major deadlines can be planned according to waterfall's detailed up-front planning requirements, the tasks within those phases can be broken down and tackled in sprints, allowing for iterative reviews and adjustments typical of scrum processes. This integrated approach encourages proactive adaptation to project needs and market changes while maintaining the overall direction and timeline integrity expected in traditional project management.

*Conflicting Priorities:*

Scrum teams prioritize tasks based on the product backlog, which is dynamically adjusted to reflect the most current business needs and customer feedback and informed by the product owner. This means what was important at the start of a project might change as the project progresses.

Waterfall teams, however, have fixed priorities that are determined at the beginning of a project and are expected to remain constant, lest a scope change and refactoring of time, resources, and budget are taken into account. This can lead to conflicts when a scrum team's shifting priorities impact the dependencies that waterfall teams might have on their deliverables.

### What do do about it

Similar to the approach to timeline conflicts, scope conflicts can begin by discussing nonnegotiables: items that, from a waterfall team's perspective must be completed in order to achieve the critical path features or functionality.

Likewise, scrum teams should communicate their sprint cadence well ahead of time so that the waterfall teams can know if and when scope conversations would be best to have. For instance, in the case that a scope change is required, the best time for both teams to make a pivot would be at the beginning of the next sprint.

*Differences in Communication Styles:*

Scrum teams typically have daily stand-ups and frequent retrospectives to ensure all members are continually aligned and can voice their insights or concerns. This constant flow of communication supports the team's ability to adapt quickly. Waterfall teams often rely on less frequent, more formal updates and milestone meetings, which can delay the communication of vital changes or decisions that affect the project's overall progress.

### What do do about it

Robust communication strategies are vital in bridging the gap between scrum and traditional project teams. Establishing regular communication channels and routines that respect both methodologies ensures that every team member stays informed about project progress and deviations. This could include integrating scrum's daily stand-ups with weekly briefings more typical of waterfall approaches, thus creating a rhythm that keeps all stakeholders aligned without overwhelming them with too frequent updates. Additionally, leveraging modern tools and technologies such as shared project management software, real-time collaborative documents, and communication platforms like Slack or Microsoft Teams can enhance transparency and ensure that updates are timely and actionable. These tools help in maintaining a continuous flow of information and assist in preempting misunderstandings or delays that might arise due to lack of communication.

Also, while work may be done in different ways and in different cadences, communication should be consistent among teams. Chapter 25 discussed the concept of the scrum of scrums for organizations where two or more teams are using Agile approaches.

While the term scrum may not be as appropriate, a similar alignment meeting to a scrum of scrums can build awareness of what different teams are working on and foster better communication in general.

*Navigating These and Other Challenges*

In addition to the specific ideas mentioned, to mitigate these challenges, organizations must foster an environment where there is respect for both methodologies.

Additionally, as demonstrated in all the examples, establishing clear communication channels that cater to both teams' styles can help ensure that important information is shared in a timely manner. Additionally, creating integrated planning sessions that allow for both up-front and iterative planning can help align the different teams' timelines and priorities.

When marketing teams using scrum work with teams employing traditional methods, establishing common ground is crucial for project success. One effective technique to achieve alignment on project goals and outcomes is to hold initial alignment sessions where both teams can present their methods, expectations, and objectives. This fosters mutual understanding and sets a foundation for cooperation.

Furthermore, shared understanding can be cultivated through joint workshops and cross-training sessions. These initiatives not only educate each team on the other's methodologies but also highlight overlapping goals and areas where collaborative efforts can yield greater results. Joint workshops particularly serve as platforms where teams can brainstorm, discuss potential challenges, and develop a unified approach to project milestones.

This hybrid approach encourages flexibility and adaptation without sacrificing the structure and predictiveness that waterfall methodologies provide, ensuring that both marketing teams using scrum and other departments using traditional approaches can collaborate effectively toward common organizational goals.

## WHAT TO EXPECT FROM OTHER TEAMS

When communicating the value of Agile to skeptics or to those who have not yet adopted Agile, here are a few things to expect:

- *Reluctance to change*: It is difficult for anyone to change habits or change behaviors that are longstanding. Be patient with those team members that may not be quite ready to adopt Agile approaches.
- *Skepticism of benefits*: It can also be difficult for those not used to Agile processes to understand how work can get done more efficiently and effectively through sprints and other scrum practices. Invite them to "sit in" on a retrospective or observe how one particular team is able to complete their work so the other team can see the benefits for themselves instead of just taking the advice of someone else.
- *"That would never work for my team."*: In other cases, other teams or departments may acknowledge that a particular team is getting great

benefits from adopting Agile practices, but that their work and processes are so different that Agile could never work for them. While these people may be hard to win over, sharing some initial struggles with them to illustrate that everyone has challenges making changes but that the changes quickly pay off.

As with any change in process and approach, it is worth taking the time to clearly communicate the value and benefits of Agile principles and approaches so they can fully understand what is in store. Don't expect immediate adoption from everyone, but build a plan to make a case for everyone involved.

## HYPOTHETICAL CASE STUDY: INTEGRATING AGILE AND WATERFALL METHODOLOGIES AT AGILECORP

It's time to return to the marketing team at AgileCorp, currently facing a unique challenge when, well into its scrum adoption, needed to collaborate with the sales team, which used traditional waterfall methods, to implement a new customer relationship management (CRM) system. This project was critical for improving customer interactions and sales tracking, requiring tight integration and cooperation between the two teams with differing project management philosophies.

There are a few initial challenges that the teams ran into when collaborating on this project while adhering to their respective ways of managing teams and projects.

First, there were some key difference in the way they planned projects. The marketing team was accustomed to planning and executing work in short, iterative sprint cycles, which allowed for adaptability and continuous improvement. Conversely, the sales team was used to the waterfall method, planning the entire project up front with a fixed scope, timeline, and budget. This fundamental difference in approach led to conflicts in project planning and execution, with the sales team feeling uncertain about the iterative nature of Agile that seemed to lack a clear, definitive end point.

Second, there were communication barriers that cropped up because of the differences in overall approaches. Each team had developed its own language and methodology for project management, which initially led to misunderstandings and misaligned expectations about project deliverables and timelines.

Fortunately, both teams acknowledged their different ways of working, as well as the need to create a strategic compromise to help solve some of these challenges. Thus, to bridge the methodological divide, both teams agreed to a series of workshops facilitated by AgileCorp's project management office to outline their processes, concerns, and needs. These discussions led to a hybrid project management approach characterized by the following compromises and solutions:

- *Defining critical requirements and paths up front*: The teams agreed to define the critical requirements and paths for the CRM implementation up front during the project's discovery phase. This approach satisfied the sales team's need for predictability and clear scope while allowing the marketing team the flexibility to adjust aspects of the project that were less critical as insights were gained during execution.

- *Educational exchange on methodologies*: The marketing team provided training sessions on Agile and scrum methodologies to the sales team, highlighting the benefits of flexibility, especially in projects involving new technology where adjustments are often necessary as more is learned during implementation. The sales team, in turn, educated the marketing team on the waterfall method's strengths, particularly in ensuring thorough up-front planning and clear documentation.

- *Iterative implementation with milestone reviews*: The teams adopted an iterative implementation approach where smaller parts of the CRM system were developed and reviewed in sprints, with regular milestone reviews that aligned with the sales team's need for structured progress assessments. This compromise ensured that there were predefined points where the project's status was evaluated against the original plan, allowing for corrective actions in a structured manner.

The results left both teams at AgileCorp more than satisfied with the results. While it was a compromise between the two philosophies, the hybrid approach led to the successful implementation of the CRM system. The marketing team was able to adapt the solution dynamically to better meet user needs discovered during the sprints, while the sales team had clear visibility into the project's progression through regular milestone reviews. The project not only finished on time and within budget but also with higher satisfaction rates from end-users, who received a system that truly addressed their needs.

This example demonstrates the potential for integrating scrum and waterfall approaches to harness the strengths of both, when both must be accounted for. By defining critical requirements up front and allowing for flexibility in less critical areas, the teams at AgileCorp ensured that project integrity and predictability were maintained without sacrificing the adaptability needed to innovate and respond to unforeseen challenges effectively.

For the company, this project serves as a model for future collaborations between different teams within AgileCorp if and until all of the teams within the organization adopt a scrum approach.

## CONCLUSION

As can be seen, while there may not be consensus within an organization on a common way to approach management and scheduling of projects, campaigns, and initiatives, there are several approaches a team can take to align marketing efforts with those of other teams in the organization that do not use a sprint-based, scrum approach.

Ideally, however, if some parts of a company are adopting scrum, there is a trend toward greater adoption. Chapter 26 concludes this part of the book by looking at some ways to implement Agile practices across an entire organization, ranging in scale from simpler working groups to a larger-scale center of excellence.

# CHAPTER 27

# BUILDING CONSENSUS AND KNOWLEDGE-SHARING

When there are multiple teams in an organization that has adopted Agile practices like scrum or made the decision to adopt Agile practices in the near future, it becomes more and more beneficial to find ways to build consensus and create opportunities to learn and grow the organization's ability to utilize Agile to benefit the business.

Historically, using methods like scrum has started its life in the software engineering or IT departments and grown from there. Increasingly marketing teams are adopting Agile methods to much success. A marketing team does not have to wait for another department to use Agile practices in order to adopt them .

In most cases, one or two departments or teams will take on scrum practices and begin utilizing them before a company-wide effort to utilize Agile is embraced. Regardless of how it originates, there are several ways to build and grow consensus around the best methods to utilize Agile.

## THREE DIFFERENT APPROACHES

If an organization is in the midst of an Agile transformation, a team may either be the first team to adopt, or one of several that adopts these approaches along the way toward full-scale company adoption. There are many ways to approach company-wide adoption of Agile, but incorporating a method of building consensus and knowledge-sharing can go a long way toward successful and consistent adoption in the long-term. Following is the exploration of three types of approaches on how an organization can build consensus and increase knowledge-sharing.

## Agile Working Group

An Agile working group is an informal assembly within an organization, designed to explore and experiment with Agile practices. This group typically comprises individuals from various departments and teams, fostering a multidisciplinary approach to understanding and implementing Agile methods, such as an implementation of scrum like the approach explored in this book. The informal nature of the group allows for a flexible and adaptive exploration of Agile principles without the pressure of formalized expectations or outcomes.

### What Makes It Unique

What sets an Agile working group apart is its low-barrier entry and informal structure, making it an excellent starting point for organizations new to Agile. Unlike more formalized committees or centers of excellence, a working group can operate under the radar, experiment with Agile practices, and innovate with minimal bureaucratic overhead.

### Benefits

The primary benefit of an Agile working group is the facilitation of grassroots exploration and experimentation, which can lead to organic growth and acceptance of practices such as scrum throughout the organization. This method allows for significant flexibility and personal initiative, enabling team members to tailor Agile practices to their specific needs without the constraints of strict guidelines. Additionally, the cross-functional nature of the group enhances knowledge-sharing and broadens the understanding of Agile across different departments.

### Potential Drawbacks

However, the informal structure of an Agile working group might also lead to its main drawbacks: A lack of formal authority and recognition within the organization can limit the group's influence on broader organizational changes. Without formal recognition, securing resources and driving significant organizational transformations can be challenging. Moreover, the dependence on an executive sponsor for visibility and impact can make the group vulnerable to shifts in leadership or strategic priorities.

*What to Know Before Getting Started*

Before launching this type of group, it's crucial to ensure alignment with an executive sponsor who understands and supports the initiative. This sponsorship is essential not just for resource allocation, but also for integrating the group's findings and practices into the larger organizational context. Additionally, setting clear, albeit flexible, goals can help demonstrate early benefits and secure wider buy-in across the organization.

An Agile working group serves as an informal, low-risk platform for initiating Agile practices within an organization. Its cross-departmental makeup and flexible structure promote an experimental approach to Agile, making it ideal for organizations just beginning their Agile journey. While the group's informal status fosters innovation and rapid adaptation, it may also restrict its influence on organizational policies without strong executive support.

## Agile Steering Committee

A steering committee is a formalized body within an organization, tasked with overseeing and guiding the adoption and implementation of Agile methodologies. Unlike the less formal working group, this committee is recognized officially within the organization and involves multiple leadership stakeholders. It serves as a bridge between Agile teams and upper management, ensuring that Agile practices are aligned with organizational goals and strategies. Additionally, it can serve as a bridge between Agile teams and non-Agile teams, such as those discussed previously in this chapter that subscribe to waterfall methods.

*What Makes It Unique*

The unique aspect of an Agile practices steering committee lies in its formal recognition and the involvement of senior leadership. This formal structure allows the committee to wield considerable influence over the adoption and adaptation of Agile principles and approaches across the organization.

The committee's authority enables it to make strategic decisions that can significantly impact the organization's approach to Agile adoption, making it an integral part of the overall corporate governance structure.

*Benefits*

The benefits of having an Agile practice steering committee include enhanced alignment between Agile teams and organizational objectives, which helps in scaling Agile practices effectively across multiple departments.

The committee facilitates consistent and coherent implementation of Agile approaches such as scrum, ensuring that all departments adhere to a unified set of practices and principles. Additionally, regular reports and findings shared with stakeholders help maintain transparency and keep all parts of the organization informed about the progress and challenges of Agile initiatives.

*Potential Drawbacks*

While this approach can strike a nice balance between the less formal working group and the more substantial center of excellence, the formal nature of the steering committee can also introduce certain drawbacks for organizations that do not have consistent buy-in from leadership.

The bureaucracy associated with its operations might slow down the decision-making process, potentially stifling the agility that Agile practices aim to promote. The involvement of multiple executives and stakeholders can also lead to conflicts or power struggles, which may divert focus from practical Agile implementations to organizational politics.

*What to Know Before Getting Started*

Establishing an Agile practices steering committee requires careful planning and a clear understanding of its scope and authority within the organization. It's essential to define the committee's roles and responsibilities explicitly and to ensure that its goals align with those of the broader organization. Additionally, selecting the right mix of members—from executives to Agile champions that have a working knowledge of scrum—is crucial to ensure the committee can effectively advocate for and support Agile transformations.

An Agile steering committee's formal status and involvement of senior leadership allow it to significantly influence organizational policies related to Agile. While the committee helps align Agile practices with organizational goals and ensures consistent implementation across departments, its formal structure can sometimes hinder the very agility it aims to promote.

## Agile Center of Excellence

An Agile center of excellence (CoE) represents the most structured and formal approach to fostering Agile adoption and consistent utilization of scrum within an organization. Positioned at the organizational level rather than within specific divisions or departments, the CoE serves as the epicenter for Agile expertise, resources, and leadership. It is designed to standardize, support, and enhance the implementation of Agile practices across the entire organization by offering guidance, best practices, and continuous learning opportunities.

### What Makes It Unique

The distinctiveness of a CoE lies in its broad organizational reach and comprehensive support structure. It not only provides a central point of leadership for Agile practices but also integrates these practices into the core operational strategies of the company.

With executive backing, the CoE wields considerable authority and resources to effect substantial and lasting changes. This allows for a more unified and coherent approach to Agile adoption, such as the rollout of scrum across diverse teams and projects.

### Benefits

The Agile CoE brings several significant benefits. It ensures a consistent application of Agile methodologies across all levels of the organization, which can greatly enhance operational efficiency and reduce friction in project execution.

By centralizing expertise, the CoE can offer substantial support and training resources, raising the competency and confidence of all Agile practitioners within the company. Furthermore, the CoE's strategic positioning allows it to effectively advocate for and implement improvements and innovations in Agile practices, thereby continuously advancing the organization's Agile maturity.

### Potential Drawbacks

Such a robust approach is not without its potential drawbacks. Establishing and maintaining an Agile CoE can be resource-intensive, requiring significant investment in terms of time, money, and personnel.

Its comprehensive and centralized nature might also lead to a certain degree of inflexibility, potentially stifling local innovations or adaptations that do not align with the established Agile guidelines from the CoE. Additionally, the breadth and depth of this type of structure's influence can make it somewhat detached from day-to-day challenges faced by individual scrum teams, possibly leading to solutions that are ideal in theory but less practical in application.

### What to Know Before Getting Started

Before establishing a CoE, it is crucial to clearly define its role, scope, and the extent of its authority within the organization. Aligning its objectives with the organization's strategic goals ensures that the CoE remains relevant and focused. It is also essential to secure ongoing executive support and to establish clear metrics for evaluating the effectiveness of the CoE in promoting and enhancing Agile practices. Understanding the resource requirements and preparing for a long-term commitment are also vital for the sustainability of the CoE.

The Agile center of excellence is a formal, organization-wide entity dedicated to enhancing and standardizing Agile practices across all departments. With significant executive support and resources, it facilitates a unified approach to Agile, ensuring consistent application and continuous improvement. While it offers numerous benefits in terms of support, training, and strategic implementation of Agile, the CoE can also be resource-heavy and somewhat rigid. Proper planning, clear goal-setting, and ongoing evaluation are essential for leveraging the full potential of an Agile CoE and ensuring its positive impact on the organization's Agile journey.

## Strengths and Weaknesses of Each Approach

This section will review the strengths and weaknesses of each of the three approaches (see Table 27.1).

**TABLE 27.1** Comparison of Approaches

|  | Strengths | Weaknesses |
|---|---|---|
| **Working Group** | Nimble and easy to adopt with minimal investments | Lacks the reach and depth of more formal solutions |
| **Steering Committee** | Has a more consistent presence from participating departments and teams; able to influence the organization in decisions | While it has some stakeholder support, it lacks the organization-wide support of a center of excellence |
| **Center of Excellence** | Can affect the most change more quickly across teams and departments; best able to retain institutional knowledge of best practices and common pitfalls | Can be costly and resource-intensive to maintain; may not be ideal for less mature organizations |

Regardless of the chosen method, some of the benefits one will reap from any of them are the information-sharing and organizational knowledge and memory of applying Agile principles and practices to their work. New teams will also be able to more quickly be able to adopt Agile and get up to speed because there is a foundation and framework to do so. Finally, common hurdles to Agile adoption will more easily be overcome because there will be a wealth of experience and first-hand knowledge that is shared and documented.

## SAFe

As mentioned earlier in the book, scrum is not the only way that Agile principles can be implemented within an organization, and there may be cases where one or more approaches are taken. A common scenario is for scrum teams to exist within an organization that implements SAFe as well.

The scaled agile framework, commonly known as SAFe, is a set of organization and workflow patterns intended to guide enterprises in scaling lean and Agile practices. SAFe was developed by author and methodologist Dean Leffingwell and was first introduced in 2011 through his book *Agile Software Requirements.*[1] It was designed to help larger organizations adopt Agile practices across multiple teams or the entire enterprise, addressing common scaling challenges. SAFe combines principles from Agile, lean, and product development flow to promote alignment, collaboration, and delivery across large numbers of Agile teams.

### Scrum and SAFe Compatibility

Scrum and SAFe can be used compatibly within an organization by employing scrum at the team level while integrating it into the larger SAFe structure for program and portfolio management. This allows teams to maintain their Agile practices and autonomy in day-to-day tasks while benefiting from SAFe's capacity for strategic planning and cross-team coordination. For instance, individual scrum teams could operate independently yet synchronize with other teams through SAFe's program implement (PI) planning sessions, ensuring alignment on larger business objectives. This hybrid approach enables organizations to adapt and implement Agile methodologies tailored to their specific needs, combining the strengths of both frameworks.

### Key Advantages of SAFe

As with any transformational effort, implementations run the risk of diverting resources from achieving key organizational objectives. SAFe offers several advantages that can make it a worthwhile investment of time and effort, and to build greater agility across departments and teams.

Some of these advantages include:

- *Scalability*: SAFe provides a structured framework for scaling Agile beyond individual teams to entire departments and enterprises. It allows for the implementation of Agile practices across multiple teams and large systems.

- *Enhanced alignment and synchronization*: SAFe promotes alignment, collaboration, and delivery across multiple teams. This ensures that organization-wide goals and strategies are effectively communicated and integrated at all levels.

- *Built-in quality practices*: SAFe emphasizes the integration of quality practices into the daily work of all teams, which is critical in ensuring that the products or services meet customer expectations and regulatory requirements.

- *Program increment (PI) planning*: One of the cornerstones of SAFe is PI planning, a regular, face-to-face event that helps teams align to the business goals, understand their dependencies, and commit to achievable outcomes over a defined time frame.

- *Transparency and visibility*: SAFe offers a clear and visible roadmap of project statuses and milestones, helping to enhance transparency across the organization and facilitating better decision-making.

### Key Criticisms of SAFe

Likewise, there are critics of SAFe that bemoan its scale and heft that can, in poor implementations, feel anything but agile. Thus, some of the common criticisms of the scaled agile framework are the following:

- *Complexity and rigidity*: One criticism of SAFe is its complexity. The framework involves multiple layers and roles, which can be daunting for organizations without prior experience in scaled Agile environments.

- *Resource intensiveness*: Implementing SAFe effectively requires significant training and organizational change management, which can be resource-intensive both in terms of time and costs.

- *Potential to overwhelm*: Smaller organizations or teams might find the extensive structure and formalities of SAFe overwhelming and not suited to their agility needs, where simpler frameworks might be more effective.
- *Risk of bureaucratization*: Due to its comprehensive nature, there is a risk that the processes within SAFe can become bureaucratic and slow, possibly detracting from the agility it aims to promote.

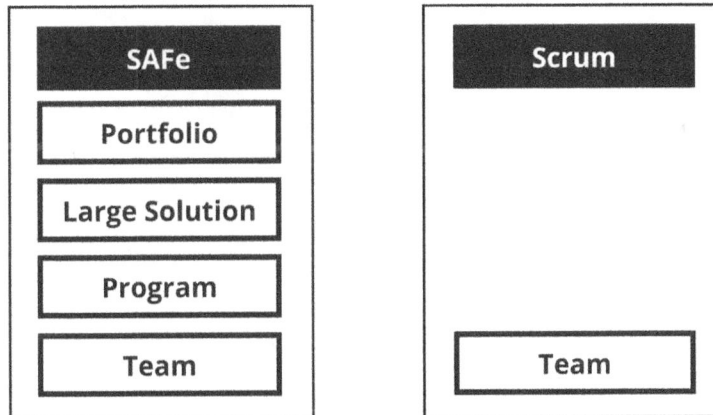

**FIGURE 27.1** The structure of SAFe versus scrum.

While scrum is focused on small teams and emphasizes simplicity and flexibility, SAFe addresses the needs of larger organizations and scales across multiple teams or the entire enterprise. Scrum provides a minimal set of rules and expects the team to develop its practices based on its unique circumstances, whereas SAFe provides a detailed and comprehensive guideline for roles, responsibilities, and processes. As seen in Figure 27.1, scrum is primarily a team-level framework, while SAFe operates at four levels: team, program, large solution, and portfolio.

## CONCLUSION

A critical component of long-term adoption of Agile principles and approaches such as scrum is consistent communication and coordination across teams. While this can take different forms, from less formal working groups or a well-resourced center of excellence, leadership buy-in and support is a must.

Additionally, an organization may choose to adopt scrum at the team level and a scale agile framework approach at the department and organizational one. While there are potential challenges with this, it can enable greater and more consistent adoption of Agile principles throughout the organization in the longer-term.

### Note

1.  Dean Leffingwell. (2010). *Agile Software Requirements.* Addison-Wesley.

# CHAPTER 28

# AGILE TEAM GROWTH AND IMPROVEMENT

As discussed previously in this book, Agile principles support continuous improvement in deliverables, process, and teamwork. Thus, teams should strive for continuous growth.

But, as experienced as some of the team members on an Agile marketing scrum team may be, they don't always have all the answers. Sometimes, just as importantly, they can be a little *too close* to some of the issues to be able to think of ways to improve them. Furthermore, sometimes, the team members can be too close to even see that the problem exists!

This is where an external advisor or coach can bring additional value. This person and their role are able to take an objective view of what is going on and offer additional insights and guidance to a team that might be struggling with an issue they are unfamiliar with or unable to even articulate enough to be able to create a solution for.

## COACHING

Coaching can be beneficial for teams of all types, whether Agile is brand new to them, if they are a seasoned Agile team, or if they have a mix of experience levels on the team. An Agile coach isn't a part of the working team per se; instead, they are brought in to guide and provide ideas that the team can take and use to improve.

Coaching is more about instilling ideas, principles, and ways of solving problems than having a "boss" that tells a team what to do. Their main strength is bringing out existing knowledge and ideas so that teams can learn how to solve their issues and improve on their own. An Agile coach is not there to tell a team what to do or how to do it.

Put another way, the 2022 State of Agile Coaching Report defines an Agile coach as the following:

> An agile coach helps organizations, teams, and individuals adopt agile practices and methods while embedding agile values and mindsets. The goal of an agile coach is to foster more effective, transparent, and cohesive teams, and to enable better outcomes, solutions, and products/services for customers.[1]

Instead of telling teams what to do, an Agile coach's role is to help teams:

- learn how to make better decisions together
- learn how to incorporate Agile principles into their daily work
- teach Agile teams to learn how to learn

## THE DIFFERENCE BETWEEN A SCRUM MASTER AND AN AGILE COACH

What exactly is the difference between a scrum master and an Agile coach? Isn't a scrum master supposed to do some of the things previously discussed? This is explored in Table 28.1.

*TABLE 28.1* Scrum Master Role Compared to an Agile Coach

| Scrum Master | Agile Coach |
|---|---|
| Focuses on a single team | Works across multiple teams |
| Responsible for a team's deliverables | Assists a team to incorporate more Agile principles |
| Works directly with their team to decide outcomes and approaches | Advises teams on best practices but never dictates a specific course of action |

- While a scrum master focuses on a single team and their objectives, an Agile coach may work across many teams simultaneously.
- A scrum master is responsible for a team's deliverables, including the sprint backlog and product backlog, as well as the project goals. In contrast, an

Agile coach is more focused on how a team is adopting Agile principles in their work.

▪ Finally, a scrum master works directly with their team to decide outcomes, approaches, and priorities, while an Agile coach works as an advisor to Agile teams on best practices, but they never dictate a specific course of action; that is for the Agile team to agree upon.

While there can be other differences between scrum masters and Agile coaches depending on the organization, these are the key ones.

## THE DIFFERENCE BETWEEN A PRODUCT OWNER AND AN AGILE COACH

Table 28.2 compares an Agile coach with another important role on a scrum team: the product owner.

**TABLE 28.2** Product Owner Role Compared to an Agile Coach

| Product Owner | Agile Coach |
|---|---|
| Focuses on a single product | Works across multiple teams and products |
| Responsible for project outcomes | Assists with improving how teams work together to deliver outcomes |
| Prioritizes items in the product backlog based on business value | Helps teams prioritize Agile principles when working together and with other teams |

▪ First, similar to a scrum master, a product owner focuses on a single product, while an Agile coach generally works across multiple teams and products.

▪ A product owner is responsible for project and product outcomes, while an Agile coach assists with improving how teams work together to *deliver* that product or outcomes.

▪ Finally, while a product owner prioritizes items in the product backlog based on their thorough understanding of the business value and how their product contributes to it, an Agile coach helps teams prioritize Agile principles when working together and with other teams.

While there can be other differences between scrum masters and product owners depending on the organization, these are the key ones.

## THE BENEFITS OF AGILE COACHING

Following a few more benefits of Agile coaching on Agile marketing scrum teams in three main categories: planning, project delivery, and culture.

### Planning

Upon obtaining the assistance of an Agile coach for sprint planning:

- Teams can leverage someone with experience in estimating velocity and potential challenges both within and outside of the team.
- The coach can guide how improvements are measured and made in estimating velocity and understanding priority. They can also help ensure clear communication with a product owner to manage expectations.
- An Agile coach's experience can play a vital role in planning, which can have several downstream impacts.

### Project Delivery

With the assistance of an Agile coach for project delivery, teams can get several benefits, including the following ideas:

- ensuring scrum practices such as standups and retrospectives are followed according to best practices and achieving maximum value
- providing best practices to ensure the product owner, scrum master, and product team are working together in the most beneficial ways
- identifying areas of improvement and methods to incorporate improvements into subsequent sprints

### Culture

With the assistance of an Agile coach, teams can get several team culture and morale benefits, including the following:

- An Agile coach can help teams as they navigate frustration with having to learn new processes.
- An Agile coach can help Agile teams work better with non-Agile teams.
- Finally, an Agile coach can be a sounding board for ideas and ways to improve things. The coach can leverage their extensive experience and knowledge of best practices to share ways in which these ideas may or

may not be successful. However, Agile coaches, in general, try not to draw direct parallels between their previous experiences and existing situations. This is a delicate balance, but important to being a successful coach.

### What an Agile Coach Is Not

This section takes on a different perspective. The chapter has explored quite a bit about what Agile coaching is and some of its benefits, and readers should understand what Agile coaching is not. Table 28.3 presents a brief summary.

*TABLE 28.3* Common Misperceptions of Agile Coaching

| Coaching is not: | Why? |
|---|---|
| **Training** | Agile coaches aren't there to teach teams how to perform scrum roles and tasks. |
| **Consulting** | While coaches have experience, their job is to help teams uncover what they already know and apply it to their work, not tell them what they should do. |
| **Facilitation** | Coaches don't bring multiple stakeholders together to have discussions; instead, they work with a team. |

### Coaching Is not Training

Agile coaches aren't there to teach teams how to perform scrum roles and tasks. This can sometimes be confusing to teams looking for practical training from a seasoned expert. Remember, there are many resources available for this type of education. A coach is not there to do this type of work.

### Agile Coaching Is not Consulting

While coaches have experience, their job is to help teams uncover what they already know and apply it to their work, not tell them what they should do. This is often a struggle for Agile coaches. While they may want to provide direct advice and tell teams what they think they should do in a specific situation, remember that coaching is more about teaching teams how to learn, adapt, and grow than it is to tell them what they should do in a specific situation.

### Agile Coaching Is not Cross-Team Facilitation

Finally, an Agile coach is not a facilitator among teams. Coaches don't bring multiple stakeholders together to have discussions; instead, they work with a single team to improve their work's dynamics, approaches, and outcomes.

## WHEN AN AGILE COACH IS NEEDED

There are many reasons an Agile coach may be needed, but here are a few that a marketing team may run into:

- A project will likely need an Agile coach if the team is transitioning from more traditional methods to an Agile approach because few team members understand Agile best practices and approaches.

- If an Agile team struggles to meet deadlines and follow scrum practices, this might also be a reason to bring in an Agile coach.

- If an Agile team needs assistance with planning and forecasting, this might also be an area where an Agile coach can help.

- Finally, if there are morale and motivation issues on the team, an Agile coach can also help here. This might be related to frustration with new processes, team members, or expectations elsewhere in the organization. An experienced Agile coach has the experience to provide insights and guidance on this and many other issues.

## ALTERNATIVES TO AN AGILE COACH

What if a team doesn't have the benefit of an Agile coach? What can teams do to grow and continue to improve? Here are a few ideas.

- Continue Agile training. Many resources are available to learn more about scrum and Agile best practices. Adopting a lifelong learning attitude and approach will make someone a great team member.

- Embrace Agile principles and review them as a group regularly. Especially as some team members are getting up to speed with Agile practices, it may be hard to keep them all in mind.

- Make sure teams are fully adopting scrum practices. Picking and choosing the ones that will work best isn't a viable approach. Each part of scrum plays a valuable role and ensures that the team continue to grow and improve.

- Embrace a continuous improvement mindset. This is a key part of Agile and critical to the continued development as a team and the results of the team's work.

- Finally, ensure that the team communicates openly about ideas, challenges, and potential solutions. Make sure to listen and contribute equally in order to benefit from the diverse views and perspectives of the team.

When some team members are new to or unfamiliar with Agile principles and practices, it can be a bit of an adjustment at first. Here are a few things to keep in mind during this transition.

- Different people learn at different paces.
- Communication styles can differ, which means an open, collaborative environment may work differently with different people.
- Make sure everyone gets an opportunity to share.
- Collaboration and cooperation are more important than fast The next chapter explores a useful tool that can help Agile marketing teams get unstuck when they run into a speed bump on their way to success.

## ADDITIONAL LEARNING AND AGILE DEVELOPMENT

Just as readers have learned about and revisited the concept of continuous improvement several times throughout this book, it is important that they adopt a mindset of continuous *learning*.

While this and the previous Agile brand guides have taught readers the fundamentals of Agile marketing and scrum, there is much more to learn and several paths available for those who would like to continue their education and training about using Agile and scrum to improve their marketing outcomes and the processes by which their teams do their work.

It is highly recommended that, similar to scrum events like retrospectives, teams incorporate Agile learning opportunities into a regular schedule. This will ensure that newcomers can catch up with an established team and that the Agile veterans on a team are ensuring they are staying current and their knowledge of Agile stays fresh.

## PROFESSIONAL DEVELOPMENT

Continuous professional development is essential for both enhancing individual performance and fostering career growth in any field, and because scrum embraces the Agile principles of continuously improving and learning, individuals should seek to continually grow their knowledge.

Thus, members of an Agile marketing team must actively seek opportunities to expand their skills and learn from their experiences to remain effective and competitive. Following is a look at some opportunities for skill enhancement and the importance of learning from both successes and failures.

## Learning from Experience

While formal training can be incredibly beneficial to individuals, there are several ways to learn on the job, and taking the time and effort to do so can benefit both individuals and teams as a whole. Here are a few of those methods:

- *Reflective practice*: Make it a habit to reflect on completed projects and campaigns. Identify what worked well and what didn't, and think about the reasons behind each outcome. This practice can transform experiences into actionable insights, enhancing decision-making and strategic planning skills.

- *Feedback culture*: It is important for leaders and managers to do their part to foster a culture where feedback is regularly sought and given. Constructive feedback from peers and supervisors can provide new perspectives and highlight areas for improvement that one might not have recognized.

- *Documenting lessons learned*: Keep a professional journal or a digital log of key projects and the lessons learned from each. This documentation can be a valuable resource for future projects, helping to avoid past mistakes and replicate successes.

- *Embrace failures as learning opportunities*: View failures as essential learning opportunities. In Agile environments, where rapid iteration and responsiveness are valued, each failure can be a step toward a more effective solution. Analyzing failures to understand their root causes can lead to significant improvements in both process and product.

## Training and Certification

It is highly encouraged to engage in formal training programs or pursue certifications relevant to role and career aspirations. For example, marketing team members might consider certifications in digital marketing, analytics, or methodologies like scrum that adhere to Agile principles. These programs not only deepen expertise but also enhance one's resumé.

There are many paths that continued education in Agile can take. While there are a few different organizations that have created sets of certification standards, there are a few general categories in which one can receive both more education and additional certifications with:

- ICAgile, one of the leading Agile and scrum organizations, has an ICP-MKG Agility in Marketing certification that can be a great next step
- The Agile Marketing Alliance is a great organization that provides education and community that is (unlike many Agile organizations and groups) specific to the marketing community
- Additionally, one can choose other areas of focus, such as:
  - leadership or business level, meant primarily for those managing organizations and large teams or departments
  - product owners
  - scrum masters
  - scrum developers, which may be the least relevant if one is in a traditional marketing role

Also, remember that both scrum and SAFe versions of several certifications are available. Individuals should make sure they do their homework to determine what certifications work best for them, their role, and their organization.

Finally, remember that once and individual knows and understands the fundamentals of scrum, Kanban, or other approaches, they can tailor their approaches to ensure they work for *their* team within *their* organization.

## CONCLUSION

Professional development in Agile marketing is not just about acquiring new knowledge and skills; it's also about applying these in real-world scenarios and learning continuously from the outcomes. By embracing both formal learning opportunities and experiential learning, team members can continually enhance their capabilities, contribute more effectively to their teams, and advance their careers in meaningful directions.

### Note

1. Scrum Alliance. State of Agile Coaching Report: Measuring the Impact of Agile. (2022). *https://resources.scrumalliance.org/Article/state-agile-coaching-report*. Retrieved January 21, 2023.

# *Epilogue*

While the initial adoption of Agile methods may need to be driven by financial reasons, its sustained adoption often depends on the teams and how valuable they find utilizing methods like scrum, Kanban, or others. Following is a transfer of focus from discussing business value to the value of Agile practices and principles.

If an organization has already formally adopted Agile practices across every team and department, there may be various perspectives about the benefits of Agile.

If a team is relatively new to Agile, or if other teams do not evenly adopt it within the organization, then other teams may not yet understand the benefits as clearly. As readers have seen in the preceding chapters, there are many benefits to taking an Agile approach with marketing efforts, and those can easily translate into other areas of the business. Here are a few things to keep in mind when talking with other teams about Agile:

- Actions speak louder than words: Demonstrate through successful implementation.
- Learn by doing: Reinforce that Agile embraces continual learning and feedback is part of the process.
- Don't evangelize: If someone is skeptical, don't try to convince them with long explanations. They will eventually see that using Agile approaches yields better results, and they will see that the teamwork and collaboration that embracing Agile principles yields improve morale and motivation.

## ARE THERE AGILE SKEPTICS OR PROPONENTS ON THE TEAM?

First, gauge the room to see what people's preconceived notions are about Agile and how open they are to go "all in" on it.

As an example, one could have the most enthusiastic scrum master on their team, but if the product team has some naysayers or those who simply don't follow through or understand what needs to get done, there will be challenges. Sometimes, this is a matter of education or coaching, and sometimes this is a matter of team dynamics and culture. Determine what the cause is and deal with it accordingly.

Even experienced Agile team members can benefit from a knowledge refresh from time to time but find ways to make learning beneficial for everyone. If challenges come down to a team member that is a bad fit for the team, this, unfortunately, may mean they need to be dropped for the team to thrive.

To work best, Agile requires a commitment from the entire team. With everyone on board, the benefits of teamwork and collaboration that Agile principles embrace will enable the most success.

## IS THERE CONSISTENCY IN THE ADOPTION OF AGILE METHODS AND PRACTICES?

With the full team on board with Agile approaches and practices, now it is time to ensure that the team follows through and adheres to their processes consistently.

Doing things right is most critical when things are stressful, when there are tight deadlines, and the stakes are high. These are never reasons to abandon the process, and it's important to think about all the time it takes to invent a new way of doing things and explain it to all parties involved!

Whatever the reasons or team members' excuses, taking shortcuts is never the right approach. Ultimately, it will incur more work, and it undermines the commitment to a common way of collaborating, creating, and improving: Agile.

## IS THERE CONTINUOUS IMPROVEMENT?

There is a sometimes-overlooked aspect of Agile, particularly by those skeptical about its benefits or who have had a less-than-positive experience in the past. This critical aspect is continuous improvement, which also happens to be one of the author's favorite parts of successful Agile implementations.

After all, Agile approaches are built on the idea that incremental work, incremental improvements, and collaborative team efforts combine to create better outcomes.

Agile's incremental nature means that, without a commitment to continuous improvement, a team will not fully benefit from all that Agile practices can offer. Keep in mind that this improvement includes the work product (such as marketing campaigns and individual marketing tactics) that is delivered deliver and the tools and methods used to deliver them. Continuous improvement needs to include both of these to deliver stellar results.

The difference between success with Agile and a disillusioned team can come down to team alignment, ensuring everyone is actively participating, and a commitment to continuously improving the work and how it's done.

## DON'T GIVE IN TO AGILE DOGMA

A lot of the text in this volume has gone through the specifics of scrum roles and practices, but there is not only one single adaptation of Agile principles that is correct. The principles can apply to many types of work and many project management methods.

Thus, don't give in to the dogma many Agile practitioners do and close the team off to improving existing practices and approaches. It helps to know the fundamentals so that the team can try those and then adjust and improve particular areas, but those fundamentals really as a starting point, not as an immovable set of rules.

## AGILE IS MEANT TO BE IMPROVED

Agile is meant to be improved over time. Whether through systems of continuous improvement, through the use of scrum practices like retrospectives, or through other means, teams should improve both their work output and the way they work.

This ability to improve both the product and the method of delivering the product is the key thing that draws many marketing teams to Agile principles in the first place. There is too much work to be done, too many expectations, and not enough time in the day to waste on work that is not optimized for both customers and the teams delivering the work. Utilizing the twelve Agile principles and applying them in meaningful ways can help teams of all sizes, disciplines, and within companies and organizations of all types to consistently and sustainably achieve their goals.

# SPRINT PLANNING AGENDA

## SPRINT PLANNING AGENDA (55 MIN.)

**Roles**

- facilitator
- note taker

**Introduction (2 min.)**

Goal: Open the session.

- Review the purpose of the meeting.

**Close Last Sprint (5 min.)**

Goal: Celebrate success and confirm work completed and yet to be completed.

- Celebrate the last achievement.
- Determine what to do with unfinished items.

**Clarify Availability (5 min.)**

Goal: Determine team availability which will affect resource allocation over the next sprint.

- Are there any upcoming outages or conflicts?

### Review Backlog (15 min.)

Goal: Review the product backlog to determine items eligible for the next sprint.

- Ensure items in the backlog are ready to be worked on.

### Start Next Sprint (25 min.)

Goal: Create the goal and sprint backlog to be completed in the next sprint.

- Agree on sprint goal.
  - What are the business priorities to achieve over the next sprint?
  - Is there an overarching goal(s) for the sprint?
- Create the backlog.
  - Based on priority and availability, create a queue.
  - Assign points/values to each item to start measuring velocity.

### Conclusion (3 min.)

Goal: Ensure common understanding of next steps.

- Summarize the meeting.
- Review action items.

# STANDUP MEETING AGENDA

## STANDUP AGENDA (15 MIN.)

**Roles:**

- facilitator
- note taker

**Introduction (2 min.)**

Goal: [Will be based on the individual project]

- Review the purpose of the meeting.

**Team Updates (12 min.)**

Goal: Gain an understanding of the current state of work progress

Each team member reviews the following:

- What did you do yesterday?
- What will you do today?
- What blockers stand in your way?

If an item requires further discussion (more than 30 seconds), it needs to be taken "offline" and can be discussed outside of the standup.

**Conclusion (1 min.)**

Goal: [Based on the individual project]

- Close the meeting.

# RETROSPECTIVE MEETING AGENDA

## MEETING AGENDA (45 MIN.)

**Roles:**

- facilitator
- note taker

**Introduction (5 min.)**

Goal: Get everyone in the room (whether in-person or virtually) and reach out to participate.

- Acknowledge the team.
- Review relevant takeaways from the previous meeting.
- Review the purpose of the meeting.

**Data Gathering (15 min.)**

Goal: Gain an understanding of each team member's perspective on successes, challenges, and learnings.

Have each team member answer the following:

- What are we doing well?
- What are we not doing well?

- What have we learned?
- What fell short?

Gather this information into themes. Chances are, there will be several that overlap. Find a method to group these together.

## Brainstorming (10 min.)

Goal: Work together to understand successes and why there are shortcomings.

Take the data you've gathered and now ask "why" to the issues:

- Why are we doing well on [item]?
- Why are we not doing well on [item]?
- Why are we able to learn from [item]?
- Why did we fall short on [item]?

## Solutions (10 min.)

Goal: Determine the area(s) to improve and use the brainstorming findings to identify solutions and the timing/process to improve.

Since there may be a lot of items that were brainstormed, the group will need to determine how to prioritize. This can be done in a few ways but having everyone pick two or three that they want to focus on is one way.

- Identify areas to be worked on.
- Identify solutions.
- Identify the next steps.

## Conclusion (5 min.)

Goal: Ensure all team members walk away with a shared purpose and set of actions.

- Summarize the meeting.
- Review action items.
- Agree how actions will be measured.

# THE TWELVE PRINCIPLES OF AGILE

The twelve Agile principles should guide your ongoing exploration and implementation of Agile marketing beyond this guide. I also encourage you to look at the Agile Marketing Manifesto principles at: *https://agilemarketingmanifesto.org/principles/* which are more specifically focused on the needs and work of marketers.

Following are definitions of each principle.

### Principle 1

Principle 1 is that the highest priority is satisfying the customer. We need to remember that, in all we do, the desired result is to serve the customer. For all the process improvements, cost savings, and improvements in quantifiable metrics, if we cannot satisfy the customer through our ongoing efforts, we cannot truly be successful. In this sense, the term "customer" could be an internal customer, in the case of many software products created internally, or it could also refer to the external end "customer."

### Principle 2

Principle 2 is that Agile processes harness change for the brand's competitive advantage. Rather than change for change's sake, this Agile principle prescribes the reason we want to continuously improve and implement processes that allow us to modify things in the first place. Being able to adapt and change quickly gives us a competitive advantage and allows us to reach our end customers more easily and effectively.

### Principle 3

Principle 3 is to deliver working output frequently, with a preference for a shorter timescale. No more do we want to create unchangeable twelve-month plans or projects whose milestones are six months or more apart. Instead, this principle dictates that we want the shortest reasonable time between delivering some type of working output so we can assess it and improve it if needed.

### Principle 4

Principle 4 states that businesspeople and developers—or, in this case, marketers—must work together daily throughout the project. This means the end of creating work in a vacuum with little to no feedback from the business at large. It is important that business stakeholders and those closest to both customers and the business needs are regularly involved in the planning and successful implementation of a project.

### Principle 5

Principle 5 is focused more on the teams doing the work. It is to build projects around motivated individuals. As we dive deeper into Agile and using it as a team and across teams, we will see how collaboration is a key component of doing Agile well. Ensuring you have the right people doing the right things who are motivated to achieve success is a critical part of Agile.

### Principle 6

Principle 6 states that direct conversation is the most efficient and effective method of conveying information. While we live in a world with remote and hybrid work, that doesn't mean we can't still have direct conversations. This principle, like the one before it, highlights the importance of teamwork and how the best approach to getting good results is to speak or communicate directly with the individuals responsible.

### Principle 7

Principle 7 states that working output is the primary measure of progress. If you've ever worked alongside an Agile software engineering team, you might have heard terms like *velocity* or *story points* used to describe how they measure their work. As much as measuring speed or hours put into a project is important, the best way to gauge how well a team is doing is to look at what they have created that is working and "in market."

## Principle 8

Principle 8 states that Agile processes promote sustainable development. While the word *sustainable* can have a variety of meanings, however in this context, we are referring to the ability to continue our work with the greatest amount of efficiency, the least amount of waste or rework, and the most potential for ongoing improvement.

## Principle 9

Principle 9 states that continuous attention to technical excellence and good design enhances agility. While these principles were originally written for software engineering teams and not marketers, I'm sure you can see the correlations here. "Technical excellence" applies to marketers just as much as engineers. For instance, how well you plan, implement, and measure a marketing campaign requires technical mastery, albeit of different tools and skill sets than creating a software product might.

Likewise, "good design" could refer to the creatives associated with your marketing effort. However, it could just as easily, and perhaps more appropriately in this case, apply to the processes you use to plan and launch campaigns, the way you build audience segments and the methods you use to provide attribution for your efforts across channels.

## Principle 10

Principle 10 states that simplicity—the art of maximizing the amount of work not done—is essential. This principle is closely related to lean principles, which often complement Agile ones. Lean principles refer to the Japanese word *muda*, which means "futility, uselessness, or wastefulness." There are seven types of muda, or waste, recognized in the lean process.

## Principle 11

Principle 11 states that the best architectures, requirements, and designs emerge from self-organizing teams. While there are a few very specific roles in Agile, the team itself is meant to be self-organizing, and this allows the flexibility inherent in the processes. Rather than being rigid or prescriptive, an Agile team can form itself to allow individuals to fill the roles they are best suited to play.

## Principle 12

The last principle, Principle 12, states that the team reflects on how to become more effective at regular intervals. This idea of reflection, to continuously improve, is a vital one to Agile and one that every Agile team must incorporate to be successful.

# INDEX